MW01273300

MY LORD AND MY GOD

MY LORD AND MY GOD

The Deity of Christ, the Perfect Man

John W. de Silva

JOHN RITCHIE LTD
CHRISTIAN PUBLICATIONS

40 Beansburn, Kilmarnock, Scotland

ISBN 1 904064 17 5

Copyright © 2003 by John Ritchie Ltd.
40 Beansburn, Kilmarnock, Scotland

All rights reserved. No part of this publication may be reproduced, stored in a retrievable system, or transmitted in any form or by any other means – electronic, mechanical, photocopy, recording or otherwise – without prior permission of the copyright owner.

Typeset by John Ritchie Ltd., Kilmarnock
Printed by Bell & Bain Ltd., Glasgow

Acknowledgements

I am very grateful to my wife Lydia for all her support;
also for the practical fellowship of the believers gathered unto His
name at Oakwood Park, Victoria;
for the cooperation of the directors of John Ritchie Ltd;
and for the editorial work of Dr Bert Cargill on the final manuscript.

(c) J W de Silva 2003

Contents

Foreword

"My Lord and my God!" This was the spontaneous and enlightened response of Thomas, a once doubting disciple of Jesus, when confronted with the wound prints in the One whom he had known and followed as the man from Nazareth. The poignant evidence before him now put beyond any doubt that this man, Jesus, was - and is - Lord and God. It became the basis of both his inner faith and his expressed worship.

This treatise on the deity of Christ is written to strengthen *our* faith and promote *our* worship. The deity of our Lord and Saviour is clearly revealed in Scripture for our unhesitating and intelligent belief. It is extremely helpful, however, when the evidences for this great truth are carefully and clearly presented so that we know why we believe what we believe. The following pages do this, providing material to clarify our own thoughts and enable us better to give an answer to those who ask about it. They will also equip us to be better able to meet the challenges of those who attack these very foundations of Christianity. The treatment is also heart warming, and honouring to the Person of Christ.

In such days as ours, a proper appreciation of His perfect humanity and true deity is as necessary as ever. In fact John de Silva undertook this work because of prevailing doubts about these vital matters, and uncertainty about their importance, which he found among young believers in his part of Australia. That such doubts and uncertainties also exist on this side of the world is regrettably all too apparent, and the publication of this thorough exposition of the truth is both timely and welcome.

I am pleased to recommend this book to all, young and old, who want to be assured of the certainty of those things most surely believed among us. In these dark days of denial by some and doubt by others, minds will be clarified and hearts uplifted as these timeless truths are examined. We will be better able to worship the Lord in the sanctuary, and to witness for Him in the world, as we are helped to understand and recognise clearly who He is in all His unique majesty. May the peerless person of our Lord Jesus Christ be magnified and all the more appreciated as a result of this publication.

Bert Cargill
St Monans
Scotland
April 2003

Preface

Since its sacred and supernal dawn, Christianity has been the target of vehement and wide-ranging opposition. The spirit of the age, however, will always attack the Person of Christ, because it is who and what He is that delights a thrice-holy God and brings salvation to man from the penalty of sin. Satan will always seek to convince man that God does not exist. But he also endeavours to have those who believe in God's existence deny His ineffable glory revealed in the Person of His beloved Son.

This endeavour became particularly evident, and a cause for growing concern over recent years during Bible-studies with young Christians. Some were unsure of the deity and perfect humanity of Christ. Others, though assured of these truths, had only a modest knowledge of where they are taught in Scripture. Many were uncertain how to study Scripture in regard to them. These truths it seemed to them, were veiled within the Bible, and to penetrate that veil they had to become schooled theologians. It was also of concern, that they had little knowledge as to why these truths are vital to Christianity and to their faith. This situation had led many to sympathise with the fatal view that Christ could sin – even though He did not sin.

As the day of grace closes, Satan's attack on the truth concerning Christ's Person will intensify. What he failed to accomplish during the earthly life of the perfect Man, he seeks to achieve through a persistent assault on those who are eternally perfected in Him. But, beloved in Christ, we are not without help, having the indwelling Spirit of truth, who has revealed in the Word of God those eternal, divine, and immutable glories of Christ, upon which our faith and eternal hope rest. His deity is fundamental to His finished work as our Redeemer, vital in His present intercession for us as our ascended High Priest and Advocate, and pivotal to His future sovereign rule as King of kings and Lord of lords. What Christ *did* was the grand truth of the Reformation; who and what He *is*, is the great consoling truth for this day.

This book does not seek to "prove" Christ's deity by debating divergent views upon it. Rather, it seeks with the deepest reverence and with a profound sense of personal inadequacy on the part of the writer, to examine and so direct the reader to those sure and superlative *revelations* of the deity of the blessed Lord in the inspired Word, which impart to it an eternal glory.

J W de Silva
Victoria
Australia

Notations and Abbreviations

The following notations have been employed in regard to major references cited in the text.

A T Robertson - *Word Pictures* - A T Robertson, A.M., D.D., LL.D. *Word Pictures in the New Testament* - Broadman Press

W E Vine - *Expository Dictionary* - W E Vine, M.A. *Expository Dictionary of New Testament Words* - Oliphants

W E Vine - *Collected Writings* - W E Vine, M.A. *The Collected Writings of W.E. Vine* - Gospel Tract Publications

Vincent - *Word Studies* - M R Vincent, D.D. *Word Studies in the New Testament* - Wm. B. Eerdmans

Wuest - *Word Studies* - K S Wuest, *Word Studies in the Greek New Testament* - Wm. B. Eerdmans

Expositors - *The Expositors Greek New Testament* - Wm. B. Eerdmans

Girdlestone – *Synonyms,* B Girdlestone M.A. *Synonyms of the Old Testament* - Wm. B. Eerdmans

AV - Authorised Version

RV - Revised Version

OT/NT - Old/New Testaments

Introduction

Who is Jesus of Nazareth, the One called the Christ of God? That He was a man who lived in ancient times, only the most obtuse and stubborn mind would question. That He was immeasurably above the very best of men in moral character only the malevolent heart would dispute. But that He is both God and man, as believed and cherished by orthodox Christianity, has brought dissent from within Christendom itself. Is Christ, as liberal Christianity would have us believe, "divine" but not Deity? Or, is He, as the cults claim, a "special creation", an angel to whom God bestowed exceptional powers and delegated eminent authority, a superior god among many gods? Perhaps He is merely one of the "holy men" of history who possessed extraordinary wisdom and prophetic insight? On the other hand, does it really matter who and what we believe Jesus Christ to be? The Lord's question to His disciples, "But whom say ye that I am?", does not invite indifference, and neither does it sanction speculation.

Through the ages, Christianity among all faiths has come under the greatest of attacks from within and without. Men do voice their opposition to other creeds. But their claims against them are comparatively muted, falling well short of the strident intolerance and virulent hostility levelled against the truths revealed in the Christian Bible. There can be no other explanation for this, except that Christianity is founded upon the two greatest and most searching truths. Jesus Christ, upon whom it rests, is both *Lord and God* and, that God, *through Christ, was reconciling the world unto Himself!* The first truth marks a confession that testifies to the coming and presence of God as man in the world. The second marks the holy character of God, declaring the purpose for which He came into the world as man. Taken together, they explain why Christianity presents the only authentic moral challenge to the proud and sinful heart of man, and why that heart becomes deeply vexed when exposed to divine revelation. They explain, too, why man has enrolled and employed every known field of investigation against Christianity with unceasing and unparalleled intensity.

The deity of Jesus Christ, the Saviour of men, is the impenetrable truth which ennobles the Christian faith. It marks the infinitely sacred divide between Christianity and all other faiths. The divine Man enjoins, enables and inspires a confession that soars in radiant emancipation above the enslaving chants of all other theology.[1]

We who take the name of Christ are often challenged to account for the hope that lives within us. We invariably begin by proclaiming the existence of God, readily enlisting the words of the psalmist, "The heavens declare *the* glory of God; and the firmament sheweth his handywork" (Ps 19:1). Appropriately we quote Romans 1:20, "For the invisible things of him from *the* creation of the world are clearly seen, being understood by *the* things that are made, even his eternal power and Godhead; so that they are without excuse."[2] However, the true basis of our glorious hope and peace is now 'within the veil'. We know that God exists because He came among men as the divine Man Christ Jesus, that He died, arose, and ascended, having vindicated a thrice-holy God.

In chapter 2 of this book we take up the biblical doctrine of Christ's Person, after dealing in chapter 1 with some common obstacles that stumble many in regard to it. In chapters 3, 4 and 5 we consider respectively, the revelation of the deity of Christ in the Gospel narratives, His majestic deity seen in His titles and names, and the explicit teaching elsewhere in the NT of His equality with God. In chapter 6 we study the priceless truth as to why God became man. How vital this is to our souls! To know why God took on humanity is to know the way of salvation. To confess it is to possess salvation.

---

[1] Yet, we observe, sadly, that some Christians fail to appreciate the singular nobility of their profession, not because they deny Christ's deity, but because that they apprehend little of its ineffable worth to the faith. For this reason they fall into the impiety of humour and irreverent familiarity when speaking about or to the Son of God most High. May we be constrained by the jealous reverence with which the Holy Spirit speaks of God's own Son, rather than be captivated by the spirit of the world, which encourages irreverence in all things, but especially in regard to the truths Christianity holds holy.

[2] These two verses point to the glory of God and are not given to prove His existence. In the Bible, God's existence is everywhere an accepted fact (Gen 1:1). The Spirit of God never sets out to prove God exists but to reveal Him as He does exist – as the Triune Godhead.

It is one thing to acknowledge the deity of Christ as a credal truth, but quite another to prize it, possess and partake of it! In chapter 7 we examine passages of Scripture that have been mishandled by those seeking to attack Christ's person. Finally, in chapter 8, we consider the Virgin Birth and its vital bearing upon the deity of Christ and His perfect humanity.

> *"No mortal can with Him compare*
> *Among the sons of men;*
> *Fairer is He than all the fair*
> *That fill the heavenly train."*
> *(Samuel Stennett)*

CHAPTER 1

"Be not faithless, but believing"

Before we study the resplendent revelation of Christ's deity in the Word of God, it is necessary to address and dispel some commonly held attitudes and opinions which have created a denial, a doubt or a perplexity in regard to it. Here are ten of these.

1. 'I cannot understand how God became man.'

Many who reject Christ's deity do so because they cannot understand how God could become man and that that Man was truly God. Strangely enough, some among them have little difficulty in believing that a man can become a god and remain a god. It was Satan himself who cultivated such hostile teaching and the false hope it advances. His diabolical lie "ye shall be as gods" brought ruin upon mankind (Gen 3:1-5). It was an appeal to man's lust, but only after he had contrived man's distrust in God: "Hath God said?" This is Satan's foremost line of attack on the beloved in Christ, evident in the tactics and beliefs propagated by the cults and the New Age Movement.[1]

Note first, the truth of Christ's deity cannot be determined according to human intellect. God therefore has never sought to reveal anything to us concerning *how* He became man and remained God, apart from the sublime revelation of the Virgin Birth. For the same reason He has not explained how He created the heavens and the earth, how

---

[1] In passing, we might note another yet related caste of unbelief. Some find it impossible to understand how the Creator could come among His own creation by way of a lowly manger and wash the feet of the creature. Such ignominy they say is inconsistent with deity. Those who stumble here stumble at the sublime setting of Calvary. There the divine Son of God gave Himself a ransom for many. He humbled Himself, took the form of a servant and became obedient unto death, even the death of the cross! Man's natural mind does not predispose him to see the glory of God in creation, or perceive His transcendent grace in redemption (1 Cor 2:14).

He raised the dead, or how He performed His miracles (miracles that are explicable cease to be miracles). To understand such supernal works of the Almighty, we would need to have the infinite understanding of God Himself. "Canst thou find out *the* Almighty unto perfection?" (Job 11:7; cf Gen 3:5).

However, man must *know* what God is. But we can only acquire such knowledge through divine revelation, otherwise we will imagine and reason about God and sink into the mire of paganism or atheism: "The world by wisdom knew not God" (1 Cor 1:21). We need to appreciate the economy of divine revelation - revealed *fact* and required *faith*, which results in restored *fellowship* with God. Divine revelation is God making something known to man that would otherwise not be known to man. Therefore only God can reveal God, and what He tells us about Himself must be accepted in trust. When the Almighty deigns to reveal such truth to us, it is never to gratify our intellectual curiosity, but to claim our obedient faith. There is nothing inconsistent or surprising then in God never setting out to explain to finite man, but rather to *reveal* according to *His* wisdom, certain hallowed and high mysteries of His Godhead.

Second, God is preoccupied with revealing His grace to fallen man, rather than explaining how He as God became man and remained God. Man can make no claim upon God apart from what He has provided through His matchless grace. When we begin to debate with God and about God, demanding explanations rather than resting upon His inspired revelation, we place ourselves outside of divine grace. It is of *faith* and, note the order - that it might be according to *grace* (Rom 4:16). An "agnostic" student once claimed immunity from divine judgement on the ground of his honest enquiry, when unable to understand and commit to certain divine truths. Surely a God of infinite justness would excuse him in the light of his sincere but failed efforts to understand the Infinite! The solemn truth is that there can be no plea of "honest doubt" before a God who has revealed Himself in creation and personally in fashion as a man, who loved us when we had no love for Him. Superstition is belief apart from divine revelation; honest doubt is pure scepticism - faithlessness in spite of it. When instructing the young in Christ, it is imperative to teach them to exercise faith in that which is written. To say to a child in the faith (or another), "I cannot explain the deity of Christ yet we must believe in it as revealed in Scripture," is not an admission of failure, but a sacred duty on the part of all who seek in faithfulness to teach Christ. The Person of Christ is beyond an individual's understanding, yet no thoughtful person can go beyond Christ for understanding in regard to sin and their salvation from its eternal judgement.

Third, we must avoid the self-serving error of "selective faith". Many who reject Christ's deity on the basis of implausibility, believe in God's capacity to create heaven and earth out of nothing, to raise the dead and perform many other miracles, despite their inability to understand how He performed these wonders. They unreservedly seek refuge within God's infinite love despite that love being incomprehensible. However, when it comes to the matter of God becoming and abiding as man, they seek to limit His infinite power. The Lord reproved the Sadducees because of their ignorance of the Scriptures, and not knowing the power of God (Mk 12:24). God does not want us to weary ourselves over the unwarranted complexities of how He became man and remains God in the person of Jesus of Nazareth.

Beloved in Christ, do you lament the lack of progress in your life for Him? Are you unremittingly downcast, your mind governed by doubt rather than by conviction? If so, then ask yourself if it is because you are seeking answers to questions that God will not answer. "Ye ask, and receive not, because ye ask amiss" (Jas 4:3). We can only know God and please Him through the simplicity of faith. For "without faith *it is* impossible to please *him*: for he that cometh to God must believe that he is, and *that* he is a rewarder of them that diligently seek him" (Heb 11:6). It is through faith in the revelation of Scripture that denial, doubt and difficulties are defeated, and strength is born out of weakness.

2. 'Portions of the Bible[2] deny the deity of Christ.'

Certain portions of Scripture, we are told, deny Christ's deity. This assertion is the product of detached biblical investigation that

---

[2] The "Bible" refers to the Old and New Testament Scriptures - once for all delivered. Expose a cult member to the incontestable teaching of Christ's deity in the Bible and see how readily he or she seeks refuge and supreme authority within some book other than the Bible, one that invariably denies the deity of the Son of God Most High! There are, of course, cults that confine themselves to the Old and New Testaments. But they systematically pervert the text so that it conforms to their false notions of Christ and God.

has abandoned grammatical principles, ignored biblical context, discarded dispensational distinctions, and failed to acknowledge the absolute holiness of God and the plight of fallen man. We will observe something of this throughout our study, but let us note here that in many instances these portions are interpreted on the *assumption* that the existence of the divine Man is implausible. This line of argument is also used by some professing Christians to deny creation: "How can God create something out of nothing and bring all things into such complex and sustained arrangements?" The creation narrative in Genesis is therefore taken as a mere myth.

This same faithless reasoning has impressed those who advance unorthodox views concerning Christ's deity and the Godhead. Because His deity (and the Trinity) lie beyond our understanding, let us interpret and invent Scripture to reveal Christ as a mere man (Unitarianism); one of three separate Beings (Tritheism); one of three divine "manifestations" (Sabellianism or Modalistic Monarchianism); an "emanation" from God (Gnosticism); one who lost His deity (Kenoticism); one who is "a god" (Mormonism, Jehovah's Witnesses and Christadelphianism).[3] All such expedient interpretations of God's Word may satisfy the natural mind, but they grieve the Spirit of God who would have us know God through faith in what He has revealed. "Faith cometh by hearing, and hearing by the [revealed] Word of God" (Rom 10:17). It is through faith in the Genesis account that we accept that the worlds were framed by the Word of God. Faith is the evidence of things not seen. By faith we understand that the things which are seen were not made of things that do appear (Heb 11:1-3). Those who interpret Scripture so as to deny the deity of Christ because this truth is beyond their understanding, fall into the line of argument employed by rationalists and humanists - the things which are seen are made of things which *do appear*. However, "we look not at the things which are seen, but at the things which are not seen: for the things which are seen *are* temporal; but the things which are not seen *are* eternal" (2 Cor 4:18). The Virgin Birth, the Incarnation, Aaron's rod that budded, the raising of the dead, and all other supernal works of

---

[3] As dealt with in later chapters and Appendix 1.

God, are unparalleled in nature and contrary to it. Yet, many seek to explain them and interpret Scripture and Christ according to natural laws and human experience. Christ anticipated this very error. "No man knoweth the Son, but the Father" (Matt 11:27). It has been well said, 'it is impossible to know fully what Christ is, but we can know what Christ is not'. Enough is revealed in Scripture concerning the Person of Christ to assure us that "he that hath the Son hath life" (1 Jn 5:11-12), and to ensure that all men should "honour the Son even as they honour the Father" (Jn 5:23).

Man's Adamic pride, too, encourages him to deny Christ's deity as revealed in the Word of God. If the man Christ Jesus is God, then all must bow before Him in all things. The cults preach that man can be saved through his righteous works. Where does such a tragic notion come from except through the pride of the Fall? This fatal doctrine denies Christ as the divine Redeemer of men, and rejects Him as the needed and accepted divine sacrifice for sin! When, therefore, many encounter the Person of Christ in Scripture, they regard Him with eyes blinded by the pride of Adam, for they, too, desire in their vain self-righteousness to be as God. Unregenerate man is foolish in his philosophy and foolhardy in his pride. Only through faith which defeats pride, can man come to know the "light of the knowledge of the glory of God in the face of Jesus Christ" (2 Cor 4:6).

God's Word *provokes* our faith, *provides* for it and *promotes* it. It also serves to *prepare* us for faith. Statements such as 'no man can know the Father save the Son'; that 'God's thoughts are not our thoughts and His ways not our ways', prepare our hearts to receive by faith the sublime mysteries of God. In our witness to men, we are *not* required to unravel and explain the mystery of the divine Man. We are called to accept the Incarnation as it is revealed in Scripture, to preach the glorious fact of it and herald the redeeming universal grace flowing from it, while we worship in obedient wonder at it!

3. 'The Bible contradicts itself.'
Some acknowledge that certain passages of Scripture clearly teach the deity of Christ, but they also assert that other passages seem to deny it. For instance, many set the claim of Christ that "I

and *my* Father are one" (Jn 10:30) against His statement that "my Father is greater than I" (Jn 14:28). Because of this apparent contradiction, they remain indifferent to the matter of Christ's deity, or side with a particular view of it on grounds other than Scripture.

Both Testaments reveal that one of the things the pre-incarnate divine Son had to do to fulfil the will of God, was to become a servant of God. The Son's declaration "my Father is greater than I", was made in accordance with His work and standing as a submissive servant of God. In this statement the Lord was not referring to His essential Person at all. Another thing the Son had to do to fulfil the will of God was to become man. So there are passages in Scripture which reveal His real manhood. Just because Christ's manhood or His work as a servant is in view, does not mean that He is not Deity. The Gospel narratives which we take up below reveal that though Christ possessed divine attributes in their totality, He willingly exercised them in a way consistent with Him being dependent upon and submissive to God as His Servant, and as Man. Consequently on occasions He withheld the exercise of His divine attributes - when for instance He allowed Himself to be taken by His enemies. But He never lost His divine attributes.

Scripture tells us that the Son must become man and a servant of God, and then records His authentic humanity and genuine humility, all that was consistent with Him being in word and deed a real man and the obedient servant of God. As we shall observe, Scripture records a great deal in the life of Christ that is compatible with Him being concurrently God, man and a servant of God. Such an account may confound the most erudite among men, but it will never stumble those who, because of their faith, are in a position to be taught by the Spirit of God to rightly divide the word of truth (2 Tim 2:15). Biblical truth can never be a blessing until it is first believed. Only upon belief, can we come to discern the glories that pertain to Christ's distinctive Person and work as the Son of God, the Servant of God, the Sovereign; and Christ as Saviour, High Priest and Advocate - our subjects in later chapters.

"Fragmentary" biblical evidence!

There are those who are unconvinced about Christ's deity because they regard the biblical revelation of His Person as fragmentary. The

25

range of subjects visited in this book, reflects the fact that the deity of Christ, like many other biblical truths, is not formulated within a single portion of Scripture. Why is this? It is because God's revelation to man has come by way of the inspired hearts and minds of men, men who lived in divergent times and circumstances. They were called to write of divine things which had a present and prospective message, impelled by the historical and spiritual conditions particular to their day (Amos 3:7). Yet, as we shall see, what they wrote composed a harmonious tapestry of truth which, while refuting all allegations of corroboration between them, testifies to the superintending work of the Spirit of God, all Scripture being of Him.

We should also understand that the revelation of divine truth answers the evolution of error among men, error that only the passage of time would reveal. The latter NT writings therefore amplify truths announced in the Gospels and early Epistles. We have in our hands the divine Canon that answers every conceivable error concerning Christ's person and work.

The divine revelation in Scripture concerning Christ, as borne out in this study, is consequently presented to us in a four-fold way: *historically* – in the deeds and words of Christ, especially recorded in the Gospel narratives; *doctrinally* – particularly proclaimed in the Epistles in their assertion and timely apology regarding His divine Person and work; *prophetically* and *typically* – both spanning the Old and New Testaments, the former underpinning and the latter confirming the sublime harmony between the historical and doctrinal teaching concerning Him.[4] Revealed divine truth was necessarily *progressive, timely* and *plenary*. And, if we are to profit spiritually in any enterprise involving Scripture, it is imperative that we accept that in the Person of God's own Son, we have the finality of all progressive and timely revelation (Heb 1:1-2).

4. 'My supernatural experiences validate my denial of Christ's deity.'

"Would God have given me that vision, that tongue, that miracle etc, if my denial of the Trinity and of the deity of Christ is wrong?"

---

[4] There are certain people, practices and precedents revealed in the OT, that foreshadow the Person and work of Christ. These are referred to as "types" or "examples", and they make up the body of biblical instruction referred to as "typical teaching" (1 Cor 10:11). We will come across a number of these wonderfully edifying types throughout this study.

What we have here is the fatal error of allowing personal experience to authenticate biblical doctrine. The Bereans have their honoured place in the inspired Word, and their conferred nobility, not because they sought signs and wonders to discover the truth. It is because "they received the word with all readiness of mind, and searched the scriptures daily, whether those things were so" (Acts 17:11). The Lord Jesus Himself declared thrice, "It is written," when tempted by Satan, expressing His conviction on divine matters. The redeemed have their names in the book of life not because of what they have experienced, but because of the One in whom they have believed - the divine Man, Jesus of Nazareth. We must forsake the need to have the miraculous works of God explained in order *to* believe, and cast aside personal experiences to support what it is we *do* believe.[5] We are to "walk by faith, not by sight" (2 Cor 5:7). Each time we determine to walk by sight, we declare the feebleness of our own faith, discourage those who seek to walk as the Spirit has directed, and deny the all-sufficiency of the Word of God.

5. 'Doctrine is not all that important.'

The lyric "too much is made of doctrine" is the first and repetitive line in the profane anthem of the ecumenical movement. Doctrine is seen as divisive. Indeed it is, and herein lies its great worth. Doctrine is vital *because* it does divide - truth from error and light from darkness – critical divides which are lost within the amorphous union called ecumenism and among churches that seek community with society. We have the importance of doctrine declared at the beginning of the church age (Acts 2:42). The local church is to be the "pillar and ground of truth" (1 Tim 3:14-15). The Christian is exhorted to know and adhere to sound doctrine. Scripture repeatedly warns against false teaching (i.e., Rom 16:17; 1 Tim 1:3,10; 4:6, 6:1; Rev 2:14-15). Doctrine is vital because it enables the child of God to be perfect, throughly furnished unto all good works (2 Tim 3:16). The thoughts of our hearts are shaped by doctrine, and our deeds are the product of our hearts (Pr 23:7).

Saul of Tarsus, the zealous and learned Jew is a prime illustration

---

[5] The folly of *empiricism* - the philosophical belief that all knowledge is derived from experiences which are from within or without (as proposed by 18th Century philosophers such as John Locke and David Hume) cf Jn 14:17.

of this truth. His tirade against the church was the outcome of his fervent Judaism. However, when he came into the school of the risen Christ and learned of Him, he was a man whose deeds were the fruit of the doctrine of Christ. Do we, as Paul, embrace the conviction to be known by our doctrine (2 Tim 3:10)? John warns, "Whosoever...abideth not in the doctrine of Christ, hath not God" (2 Jn 9). The belief that doctrine is not important is itself a doctrine.[6] May we regard Paul's exhortation - "Take heed unto thyself, and unto the doctrine; continue in them: for in doing this thou shalt both save thyself, and them that hear thee" (1 Tim 4:16).

6. 'So many opinions - who can I believe?'

Chronic conflicting opinion concerning the Person of Christ has caused despair and denial among many professing Christians, and it has also stumbled unbelievers. The first step towards assurance and assent is to place unswerving faith in the inspired Word of God, and thereby submit to the teaching of the Spirit of truth. Let God be true but every man a liar (Rom 3:4). Also we must reject any doctrine which is:

• the result of some "supernatural revelation" foreign to the completed Canon of Scripture;
• sourced and founded on any text other than the completed Canon of Scripture which has been "once [for all] delivered" (Jude 3);
• the outcome of any one person's understanding of the Word of God - we are warned about "private interpretation" (2 Pet 1:20);[7]
• inconsistent with any doctrine that has been proved by comparing Scripture with itself. Within the professing contemporary Church there is an endemic failure to rightly divide the truth, evident in the admixture of law and grace, the failure to distinguish between the Church and Israel, the Redeemer and the redeemed, and between the Creator and the creature!

The cults that profess Christianity fail one or more of these tests. But there is a vital question we must put to all who teach about the Person of Christ: "What is the way of salvation?" If their answer is

---

[6] The 'deeds' of the Nicolaitanes which the Lord hated soon became a doctrine (Rev 2:15).
[7] Arius, Sabellius etc, and more recently, Joseph Smith (Mormons), C T Russell ("Jehovah's Witnesses"), John Thomas (Christadelphians).

anything other than salvation *solely* through faith in Christ and His shed blood, then we must reject *all* they say in regard to Christian creed. Those who base their salvation in any measure upon themselves deny the all-sufficiency of Christ's saving work, which rests upon His deity and perfect humanity. Such persons cannot be ministers of the Gospel of God's grace, for sadly they have never partaken of it unto salvation. There can be no light shed concerning Christ, if the person professing to teach has no life in Christ, who is alone the Source of life.

When facing the tide of contradictory teaching concerning Christ, it is tempting to seek refuge in popular opinion. Here the young in Christ are particularly susceptible. They have a greater need of assurance and a desire to be accepted among peers. These feelings often override the importance of holding truths that are biblical, yet unpopular with the majority. But the popularity of a doctrine is never a test of its truth, for the simple reason that the truth is never popular! The Lord pointed this out to the Jews. "Because I tell *you* the truth, ye believe me not" (Jn 8:45). We can be encouraged that Scripture speaks highly of a faithful remnant amidst a faithless majority. We are inspired by men such as Joshua, Caleb, Gideon, Daniel and his steadfast companions, and the martyrs of the Reformation, not simply because they held to the truth, but because they held it amidst a vast and often vilifying multitude who rejected it. The Lord Himself is 'by the few enthroned', having been rejected by the world - but 'the crowning day is coming bye and bye!' Popular opinion can never be a source of abiding assurance because it sows the seeds of its own demise.

7. 'Church history denies Christ's deity.'
A controversy over Christ's deity (and the Trinity) arose within the church during the 4th century, instigated by a Christian cleric named Arius.[8] Christ, he said, was a created being through whom God created the world.[9] To address this challenge, Constantine,

---

[8] Arianism was a Christian heresy first proposed early in the 4th Century by Arius. The Council of Nicea condemned Arianism and issued a creed to safeguard orthodox Christian belief (i.e. the deity of Christ). The believers in Christ's deity at the Council of Nicea were not there to debate the deity of Christ, but to defend it! Arius was regarded as a heretic by the Church well before the Council of Nicea was convened.

the emperor of the day, established the Council of Nicea I (325 AD), which affirmed that the Son is of the *same* substance [*homoousios*] of the Father (the Nicene Creed). The Son is very God; He is *homoousion to Patri* - He is all that the Father is![10] The Arian view, that Christ is of a *similar* or *like* substance to the Father [*homoiousios*], was repudiated.[11]

Some assert that the early Christians never held the doctrine of Christ's deity, that it was "invented" to meet and end the Arian challenge. There is no substance at all to this assertion. Firstly, it is based upon a misunderstanding of ecclesiastical and biblical history. The truth concerning the Person of Christ was defended in biblical times, well before the 4th Century. In his Colossian Epistle (AD 61-63), Paul resolutely opposes the Gnostics who, when they embraced Christianity, denied Christ's deity and His real humanity. These Gnostic ideas did not originate from within the Church. They represented error that entered the Church from without, and tried the faith of some within it.

Just prior to Paul's second missionary journey, a controversy did develop within the Church, but it was not in regard to Christ's person. It was over the relevance of Jewish practices such as circumcision in the life of the Christian (Acts 15; Romans & Galatians). It is significant that throughout this controversy the Judaizers never brought Christ's person into the debate.[12] It would have greatly helped their cause to present Christ as inferior to God, for it was Jehovah-God who ordained the covenant rite of circumcision and gave the law to Moses (Gen 17:11; Acts 15:5). This is all the more striking because some of the Judaizers were converted Pharisees (Acts 15:5). In support of their case for circumcision, they never referred to the blasphemy of Christ alleged by their former associates - that He made Himself equal with God. These were Jewish-Christians who knew and revered

---

[9] In this, Arius was the father of falsehood evident among the cults - Mormonism; Christadelphianism; "Jehovah's' Witnesses", who regard Arius as the fore-runner to their founder, Charles Taze Russell; Unitarianism.
[10] Consubstantial – of the same substance.
[11] Athanasius (AD 298 c -373) led the defence of Christ's deity against Arius, and for over half a century this dour defender honoured God in fighting Arian false doctrine.
[12] The Judaizers were those early Jewish Christians who sought to retain aspects of Jewish law and custom, such as circumcision.

Jehovah's jealousy, yet they served and worshipped Christ as God.

Secondly, the timing of the decisions of councils and men, irrespective of their persuasion, have no bearing whatsoever on the origin of divine truth.[13] Thirdly, it is sheer naivety to believe that "Church leaders" of the early post-apostolic centuries spoke for all Christians, any more than present church 'leaders' speak for the Church today. Finally, we must not place the interpretations of historians with unregenerate hearts and uninspired pens above the Word of God. It is to Scripture that we turn to interpret history.

8. 'Modern 'scholarship' denies Christ's deity.'

From their clinical and Christ-less reasoning, certain contemporary scholars inform us that Jesus of Nazareth was, like other notable persons of history, merely a product of His time. Scripture declares their sad state of mind and soul - "ever learning, and never able to come to the knowledge of the truth" (2 Tim 3:7).

The Person and life of Jesus of Nazareth was never the product of His or any other age. What much of contemporary religious and secular scholarship fails to see, or does not wish to see, is that Jesus of Nazareth singularly meets the need of every age. Its exponents ignore or are ignorant of the truth that Jesus Christ is not only the centre-point of NT revelation, He is also the pivotal theme of OT prophecy. The coming and commission of Christ was according to the determinate counsel and foreknowledge of God (Acts 2:23). In the OT Christ is *announced* and *anticipated*; in the Gospels He *arrives*, and dwells *among* men; in Acts He is *ascended* and *adored*, and in the Epistles He is *affirmed* and *awaited*. In Revelation He again *arrives* and is *acclaimed*. The predictable failing of the popular quest to find the 'historical Jesus', is its ignorance of the fact that the Eternal God was, in Christ, reconciling the world unto Himself, and that this sublime matter brooded in the heart of the Triune Godhead in eternity past!

Let no one suppose however, that the Christian decries honest scientific investigation into the material world, for the results of such enquiry will never conflict with biblical revelation of the One

---

[13] The earth was a ball hanging in space long before Galileo demonstrated it to be so.

who created and sustains that world. But the truth is that if we are unable to find sufficient evidence of Christ's deity in the Bible, then we will not find it anywhere else. "Search the Scriptures", exhorted the Lord, "for .... they are they which testify of me" (Jn 5:39). What a day of radiant delight dawned upon Nathanael, when Philip declared - "We have found Him, of whom Moses in the law, and the prophets, did write, Jesus of Nazareth" (Jn 1:45). His "goings have been from old, from everlasting" (Mic 5:2).

9. 'Christ never said He was God.'

A frequent claim made by those who deny the deity of Christ is that He never explicitly claimed to be God. There are at least two errors here. First, Christ did indeed explicitly declare His deity, so explicitly that His opponents sought to kill Him because of it. This is a matter of record and *not* interpretation. And, concerning plain statements, where are the explicit statements in Scripture which declare that Christ is *not* God; that God *created* His Son; and that we are *not* to worship the Son as God? Where hearts abide in unbelief, the most transparent of truths will be rejected.

It is true, Scripture does not record Christ stating "I am Jehovah" – a sequence of words which some doubters require. But then neither does it record the Father uttering these same words. Is the Father therefore not God? Scripture does reveal that Christ declared Himself to be the "I am". When this expression is viewed within the whole compass of Scripture and we acknowledge to whom He spoke, there is no doubt He was declaring Himself to be Jehovah! The expression "I am" is the most emphatic statement Christ could employ to proclaim His deity before the Jews, and later we note why. Apart from the explicit "I am", we have in Scripture the recurring and inimitable "I am He": "I *am* he that liveth, and was dead; and, behold, I am alive for evermore" (Rev 1:18, see also Rev 2:23 - Jn 8:24; 9:9; 13:19). Jehovah frequently identifies Himself as God using this expression. "Understand that I *am* he: before me there was no God formed, neither shall there be after me" (Isa 43:10, cf Deut 32:39; Isa 41:4; 43:25; 48:12 etc).

Let us not forget, too, the explicit statements of Christ's deity made by the Holy Spirit through inspired men: the Word was God (Jn 1:1); Christ, as according to the flesh, the One who is over all,

God blessed forever (Rom 9:5); the great God and our Saviour Jesus Christ (Titus 2:13); "My Lord and my God" (Jn 20:28). It is also instructive to note the motive and manner in which the Lord often revealed His deity. Consider first His *claim* upon men. He did not confront individuals and crowds with bold assertions proclaiming who He was, and so try to cultivate allegiance as would a Caesar. Rather, He sought a work within the hearts of men, for it is with his heart that man believes unto righteousness. We see Him therefore composing words and questions to draw a conviction and then a confession of His deity from within, as seen in His conversation with the woman of Samaria; the young man who called Him "good master"; the Jews (Matt 22); and, most notably, His post-resurrection encounter with Thomas. He desired to lead all along the way of conviction, confession and faith, so that all may have faith's reward, according to divine grace.

Consider second, the Lord's use of *context*. In many instances when He spoke of His deity, He deliberately associated it with some vital aspect of the history and theology of the OT. This is because His deity could not be considered apart from the framework of divine revelation - historical, covenantal and prophetic. For this reason also, the Lord did not utter isolated assertions of His deity. When He spoke of it, it had to be within this threefold context in order to establish divine fulfilment, communicate divine purpose, and enhance its acceptance among the Jews. He therefore preferred to ask, "Whom do men say that I the Son of man am?"; "What think ye of Christ [the Messiah]?"; " whose son is He?" And, for this reason, too, He preferred to declare "Before Abraham was I am" - which provided a greater lesson as to His identity than if He had simply declared, "I am Jehovah-God." He did not confront His disciples declaring, "I am your Lord and God." It was more edifying to them and glorifying to God to have one who doubted His resurrection confess it, and in so doing connect His personal divine glory with His resurrection glory. And, it is because of context that He often selected the Sabbath and the precincts of the synagogue to manifest and declare His deity. The Lord's manner and motive in revealing His deity was entirely consistent with One who was the Son of God come of a woman - as God revealing His humanity; and as One come under the law - as a Jew revealing His deity (Gal 4:4).

10. 'The Bible must be interpreted in a contemporary fashion.'

There are people within the professing church who seek to persuade us that in view of today's advancements in science, knowledge and social insight, to adhere to the venerable truths of the Bible is to consent to childish credulity and cultivate narrow-mindedness. The increasing defection from Christianity they say, is due to dated and conservative Christian dogma. To arrest and reverse this trend we must "interpret the Bible to accommodate the mind of the age", a notion that, ironically, has its impious origins at the beginning of man's history.

It is vital to identify the insidious cunning of those who advance such treacherous notions and so avoid their beguiling influence. These false teachers, schooled in secular and religious matters, know only too well that to deny Christ's deity within today's liberal society would scarcely raise yawning attention. They therefore commingle their false doctrine with the popular causes of the day. This ensures that their denials of Christ enjoy the patronage and applause of the present age, which consents to a God of love, but rejects a God of holiness! The Christianity they preach is socially valued, but spiritually bankrupted, seeking mercy apart from truth and peace without righteousness.

These articulate false professors are revered by society because the branded religion they peddle is perceived to be 'in touch' with contemporary thought. The Bible in its time-honoured relevance views them quite differently, as scoffers, walking after their own lusts and giving heed to seducing spirits, causing many to heed the doctrines of demons (2 Pet 3:3; 1 Tim 4:1-2). Paul gave a certain warning centuries ago: "For I know this, that after my departing shall grievous wolves enter in among you, not sparing the flock. Also of your own selves shall men arise, speaking perverse things, to draw away disciples after them" (Acts 20:29-30). They have "a form of godliness" but deny its power - from such turn away (2 Tim 3:5). What relevance these timely words have for those who seek to hold fast the truth today!

In their profane arrogance, these apostles of dark denial charge the Almighty God with moral, social and spiritual myopia, in that He inspired a Book that is inadequate to meet man's need in every age. They seek to rob man of the true moral constant given in the

Person of the divine Son of God. Their hearts are consumed by intellectual apprehension, but void of spiritual appropriation. They know nothing of the omniscient God, the One who stands astride the ages who, when He inspired the enduring truths of Scripture, knew the end from the beginning. The "once delivered" timeless truths of Scripture (Jude 3) were never revealed by God to be *adapted* to the age, but to be *applied* in absolute faithfulness and wisdom to the sin-cursed hearts of people in all ages, for sin abides in every age! "Let God be true, but every man a liar."

Finally, we note that accompanying the speculation emanating from apostate thought and, no doubt giving it impetus, is the notion that the Gospels are merely idealised histories, and that the declarations of Christ's deity in the Epistles are, in turn, simply idealised accretions on the Gospel and OT accounts. What is plainly intelligent to faith, has in the instance of those who make such allegations, been confounded by the impious science of rationalism, which the god of this world has employed to blind men to the truth, that all Scripture is given by inspiration of God.

CHAPTER 2

The Biblical Doctrine of the Deity of Christ

"And he said, Draw not nigh hither: put off thy shoes from off thy feet, for the place whereon thou standest is holy ground" (Ex 3:5).

Biblical revelation is given to us through a number of unique terms and expressions. These must be clearly understood by discerning the distinction and the alliance between them. Now it must be said that certain terms used in relation to our subject are not found in Scripture. However, they serve us admirably by effectually representing the truths that are given in Scripture. These terms too must be clearly understood, and their legitimacy firmly established from the Word of God. It is not a case of using them to 'invent' doctrine, as some mischievously assert, but one of applying them to make biblical doctrine more communicable.

The terms "divine", "divinity", and the attributes of God
A person's attributes are those things that characterise that person. They serve to describe that person and, where they are unique, they also serve to distinguish that person. A person's name often reveals their attributes, as we note in regard to Christ in chapter 4.

In the NT, the Greek word *theiotes* (divinity), refers to God from the point of view of His attributes, the qualities that *describe* Him and *declare* His existence in all His uniqueness as God. The use of this term is illustrated in Romans, cited above - "his [God's] eternal power and divinity [divine characteristics]."[1] The existence, nature

---

[1] It is not "Godhead" as in the AV, but *theiotes*, attributes, God's "divine nature and properties" W E Vine, *Expository Dictionary* p 329. Wuest - *theiotes*, "His divinity, namely, the fact that He is a Being having divine attributes". *Word Studies*, Ephesians and Colossians, Vol 1 p 203. His *Godhood*, for Godhead refers to His deity (*theos*) and His *Godhood* refers to His divinity (*theiotes*) (see Vincent *Word Studies* Vol III p16).

and the glory of God are evident in His work of creation. In this fact alone Christ's deity is declared, since Scripture teaches that Christ created all things. Christ must indeed be God, for how can the heavens declare God's attributes and glory if they are not the work of God Himself (Ps 19:1; Isa 40:25-26; 45:12)?[2]

What are the attributes of God?

Using the passages in Scripture which describe and distinguish God, we can, as others have shown, classify His attributes into two categories - *natural* and *moral*. His natural attributes refer to the nature of His existence. His moral attributes refer to His character. While this is a useful classification, it must never be taken to deny the truth that the natural and moral attributes of God abide in Him as an inseparable unity.

God's natural attributes are:
• Omnipotence - He is all powerful (Gen 1; Matt 19:26; Rom 1:20);
• Omniscience - He is all seeing, knowing all things (Ps 139:1-12; Ps 147:5; Matt 10:29-30);
• Omnipresence - He is all present (1 Kings 8:27; Isa 57:15; Ps 139:5);
• Self-existence - He is from everlasting to everlasting - uncreated or unoriginated (Ps 90:2; Hab 1:12).

God's moral attributes are:
• Absolute holiness (Ex 15:11; Rev 4:8);
• Absolute righteousness (Ex 9:27);
• Infinite love, light, life, grace, goodness, mercy, truth, faithfulness etc.

God is Love, Light and Life (1 Jn 1:1;5; 4:8). Love is not God, rather, God is love (1 Jn 4:8,16). To say love is God is wrong because it deifies an attribute. God is not a "divine principle" nor is He a "divine power". He is a Being who has divine principles and

---

2 Amos 4:13; Acts 4:24

possesses divine power. He is the great "I AM", the One we entreat, importune and praise as the Living God!

In what way does God possess the divine attributes?
Scripture reveals God is God because He possesses the divine attributes in a four-fold manner - entirely, equally, eternally and exclusively.

• *Entirely*: God possesses all the divine attributes in their entirety - totally. If His possession of them were to be diminished in number, then He would cease to be God. Those properties that constitute His exclusive divine nature and morality would be compromised. God is what He is because He never changes. He never changes for He is Jehovah who changes not (Mal 3:6; Ps 102:27); He is the Father of lights, with whom there is no variableness, neither shadow of turning" (Jas 1:17). Christ, too, possesses the divine attributes in their entirety (Col 1:19; 2:9).
• *Equally*: God possesses all the divine attributes equally, He never possesses any one attribute to a lesser degree than another. Neither can one divine attribute gain predominance at the expense of another. To be otherwise is to have God naturally and morally unbalanced. Scripture speaks of God's infinite love but His love is never at the expense of His infinite righteousness. Surely, if it were possible for God to abandon one iota of His righteousness to His love, it would have surely happened in Gethsemane's garden when His Son declared - "O my Father, if it be possible, let this cup pass from me: nevertheless not as I will, but as thou wilt" (Matt 26:39, 42, 44). God is indeed love, but He is also light – so He spared not His own Son (Rom 8:32). He is merciful but rejoices in the truth. Divine grace is always in perfect accord with divine righteousness. Grace reigns through righteousness (Rom 5:21). God is omnipotent, yet He cannot lie because of His absolute holiness. He is omniscient, but He is of purer eyes than to behold evil, and can not look upon iniquity (Hab 1:13). His omnipotence cannot exist apart from His omnipresence and omniscience. How can He be all-powerful if he is not all-present, all-seeing and all-knowing? The divine attributes complement each other absolutely, and are exercised by God in sublime harmony, one attribute never competing with another.

Being absolutely complementary, the divine attributes are possessed by God equally.

• *Eternally*: The divine attributes are eternal - infinite. They are eternal because God is eternal (Gen 21:33; Deut 33:27; Ps 90:2; 93:2 etc). Therefore they permanently reside in Him, as they reside permanently in His Son (Col 1:19; 2:9). The divine attributes can never *cease* to exist where they do exist. Neither can they *begin* to exist where they did not previously exist. Deity therefore can never cease to exist where it does exist, and neither can it begin to exist where it previously did not exist. The first idea denies that Christ 'lost' His deity; the second idea repudiates the notion that created beings can become Deity. Further, if one divine attribute is eternal then all the others are eternal. This must be true if all the divine attributes are absolutely complementary and abide in an eternal God entirely and equally. God is immutable. His Person, strength, mercy, righteousness, are everlasting (Ps 93:2; 100:5; 103:17; 119:142; Isa 26:4; 60:19; 63:16 etc). The attributes of God are infinite and cannot be limited by time.

• *Exclusively*: This obvious point needs to be stated because it is vital not only in determining what is of God, but what is *not* of God. "*there is* none like unto the LORD our God" (Ex 8:10; Deut 4:35; 6:4 etc). As one Being, the Father, the Son and the Holy Spirit possess the divine attributes exclusively.

Possession of all or none possessed at all

It is clear from these four truths that one divine attribute (or divine property) cannot exist independently of any other divine attribute. It is a case of the divine attributes all being possessed, or none being possessed at all.

God is what He is because He possesses the divine attributes *entirely*. Given that God is eternal, *each* divine attribute must be *eternal*. If all the divine attributes are eternal, then they must all be possessed by God *equally* and be *exclusive* to Him - for only God is eternal. Therefore, to possess one divine attribute is to possess them all - equally, eternally and exclusively. This is the essential nature of Deity according to God's Word. We will note the critical importance of this truth later in discerning Christ's deity as it is revealed in Scripture.

Is not man divine?

In view of the rampant error concerning the Person of Christ, it is understandable, though not commendable, that some Christians assert that we should speak less of Christ's divinity and more of His deity. It would be more profitable to exhort that we speak nothing of man's divinity and more of his depravity before a thrice-holy God. Man's finite and sin-tainted natural and moral attributes are in dire contrast to the infinite and holy attributes of God. Man is altogether short of the glory of God (Rom 3:23).

However, when we are redeemed in Christ, we become "partakers of [partners in] the divine nature" (2 Pet 1:4, cf 1 Pet 1:23).[3] Having been 'born again' we have the Spirit of God dwelling within us who imparts to us the new nature, one which seeks to grow according to the moral example of Christ, the divine Man. "That which is born of the Spirit is spirit" (Jn 3:6).[4]

The terms 'likeness', 'image' and 'fashion'
Likeness

Scripture never speaks of Christ being in the 'likeness of God'. Likeness is a relative term used to compare two things that display similar characteristics, but are in themselves very different. Therefore, only one who is *not* God can be said to be like God. It is meaningless to say "God is like God", because God is God. For this reason Christ is never referred to in Scripture as God's likeness. Man is not God, and we can say that man is God-like. Scripture itself declares that man as a moral being was at creation made in the "likeness of God", to the extent that man was created innocent and without evil (Gen 1:26; 5:1).[5]

We do read however, of Christ having become in the "likeness of men" (Phil 2:7) and that He came in "*the* likeness of sinful flesh" (Rom 8:3). The first statement brings two truths before us. First, it

---

[3] In this, regenerate man is exceedingly blessed above all angels (who are created beings), whose life is dependent upon the "upholding power" of the Son (Heb 1:3). They never partake of that blessed redeemed eternal life "in Him". Therefore they never partake of His divine nature that is consequent upon it.
[4] Believers in Christ have become "the righteousness of God in Him" (2 Cor 5:21). This does not mean that the believer inherently possesses Christ's righteousness - this is a divine attribute. It refers to the *standing* believers have before God in Christ.
[5] This moral likeness ceased when in Adam man fell. We read therefore that Seth was begat in Adam's likeness, not God's (Gen 5:3).

tells us that although God, Christ *became* what *men* are.[6] It is not that He simply took on the appearance of *a* man, but took up the nature of *men*. He did not take on the mode of existence of angels or some other celestial creature. Second, He is said to be in the "*likeness* of men" for though a real man He is not identical to other men. The difference is that He is both man *and* God. His deity makes Him unique among men so the Spirit can say that He is in man's "likeness". It is *because* of His deity, which the Spirit guards here, that He is said to be 'in the likeness of men'.[7] To assert that Christ lost His deity and was not God, is to say that He was just a man. If this was so, the biblical expression "in the likeness of men" used in regard to Christ becomes nonsensical.

The second statement is essentially "in likeness of the flesh of sin". The term "flesh of sin" characterises man's sinful nature since the Fall. As part of Adam's fallen race we came "in the flesh of sin". This is not so in regard to the Son of God. He was indeed born of Mary who was in the flesh of sin, but His deity and divine conception means that He came in *likeness* of the flesh of sin. His pre-incarnate deity and Virgin Birth rule out the expression that He came '*in* the flesh of sin'. He is holy, sinless, and in this sense, too, He is unlike all other men. Because He is not *in* the flesh of sin, He is said to be in its likeness, which is proved by the moral context of this passage. How can One who comes "in the flesh of sin" condemn sin in the flesh? We have here one of a number of revelations of the vital connection between Christ's holy Person and His efficacious work of reconciliation. Again the Spirit of God carefully preserves His deity and holy manhood. We may bring together the truths concerning Christ's Person given in these two expressions as follows:

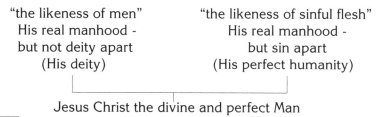

"the likeness of men"	"the likeness of sinful flesh"
His real manhood -	His real manhood -
but not deity apart	but sin apart
(His deity)	(His perfect humanity)

Jesus Christ the divine and perfect Man

[6] Not "made" in the likeness of men as in the AV.
[7] Cf Acts 14:11- "The gods are come down to us in the likeness of men." Paul and Barnabas were regarded as god-men (Mercurius and Jupiter respectively).

Image
The term "image" is applied to both man and Christ in Scripture but with a vital difference. The word itself can mean "visible representation". Man as the image of God is the visible representation of God and, so too, Christ as the image of God is the visible representation of God. But it is never said in Scripture of the Son as it is said of man that He was *made* in the image of God (Gen 1:27). Image can also mean a 'stamp' or a 'replication' of another thing. In the Hebrews Epistle Christ is spoken of as the *"express image"* of God. He is not 'godlike' as noted above, but He is the 'exact replication' of the nature and character of God (Heb 1:3), for He is God. Such a description is never attributed in Scripture to any other being, human or angelic.

Fashion
In Philippians 2 we read that Christ was 'found in fashion as a man'. The term *fashion* refers to His outward presentation, that which appears to the eyes of men. We consider this expression and the context in which it occurs in chapter 7, noting here that in no manner does it teach a limitation to Christ's real humanity.

The term 'deity'
Deity is from the Greek word *theos*, and refers to God not in regard to His qualities, but as He Himself is.[8] *Theos* speaks of God's very substance or essence, as given in Colossians 2:9. "For in Him [Christ] dwelleth all the fulness of the Godhead [*theotetos*] bodily."
There are two convergent lines of truth that Scripture insists upon in regard to Christ's deity:
• Christ possesses the attributes of God entirely, equally, eternally

---

[8] W E Vine-*Expository Dictionary* p 160. The distinction in the terms divinity and deity is also seen according to their particular use in Scripture. In two instances Paul has Deity in view (the Godhead) but prefers to use *theiotes* rather than *theos*. He does this to accommodate the way in which pagans view their gods - through their divine attributes. This he does at Mars' Hill before the philosophers (*to theion*, Acts 17:29), and in Romans 1:20 (*theiotes*), when he speaks of the invisible things of God, His eternal power and divinity. However, when he addresses the Gnostic heresy at Colossae and speaks to believers, he employs *theos*, for he wishes to bring before them the very essence of God in Christ - in whom all the fullness of the Godhead dwells bodily, for it is in such a One that all their hope and security in redemption exists. (See Wuest *Word Studies* Vol 1 Ephesians and Colossians pp 202-203).

and exclusively. *Therefore* He is God, the essence of Deity, particularly revealed through His deeds and claims recorded in the Gospel narratives.

- Christ is God, i.e., as given in John 1 and the Epistles. *Therefore* He possesses the attributes of God entirely, equally, eternally and exclusively.

Scripture declares Christ to be God whether it speaks of His "divinity" or His "deity". It is *scriptural* to refer to Christ as the "divine Man" and, in doing so, mean that He is God in all His essential nature. Modernists however, always poised to exploit a liberal interpretation of biblical grammar to serve their purpose, have sought to dilute the term "divinity". They deny the deity of Christ but are prepared to agree to His "divinity", thereby imparting to the term a lesser worth than accorded to it in Scripture. They admit and appeal to the exemplary moral qualities of Christ, but are not prepared to acknowledge Him being truly God.

Five vital truths concerning the Person of Christ

1. *The eternity of Christ.* Christ's deity means that He is *eternal*, and therefore He existed before time and all creation and He is equal with God in essence and power (Jn 1:1; Mic 5:2 etc). It means, too, that He was never part of creation. He is the Creator (Jn 1:3; Col 1:16; Heb 1:2-3 etc). [9]

2. *The humanity of Christ.* Christ is the "divine Man". The Incarnation refers to God *becoming* man.[10] The Virgin Birth tells us *how* the Incarnation took place. The Second Person of the Trinity became something that He was not previously. He did not become a new Person, only the manner of His prior existence altered. Deity took on humanity. Christ's humanity is *real*, He does not have a 'phantom' body. God took part of flesh and blood (Heb 2:14). The Fourth Gospel makes it abundantly clear that the Word *became* flesh that speaks of *incarnation*, not "inhabitation". He did not come "into flesh" (Jn 1:14; 2 Jn 7). Christ is not God inhabiting a host human

---

[9] The expression "equal with God" used here and throughout this volume in regard to Christ, has its basis in Scripture (Jn 5:18; Phil 2:6 etc). Christ is "equal" with God in regard to what makes God what He is.

[10] The Incarnation is not a Christophany or Theophany - God taking on the *appearance* of a man (Gen 28:13-15 cf Gen 31:13; Gen 48; etc). It is God taking on actual humanity.

body. The Lord explicitly declared His real humanity - "A spirit hath not flesh and bones, as ye see me have" (Lk 24:39). Though conceived by the Holy Ghost He was born naturally, and He manifested the marks of humanity - sin apart. Being truly man, He comprises body, soul and spirit - His *body* (Jn 4:7; 19:28; Heb 10:5;10 etc); His *soul* (Matt 26:38; Jn 11:35 etc); His *spirit* (Mk 2:8; Lk 23:46).

3. *The immutability of Christ.* Christ's deity means that He cannot cease to be Deity. He possesses the divine attributes entirely, equally, eternally and exclusively. He is therefore unceasingly the divine perfect Man.

4. *The unity of Christ.* Christ is both God and man, not in the sense of two separate natures side by side, but as one essential unity. The two natures are distinguishable yet combined perfectly in an inseparable oneness. Scripture never reveals Him as "part God" and "part man", acting in some instances only as God and in others only as man. If Christ could act as man apart from His deity, then it is possible for Him to act apart from the divine attribute of absolute holiness. This casts doubt on what He said and did, for when did he act apart from absolute holiness? On some occasions Scripture *focuses* upon Christ's humanity (Jn 11:35). On other occasions His deity is the dominant view (Jn 11:43). In such instances it is a matter of 'prominence' in one nature, not the 'predominance' of it. He is revealed in Scripture as the "undivided" divine Person.

5. *The purity of Christ.* His manhood is perfect, spotless and undefiled. His divine nature meant that sin was not just abhorrent, but that it found no response within Him. "The prince of this world cometh, and hath nothing in me" (Jn 14:30). He did not come by the way of Adam's generation. He came through divine conception as the 'seed of the woman'. "*That* Holy thing which shall be born of thee" (Lk 1:35; Matt 1:18, 20). His pre-incarnate and abiding deity imparts *absolute* and *abiding* moral perfection to Him.

The Trinity
The term "Trinity"[11]

This term was adopted by the early church to *represent* the biblical

---

[11] The *term* "Trinity" is not found in Scripture. But this does not mean that the *teaching* of One Being comprising three Persons is not revealed in Scripture. The term "incarnation" is not found in Scripture, but it well represents the biblical teaching in regard to the birth of Christ.

revelation of the Godhead as One Being yet Three Persons. It does not explain it. No single or multiple of words can do so. Yet, ingenious notions have been advanced to do this very thing – the three states of water; the three corners of a triangle, and the three parts of an egg, number among many. All attempts stumble, for to whom shall we liken God who sits upon the circle of the earth? (Isa 40:18-22). Man is required to accept by faith God's Triune Being revealed in Scripture.

The doctrine

Though the doctrine of the Trinity is not our prime focus, it is important to give some attention to it here because of its centrality to true Christianity. If Christ's deity is denied, the doctrine of the Trinity is also denied.[12]

The plurality of Persons within the Godhead is clearly given in the OT. For instance, the frequently used word for God in the OT, is on occasions given in the plural - *Elohim*, but associated with the verb in the singular, indicating a plurality of Persons yet the oneness of God. These instances intimate the distinction yet the equality of the Persons within the Godhead. In Genesis 1:1 we have "In the beginning God [plural] created [singular] the heaven and the earth", which speaks of the plurality of Persons within the Godhead exercising unity in purpose. "As long as the passage … [Gen 1:26] stands on the first page of the Bible, the believer in the Trinity has the right to turn to it as a proof that the Plurality in the Godhead is a very different thing from Polytheism, and as an indication that the frequent assertions of the divine Unity are not inconsistent with the belief that the Father is God, the Son is God, and the Holy Ghost is God."[13] (cf Gen 3:22; 11:7; Isa 6:8). In Deuteronomy 6:4 the Lord [Jehovah] is declared to be "one" Lord. The word "one" - *echad*, means a compound unity, one but a company of more than one. *Echad* emphasises unity/oneness, but recognizes diversity within that oneness.[14] Adam and Eve were two distinct persons yet they were "one" (*echad*, Gen 2:24).[15]

---

[12] The deity of Christ is a necessary but not sufficient truth in regard to the doctrine that God is a *Triunity* i.e. that the Godhead comprises *three* Persons.

[13] Girdlestone *"Synonyms"*, p 22.

[14] See Strong - *Hebrew and Aramaic Dictionary*.

[15] In contrast the word *yachid* refers to "only one" – solitary (Gen 22:2, 12 etc). W E Vine *Expository Dictionary* p 140. God is the only God – the only *one* God, besides Him there is no other (cf Christ as the only Begotten Son of God).

These examples are a few among many embryonic references to the Trinity in the Bible. The complete revelation of the Trinity had to wait the coming of God Himself among men. The Incarnation and the personal ministry of Christ brought the revelation of the Trinity into its radiant and blessed maturity. In the NT we have the *One Being* - God, explicitly revealed as three distinct *Persons*, the *Father*, the *Son* and the *Holy Spirit*, each possessing their own *identity*. God is One yet He is Three - Three in One and One in Three. They "permeate each other" as said by another. Each Person exercises a distinct *responsibility*, which is never exercised without absolute *unity* and *harmony* between Them. Christ Himself teaches this very thing. For instance, His disciples are exhorted to go forth, to teach and to baptise in (not into) the "name of the Father, and of the Son, and of the Holy Ghost" (Matt 28:19). Here the word "name" is singular, declaring one Being, yet there are three distinct Persons. The distinction is given in that each Person is identified by a conjunction and the definite article. It is not Tritheism - three separate Persons, which would be implied if it were "in the *names* of...". Tritheism denies the 'oneness' of God revealed in Scripture. Neither is it Sabellianism - three manifestations of the one God, which would be suggested if it were "in the name of the Father, Son and Holy Spirit".

Any honest reading of Scripture will show that the Father is revealed as God, and so, too, the Son and the Spirit are revealed as God. It will also show that there is but one God. These two truths cannot be reconciled apart from the existence of One God yet three Persons within the Godhead, all of whom are equal in divine essence.

The attributes, prerogative and glory of God
The three marks of deity
There are three aspects of God's being revealed in Scripture which we may refer to as the 'three marks of deity':
- God's attributes — determine what only God *can* do
- God's prerogative — defines what only God can *choose* to do
- God's glory — declares what only God *has done*

There are certain things that only God can do because of His exclusive natural and moral attributes. God's prerogative speaks of those things which only He can choose to do because He possesses those exclusive attributes. Only He can exercise divine will. God's glory we may define as the revelation of His character or "reputation", seen through what He, as God has done. His glory is exclusive to Himself because it depends upon what only He as God can do and upon what only He as God has chosen to do. Accordingly, the glory of God, the wonder and majesty of His Being, can be viewed in terms of His exclusive *works*, His -

- Creatorial glory   - His reputation as *Creator* of all things
- Redemptive glory   - His reputation as the *Redeemer* of men
- Judicial glory   - His reputation as the *Judge* of all things[16]

There is also however, His unique personal glory - that which is in regard to His essential Being - who and what He *is*!

The three marks of deity are interdependent
Consider the divine work of creation. The glory of the Creator can only be seen in the One who is able to create - the One who indeed did create! Here God Himself declares the interdependence between the three marks of deity. "To whom then will ye liken me, or shall I be equal?" saith the Holy One – *His exclusive divine attributes*; "Lift up your eyes on high, and behold who hath created these *things*, that bringeth out their host by number: he calleth them all by names by the greatness of his might" - *His exclusive divine prerogative*; "for that *he is* strong in power; not one faileth" – *His exclusive divine glory* (Isa 40:25-26).

In this instance we also have the personal glory of God inextricably linked to His divine attributes and prerogative. Who can create life from nothing and choose to do so except One who is Himself uncreated and eternal? When the psalmist proclaims that the heavens declare the glory of God, he is surely referring to God's personal glory as much as he is referring to His creatorial

---

[16] There are particular facets of the glory of Christ such as His glory as the Son of man, the Son of God, the Head of the Church, the Second man and as our Great High Priest. In addition, there is the particular glory of Christ in resurrection that, as the Son, He receives from the Father (Jn 17:22-23 cf 1 Pet 1:21), God, that raised him up from the dead, and gave him glory in victory.

glory. And, speaking of His personal glory, who can reveal and choose to reveal Himself as the "I AM", save One who is uncreated?

Divine redemption also reveals the interdependence between the three marks of deity. Here, too, man must acknowledge the "finger of God" (Ex 8:19), for who can redeem man and execute perfect judgement except One whose prerogative is based upon the divine attribute of absolute holiness. Who is like unto thee - glorious in power and holiness? (Ex 15).

In the NT, notable examples of the inextricable interdependence of the three marks of deity are seen in Christ - when He turned water into wine, healed the leper and raised Lazarus. Paul uses the inextricable interdependence between the three marks of deity when he defends the deity of Christ in the face of Gnostic error, presenting Him as the Creator of all things (Col 1:16-17). These and many other examples in Scripture reveal the interdependence between the divine attributes, divine prerogative and the glory of God. We can therefore refer to them as *'the three interdependent marks of deity'*.

The significance of this interdependence

It is impossible to possess one mark of deity without possessing the other two marks of deity. All marks must be possessed or none at all can be possessed. For instance, to create is to exercise the divine prerogative to create, which can only be done by One who possess the attributes of God that enable the act of creation. In turn, the act of creation manifests the glory of the One who has chosen to create. Approach creation from the aspect of divine glory and we have the same inextricable link. To possess and manifest the glory of the Creator, One must have exercised the prerogative to create, which can only be possible if One had the divine natural attributes that enable creation. Consider, too, divine redemption. The needed and acceptable sacrifice for sin must be absolutely holy. Only God Himself can be that perfect Sacrifice because He only is absolutely holy. The putting and taking away of sin is therefore a divine prerogative that God exercised through the Second Person of the Trinity. God the Son came down to put away sin by the sacrifice of Himself, and in so doing He revealed His exclusive divine redemptive glory.

Ascertaining Christ's deity from Scripture

When faced with a study of Christ's person in Scripture, many younger Christians express difficulty in knowing where to begin, while others wrongly regard the matter as being too profound and best left to theologians. The interdependence between the three marks of deity is a useful vantage point from which to view and begin a study of the biblical revelation of Christ's deity. It will enable us to apprehend something of the profound extent to which His deity pervades Scripture.

Distinguishing deity

If a Person possesses the attributes of God, exercises the prerogatives of God and manifests the glory of God, then that Person is God - Deity. We may illustrate this interdependence.[17]

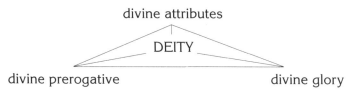

The Son of God came to earth to declare God to man. To accomplish this, He had to manifest the attributes of God, exercise the prerogatives of God and display the glory of God.

Discerning deity

Some professing Christians believe that Christ was never God. Those of the Kenosis persuasion believe He was God but there was a time when He ceased to be God. On the other hand, Gnosticism and New Age theology assert that deity can exist in degrees - Christ was an emanation from God. The task before us therefore, is not simply to determine if Scripture reveals Christ to be God, but whether or not it reveals Him to be God in His *undiminished* and *unceasing* deity. There are, of course, specific passages of Scripture that categorically declare Christ's everlasting deity, which we examine later. But in what follows, we formulate a biblically validated rule that will help us to identify the many other

---

[17] This is *not* an attempt to explain Deity. It is only an illustration of the connection between the three marks that identify it.

occasions in the Word of God, particularly in the Gospels, where Christ's undiminished and unceasing deity is revealed. This will help us to corroborate those specific passages in the Word of God that declare His everlasting deity, and provide further repudiation of the notions that He was never God or that He ever became less than God.

Recall that to possess just *one* divine attribute is to possess them all - equally, eternally and exclusively, which speaks of the undiminished and unceasing nature of Deity. Therefore, wherever Christ is shown in Scripture to possess any *one* of the divine attributes, there we have a revelation of His undiminished and unceasing deity. This line of inquiry can be illustrated as follows.

the biblical *observation* - of Christ possessing *a* divine attribute.

the biblical *conclusion* - that Christ therefore possesses *all* the divine attributes - *equally, eternally* and *exclusively.*

the biblical *revelation* - of Christ's *undiminished* and *unceasing* deity.

The interdependence between the marks of deity means we can apply this line of inquiry each time Scripture reveals Christ exercising (or claiming) a divine prerogative, or manifesting the glory of God. For instance, when Scripture reveals Christ exercising a prerogative of God, it also confirms His possession of the divine attributes, which, of course, He must possess entirely, equally, eternally and exclusively. In this case we trace His possession of the divine attributes and the undiminished and unceasing deity it confers upon Him, from a revelation of His divine prerogative. We will arrive at the same conclusion concerning His undiminished and unceasing deity if we begin with a recorded revelation of His divine glory, as illustrated below.

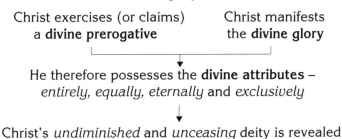

Christ exercises (or claims)   Christ manifests
a **divine prerogative**   the **divine glory**

He therefore possesses the **divine attributes** –
entirely, equally, eternally and *exclusively*

Christ's *undiminished* and *unceasing* deity is revealed

These principles can be combined into a simple rule, which will enable us to readily identify the occasions in Scripture where the undiminished and unceasing deity of Christ is revealed.

Any one divine attribute or any one mark of deity revealed in Christ, is a necessary and a sufficient revelation of His undiminished and unceasing deity.

Is this not true of the Father and of the Holy Spirit? Applying this rule means that whenever we find in Scripture a divine attribute possessed by Christ, His exercise of or claim to a divine prerogative, or a manifestation of divine glory by Him, whether in prophecy, in title and name, in doctrine or in His deeds, we have an emphatic scriptural repudiation of modernism that prefers His "divinity" to His deity; of Gnosticism and its contemporary offspring that asserts He is a diluted emanation from God; of Kenoticism that teaches He emptied Himself of His deity; of the teaching that He was "a god", and of all the false doctrines that deny His perpetual perfect humanity. This rule will help us to identify and enjoy the fragrant and variegated testimony of Christ's undiminished and unceasing deity which permeates the Word of God - the very breath of the Spirit of truth.[18] If Christ is God at any one moment of time, which Scripture reveals is true, then He is God before and after all time.

---

[18] This rule suggests another line of enquiry that will enrich our knowledge and appreciation of the Lord's Person. For instance, when we come across an occasion where Christ's glory is given - in His titles, His words or His works, it will prompt us to ascertain from Scripture the divine attributes and prerogatives particularly associated with it. One such instance is John 1:14.

CHAPTER 3

Christ's Deity Revealed in the Gospel Narratives

The Gospel narratives in their pure and varied historical accounts, unfold a particularly blessed revelation of Jesus of Nazareth. The Spirit of truth invites us to draw near to the Man and listen to His words for 'never man spoke like this man'. We are to observe His marvellous deeds, for with His words they compose a sacred portrait of His deity and perfect humanity. We are obliged to note the vibrant manifestation of His divine attributes, divine prerogatives and divine glory as He walked as a man among men, ever commanding, challenging and convicting their hearts according to immanent divine grace and truth. And, having this revelation before us, we are well placed to appreciate the convergent doctrine concerning His divine Person declared in the Epistles.

The line of investigation
A rule of methodology
We are interested in what the Gospels have to say regarding the *undiminished* and *unceasing* deity of Christ. To this end we will apply the rule stated before - *any one divine attribute or any one mark of deity revealed in Christ, is a necessary and a sufficient revelation of His undiminished and unceasing deity.*

The divine prerogative - a clarification
It is not our task to examine why certain matters fall within God's prerogative, although we will inevitably see something of this in the earthly ministry of the Son of God. The Jews, through their

history and possession of the Holy Oracles, had a sound knowledge of the prerogatives that belonged to God. It was this knowledge that brought them into headlong conflict with Christ when He claimed those prerogatives for Himself.

To possess the prerogatives of God is a mark of deity. Where the Lord exercised a divine prerogative, we have a tangible revelation of His deity. In some instances however, divine prerogatives are *claimed* by Him but have no recorded demonstration, such as those relating to His divine sovereignty in future judgement, or His claim to authority over the Sabbath. Speaking generally, a mere *claim* to possess a divine prerogative by itself, can never be proof of deity. Scripture warns of false prophets who will come professing to be God. However, the moral integrity of the person who makes the claim bears on its truth. When we begin with the undeniable truth of Christ's moral perfection, we are bound to accept all that He says, even the claims He makes to own the prerogatives of God. The alternative is to cast Him as a charlatan. Nevertheless our task involves noting the occasions in Scripture where Christ *demonstrated* and *claimed* divine prerogative.

A rule of morality

It can never be man's task to prove the moral purity of Christ. His moral perfection was affirmed at the highest level of approbation. The Father declared it at His baptism (Matt 3:17) and at His transfiguration (Mk 9:7, cf Jn 5:37; Phil 2:9). His present place at God's right hand is an emphatic vindication of all that He did and claimed concerning Himself (Acts 2:32-33; Rom 6:4; Heb 1:3; 10:12 etc). Any credible apologetic study concerning Christ's person however, must embrace His moral virtue as a cardinal tenet. There is a moral principle given by James that will assist us to mark (not to prove) Christ's moral perfection: "To him that knoweth to do good, and doeth *it* not, to him it is sin" (Jas 4:17). This principle will bring into relief the moral legitimacy of Christ's claims and deeds. It will emphasise the doctrinal importance of His claims and challenge those who deny His deity yet avow His moral perfection. In its plain meaning, this moral principle refers to "sins of omission" - knowing what is good and proper yet refusing to do it is wilful deceit! Can it be said of Jesus of Nazareth that He knew to do good, but did not do it? Was He an imperfect man who offended in word (Jas 3:2)?

Christ-centred narratives

Christ's identity is integral to the Gospel narratives, *historically, contemporarily, prophetically* and *theologically*. They reveal that God, the Eternal Son, stepped into time and history; that He walked in fashion as a man to declare the Father's glory before men; that His coming among men was the fulfilment of the prophecies concerning the Messiah and One who is the Light to lighten the Gentiles (Isa 49:6; Acts 13:47). The Gospels reveal Jesus of Nazareth as the Divine Light shining in darkness, the Living Beacon who radiated the glory of God to the world.

Christ's person gives the Gospel narratives their distinctive divine character. They record Him as One who continuously drew attention to His divine identity, who frequently challenged others in regard to it. He was One greater than the temple (Matt 12:6); One greater than Jonas (Matt 12:41) and One greater than Solomon (Matt 12:42). "Whom say ye that I am?" (Matt 16:15); "What think ye of Christ? whose son is he?" (Matt 22:42); He brought the matter of His identity into intense focus through His miracles (Jn 20:30-31). He enjoined all men to place absolute dependence upon *His* words, words which He claimed to be of ultimate authority (Matt 24:35; cf Jn 5:46; 12:48; 14:23; 15:7). He required a confession of His identity from His disciples, from the Jews and their leaders, and from the Gentiles. To what purpose? He wanted all to acknowledge who He was, but more, to *believe* in Him because of who He was - *very God*, for in His deity and perfect humanity lie the hope and salvation of man.

The centrality of Christ in the Gospels is in accord with His centrality in regard to the entire Word of God. The Jews rightly believed Jehovah to be the sole object of biblical revelation, but Christ unreservedly declared that the Scriptures "testify of me" (Jn 5:39 cf Lk 24:27), teaching that He and Jehovah are One, both being the principal object of biblical revelation.

All four Gospels

Our study involves all four Gospels and we particularly note the categorical revelation in the three Synoptic Gospels of the deity of Christ. This is evident in the Lord's possession and exercise of the divine attributes and prerogatives recorded within them (Matthew, Mark, Luke). The marks of deity revealed in Christ in each Gospel, is proof positive against the claim that the deity of Christ is merely 'implicit' in the Synoptics, and is only revealed explicitly in the fourth Gospel (where we acknowledge it is particularly celebrated and declared). The revelation of Christ's deity in the Gospels is also an emphatic repudiation of the claim that His deity revealed in the Epistles is mere accumulation of idealised impressions of the Gospel accounts.

Having considered these preliminary matters, we can now study the Gospel narratives with a defined purpose. In terms of chronology and content it would be appropriate to begin with Christ's birth; but this subject is in chapter 8, where we specifically consider His virgin birth in regard to His person. So now we will look at thirteen examples in the Gospels where Christ *demonstrated* and *claimed* divine prerogative.

1. Christ as Jehovah Ropheca (my Healer)
Mark 1:40-45 (Matt 8; cf Luke 4)

40. And there came a leper to him, beseeching him, and kneeling down to him, and saying unto him, "If thou wilt, thou canst make me clean."

41. And Jesus, moved with compassion, put forth *his* hand, *and* touched him, and saith unto him, "I will; be thou clean."

42. And as soon as he had spoken, immediately the leprosy departed from him, and he was cleansed.

43. And he straitly charged him, *and* forthwith sent him away;

44. And saith unto him, "See thou say nothing to any man: but go thy way, shew thyself to the priest, and offer for thy cleansing those things which Moses commanded, for a testimony unto them.

45. But he went out, *and* began to publish *it* much, and to blaze abroad the matter, insomuch that Jesus could no more openly enter into *the* city, but was without in desert places: and they came to him from every quarter.

To identify the purpose and appreciate the profound significance of this miracle, we must understand the background against which it is performed. It was notable historically because this was the first known occasion of a Jew being cured of leprosy since the law of leprosy was given centuries earlier. It was morally significant in that leprosy was regarded as divine judgement against sin (Miriam and Uzziah, Num 12; 2 Chron 26). For this reason leprosy was referred to as "the finger of God" or "the stroke", and it had no remedy in Jewish medicine. The moral-dispensational significance is seen in that the leper's uncleanness and separation represented the spiritual condition of God's chosen people at that time. Of deepest significance is the theological context. Leprosy had no cure among men.[1] If a person was cured of leprosy, it was a sign that God in sovereign grace and divine power had done the healing. This was acknowledged by the King of Israel when he was asked to cure the leprous Naaman: "And it came to pass, when the king of Israel had read the letter, that he rent his clothes, and said, *Am I God, to kill and to make alive, that this man doth send unto me to recover a man of his leprosy?"* (2 Kings 5:7).

The man kneeling before Christ was "full of leprosy", but his yielded heart barred any doubt that Christ could heal him. In an expression of pure faith, the helpless leper never propositioned Christ's power but pleaded His divine prerogative - "if thou wilt, thou canst...". This Christ did by exercising His *own* divine will and through His *own* divine power (v.40-41). Matthew tells us the healed leper worshipped the Lord, worship that was accepted by Him for He was God.

Here, then, is the divine intent and deep significance of this miracle. It is a clear demonstration of the particular manner in which Christ revealed His deity before men, in that He declared it within the historical, prophetical and theological framework of the OT. The Jewish leper was healed by Christ as a "testimony unto them" – the Jews, that He was *Jehovah Ropheca*, who had moved in divine power and prerogative; that He was *Emmanuel*, God with us, the divine *Messiah* who had come as prophesied to restore to God a separated and disobedient people.

This miracle reveals that Jesus of Nazareth possessed the marks of deity. He chose to do and did what only God could do, thereby manifesting His divine glory. Luke records the Lord healing another ten lepers, each one is an emphatic revelation of His undiminished

---

[1] The Levitical laws had nothing whatsoever to do with curing the leper. They related to ceremonial cleansing, which was to demonstrate that the cured person was fit to re-enter society. Accordingly, when He had healed the leper, the Lord commanded the man to do what the law required - to go to the priest and be declared clean.

and unceasing deity, of His divine power, prerogative and glory (Lk 17:11-19). But, like so many today, the Jews were blinded in their unbelief in regard to His divine Majesty.

The Miracles of Christ - manifestations of deity
Christ's deity was pivotal to His earthly ministry concerning the kingdom of God, Israel and the gospel of eternal life to all men. Many of His miracles therefore were performed to reveal and convict men that He was God – Emmanuel, God with us. Who but the Divine Physician could heal the "sick unto death" with a word or a touch? Only the word of the Divine Judge could cause the predacious mob to fall backwards, or cause the fig tree to wither and dry up from its roots. Only the Omnipotent Creator could still the wind and the waves. Who but divine Omniscience could see into the heart of a demoniac and free him from spiritual bondage? Who except the divine Life had the authority and power to Himself raise the dead?

Consider again the leper's healing and how it typified the Lord's miracles, revealing His possession and exercise of the attributes of God. The miracles performed by the prophets and apostles were done in the permissive will of God, through the power of God and in God's name – even the name of Christ! The miraculous power involved was not inherent in these men. Peter makes this clear when he healed the lame man at the gate Beautiful. "Ye men of Israel, why marvel ye at this? or why look ye so earnestly on us, as though by our own power or holiness we had made this man to walk?" (Acts 3:12). If Peter claimed to have performed this miracle himself, he would be claiming to possess the attributes of God. He could not, of course, claim such a thing, but Christ did! His miracles were done in His own name, through His own power and according to His permissive will: "I will" (Mk 1:41); "I charge thee" (Mk 9:25); "I say unto thee, Arise" (Lk 7:14); "I will come and heal him" (Matt 8:7); "Believe ye that I am able to do this?" (Matt 9:28). Each authoritative utterance is a sacred witness to His possession of the divine attributes - the ability to do what only God can do; His divine prerogative - to do what only God can choose to do; His divine glory - the result of having done what only God could have done, revealing His undiminished and unceasing deity.

2. Christ as Saviour-God
Mark 2:1-12 (Luke 5:17-20)

1. And again he entered into Capernaum after *some* days; and it was noised that he was in the house.

2. And straightway many were gathered together, insomuch that there was no room to receive *them*, no, not so much as about the door: and he preached the word unto them.

3. And they come unto him, bringing one sick of *the* palsy, which was borne of four.

4. And when they could not come nigh unto him for the press, they uncovered the roof where he was: and when they had broken *it* up, they let down the bed wherein the sick of the palsy lay.

5. When Jesus saw their faith, he said unto the sick of *the* palsy, "Son, thy sins be forgiven thee."

6. But there were certain of the scribes sitting there, and reasoning in their hearts,

7. "Why doth this *man* thus speak blasphemies? who can forgive sins but God only?"

8. And immediately when Jesus perceived in his spirit that they so reasoned within themselves, he said unto them, "Why reason ye these things in your hearts?

9. Whether is it easier to say to the sick of the palsy, 'Thy sins be forgiven thee;' or to say, 'Arise, and take up thy bed, and walk?'

10. But that ye may know that the Son of man hath power on earth to forgive sins, (he saith to the sick of the palsy,)

11. "I say unto thee, Arise, and take up thy bed, and go thy way into thine house."

12. And immediately he arose, took up the bed, and went forth before *them* all; insomuch that they were all amazed, and glorified God, saying, "We never saw it on this fashion."

Again the Lord seeks to reveal His messianic deity through a miracle performed within the theological context of the OT. What the previous miracle gave in type - cleansing from sin, is now demonstrated in reality. Here it is not "Who can cure leprosy save God only?" It is "Who can forgive sins save God only?" (v.7; Ps 32:1-5; 51:1-2).

The Jewish religious leaders rightly believed that only God can forgive sins. It was God who held the nation accountable for sin, as seen in the OT economy of sacrifices and offerings. David's confession taught them that sin is against God even when transgressing against man - "Against thee, thee only, have I sinned, and done *this* evil in thy sight" (Ps 51:3-4; Lk 15:21; cf Jer 31:34). Sin is against God because God is man's Creator and He is absolutely holy. Christ is man's Creator and He also possesses the divine attribute of absolute holiness. Paul declares that sin is against Christ (1 Cor 8:12). The Jews knew from the Holy Oracles, that God has the exclusive authority to forgive sins because God is the only One who is absolutely holy. When therefore the Lord claimed authority to forgive this man's sins, He was claiming to possess the attribute of divine holiness and to possess the associated divine prerogative to forgive sins.[2] Little wonder why the Jews considered His words blasphemous.[3]

Yet, knowing why He was being accused of blasphemy, the Lord never withdrew or tempered His claim to possess the prerogative to forgive sins. Indeed, He proceeded to confirm His undiminished and unceasing deity by healing the man, His words also justifying His claim to it. Which authority is easier to claim, "to say to the sick of the palsy, '*Thy* sins be forgiven thee', or to say, 'Arise, and take up thy bed, and walk'?" Both actions fall exclusively within the prerogative of God and call upon His divine attributes. By demonstrating the latter He proved His possession of the former.

There is a further revelation of Christ's undiminished and unceasing deity here, in that He knew the thoughts and perceived the inner reasoning of the scribes.[4] This is the preserve of Omniscient Deity, "for thou [Jehovah], *even* thou only, knowest the hearts of all the children of men" (1 Kings 8:39). The leper was healed "for a testimony unto them". Here the healing was done "that ye may know" (Mk 2:10). Know what? It was that the Son of Man had authority on earth to forgive sins and He is God. This divine title is associated with divine universal authority (Dan

---

[2] The word "power" in the AV (v.10) is "authority" - the *right* to forgive sins.
[3] Cf John 20:23. Here the Lord bestows to the disciples (and to all who minister the Gospel) the authority of assuring others that their sins are forgiven, providing of course that they believe in the gospel of Christ, which is the "power of God unto salvation" (Rom 1:16). It can never be, as some assert, that certain men have the authority to forgive sins. The fact that the Lord did not in any way deny the doctrine that only God can forgive sins, is proof of His claim to deity and also that He cannot mean, in John 20, that His disciples in themselves possessed such authority (so, too, Matt 16:19; 18:18).
[4] The Synoptic accounts carefully avoid the notion that the Lord "read their faces" and therefore He made an assumption about their thoughts. He *knew* the *thoughts* of the scribes. He also *understood* the *reasoning* in their hearts.

7). Here again it was Emmanuel, "God with us", but the conceit of the Jews blinded them to the reality of it.

3. Christ as God Jehovah - the Lord of the Sabbath
Mark 2:23-28
23. And it came to pass, that he went through the corn fields on the sabbath *day*; and his disciples began, as they went, to pluck the ears of corn.
24. And the Pharisees said unto him, "Behold, why do they on the sabbath day that which is not lawful?"
25. And he said unto them, "Have ye never read what David did, when he had need, and was an hungred, he, and they that were with him?
26. How he went into the house of God in the days of Abiathar the high priest, and did eat the shewbread, which is not lawful to eat but for the priests, and gave also to them which were with him?"
27. And he said unto them, "The sabbath was made for man, and not man for the sabbath:
28. Therefore the Son of man is Lord also of the sabbath."
Matthew 12:5-8
5. "Or have ye not read in the law, how that on the sabbath *days* the priests in the temple profane the sabbath, and are blameless?
6. But I say unto you, That in this place is *one* greater than the temple.
7. But if ye had known what *this* meaneth, I will have mercy, and not sacrifice, ye would not have condemned the guiltless.
8. For the Son of man is Lord even of the sabbath *day*."

On this summer's day the Lord and His disciples walked through the cornfields. To satisfy their hunger, the disciples plucked the wholesome ears and rubbed them between their hands separating the grain from the chaff. It was the Sabbath, and the ever-vigilant Pharisees censured the Lord for allowing His disciples to act in such a manner, and in their judgement to desecrate this holy day.

Through their stony self-righteousness, these Jewish leaders had misinterpreted the divine intent of the law of the Sabbath. The Sabbath was no longer a blessed "day of rest", it had become a day of burden. The Lord advanced several arguments in reply to their censure, firstly to repudiate the self-righteous traditions they had appended to the Sabbath law.[5] However, He raised the following

---

[5] *patriarchal*: they should look to the spirit of the law rather than to its letter, as seen through the physical need of their revered patriarch, king David, who ate of the sacred shewbread: *priestly*: they should remember a "proper" requirement of the Law - the holy service of Israel's priests on the Sabbath: *preceptive*: they must learn the moral superiority of mercy over sacrifice.

matters to bring His deity into view, since they spoke of His divine prerogative over the Sabbath:

- *prophetical*: the reference to Himself as the Messiah (Matt 12:6-7);
- *prescriptive*: His ruling concerning the purpose of the Sabbath "the Sabbath was made for man, and not man for the Sabbath" (Mk 2:27 etc);
- *presidential*: His claim to be Lord of the Sabbath (Mk 2:28; Matt 12:8; Lk 6:5).

The institution of the Sabbath was God's prerogative in creation; its order was His prerogative in legislation. The Day was instituted and ordained by God and its holiness inscribed by the "finger of God" (Ex 31:18). It was God's sole possession - "my sabbaths" (Lev 19:3). The Lord clearly spoke as *the* One who instituted the Sabbath and who had authority over its order. In this He claimed equality with God, which He did as the Son of man, who, as we noted, is One who possess divine universal authority. He is Lord *also* of the Sabbath (Mk 2:28).

The Lord claimed this same divine authority when He healed the woman with a spirit of infirmity (Lk 13). Again He spoke as One having authority over divine law (vv.15-17), an authority He repeatedly declared through His words, "but I say unto you" (Matt 5:21-44). Jehovah had expressly forbidden any "addition or diminishing" of His commandment (Deut 4:2). Clearly, Jesus of Nazareth was not bound by such an interdiction, for He is the Divine One.

Other Sabbath healings did nothing to assuage the growing rancour against Him. In fact it fuelled the desire to destroy Him (Matt 12:14). Yet, He never retreated from or changed His claims. Was it a case of callous indifference to the truth? Did He, through whom came grace and truth, know to do good but did it not (Jn 1:17)?

4. Christ as the God of life
Luke 7:11-16

11. And it came to pass the day after, that he went into a city called Nain; and many of his disciples went with him, and much people.

12. Now when he came nigh to the gate of the city, behold, there was a dead man carried out, the only son of his mother, and she was a widow: and much people of the city was with her.

13. And when the Lord saw her, he had compassion on her, and said unto her, "Weep not".
14. And he came and touched the bier: and they that bare *him* stood still. And he said, "Young man, I say unto thee, Arise."
15. And he that was dead sat up, and began to speak. And he delivered him to his mother.
16. And there came a fear on all: and they glorified God, saying, That a great prophet is risen up among us; and, That God hath visited his people.

This instance recorded only by Luke, is one of three where the Lord raised the dead. It appears to be the first of such momentous occasions, followed by the raising of Jarius' daughter and of Lazarus. Some nine hundred years had passed since the hand of God moved in such divine grace and power among men.[6]

What moved the Lord to go to Nain? There was no guiding vision or beseeching messenger. In His omniscience He saw the grieving widow in that procession of death. On arrival His first words were authoritative yet consoling, "Weep not!" He then commanded the dead son - "Young man, I say unto thee, Arise". The strong man's house was spoiled and death released its captive. Who was this Emancipator? He was Jesus of Nazareth, the Resurrection and the Life in all His undiminished and unceasing deity. He exercised His divine attributes and His prerogative over life and death, and manifested the glory of God. His omniscience is complemented by His omnipotence, for He *Himself* commands death to release its prey - *"I say unto thee, Arise"*. Elijah, Elisha and Peter could only prostrate their hearts in intercession unto God for those taken in death.

5. Christ the Son as the Father's equal
John 5
1. After this there was a feast of the Jews; and Jesus went up to Jerusalem.
2. Now there is at Jerusalem by the sheep *market* a pool, which is called in the Hebrew tongue Bethesda, having five porches.
3. In these lay a great multitude of impotent folk, of blind, halt, withered, waiting for the moving of the water.
4. For an angel went down at a certain season into the pool, and troubled the water: whosoever then first after the troubling of the water stepped in was made whole of whatsoever disease he had.

---

[6] The son of the widow of Zarephath (1 Kings 17:20-21) and the Shunammite's son (2 Kings 4:34-35;).

5. And a certain man was there, which had an infirmity thirty and eight years.

6. When Jesus saw him lie, and knew that he had been now a long time *in that case*, he saith unto him, "Wilt thou be made whole?"

7. The impotent man answered him, "Sir, I have no man, when the water is troubled, to put me into the pool: but while I am coming, another steppeth down before me."

8. Jesus saith unto him, "Rise, take up thy bed, and walk."

9. And immediately the man was made whole, and took up his bed, and walked: and on the same day was *the* sabbath.

10. The Jews therefore said unto him that was cured, "It is *the* sabbath *day*: it is not lawful for thee to carry *thy* bed."

11. He answered them, "He that made me whole, the same said unto me, 'Take up thy bed, and walk'."

12. Then asked they him, "What man is that which said unto thee, Take up thy bed, and walk?"

13. And he that was healed wist not who it was: for Jesus had conveyed himself away, a multitude being in *that* place.

14. Afterward Jesus findeth him in the temple, and said unto him, "Behold, thou art made whole: sin no more, lest a worse thing come unto thee."

15. The man departed, and told the Jews that it was Jesus, which had made him whole.

16. And therefore did the Jews persecute Jesus, and sought to slay him, because he had done these things on *the* sabbath *day*.

17. But Jesus answered them, "My Father worketh hitherto, and I work."

18. Therefore the Jews sought the more to kill him, because he not only had broken the sabbath, but said also that God *was* his Father, making himself equal with God.

19. Then answered Jesus and said unto them, "Verily, verily, I say unto you, The Son can do nothing of himself, but what he seeth the Father do: for what things soever he doeth, these also doeth the Son likewise.

20. For the Father loveth the Son, and sheweth him all things that himself doeth: and he will shew him greater works than these, that ye may marvel.

21. For as the Father raiseth up the dead, and quickeneth *them*; even so the Son quickeneth whom he will.

22. For the Father judgeth no man, but hath committed all judgment unto the Son:

23. That all *men* should honour the Son, even as they honour the Father. He that honoureth not the Son honoureth not the Father which hath sent him."

This is another Sabbath healing performed by the Lord. He was in Jerusalem at the time of the Feast of the Jews. Here, too, through the timing, location and nature of this miracle, He wanted to convict

His people of His messianic credentials and deity. He therefore did what the Jews considered to be forbidden. He healed and directed the healed man to "take up his bed and walk" on the sacred Sabbath (vv.8,10,16).[7] As a result, the Jews marked Him as a defiler of God's law and sought to slay Him (v.16). The penalty for the breach of the Sabbath was death. (Ex 31:14-15).

In His defence the Lord again claimed to be the One who instituted the Sabbath. Here it was based upon His divine *sonship* rather than upon His divine *lordship* - "My Father worketh hitherto, and I work" (v.17). The Jews correctly interpreted these words to mean that He had said God was *His* Father, "making Himself equal with God" (v.18).[8] They then accused Him of blasphemy and accordingly sought "the more to kill Him".[9]

Observe firstly that the Lord's words and the Sabbath miracle created the sure belief among the Jews (and no doubt among the disciples), that He was declaring Himself to be God. Secondly, the Lord said nothing to overturn their clear understanding of what He had claimed. Thirdly, and most significantly, the equality He claimed with God, as rightly understood by the Jews, was in regard to divine *essence.* This is clear from the charge of blasphemy and from the wording of the accusation against Him. The Jews knew that the expression "my Father" meant that God was His *own* Father, that He was *the* Son of God, His *own* Son (Rom 8:32). The Son is of the same substance (*homoousios*) of the Father.[10] The Lord's defence to the indictment against Him as a Sabbath-breaker was that he was God, who had prerogative over the Sabbath.

---

[7] Seven Sabbath healings by the Lord are recorded in Scripture: The Demoniac, Mk 1:21-27#; Peter's wife's mother , Mk 1:29-31: the man with the withered hand, Mk 3:1-6#; the woman with an infirmity, Lk 13:10-17#; the man with dropsy, Lk 14:1-6; the impotent man, Jn 5:1-9; the blind man Jn 9:1-14. Each occasion illustrates how the Lord used the divine framework of the OT to reveal His deity. The provocative intent of the Lord in regard to His divine prerogative, is seen in that three of these Sabbath instances were within the very precinct of the synagogue (#).

[8] *Isos* means *equal.* In Philippians 2:6 Paul refers to Christ as *isa theoi* - "equal to God". A T Robertson *Word Pictures* Vol V p 83.

[9] Let us observe further verification of this. In Exodus we are informed that the works of God bear the mark of the "finger of God" - seen in God's miraculous hand before Pharaoh and in God giving the law (Ex 8:19; 31:18). Jesus of Nazareth claimed to do *His* works by the same divine power and prerogative. "But if I with the finger of God cast out devils, no doubt the kingdom of God is come upon you" (Lk 11:20).

[10] In verse 17 the Lord said "My Father" not "our Father". There is a clear distinction in these expressions which did not go unnoticed by the Jews. In verse 18 they correctly identified the Lord's claim to deity in them, for they charge Him as having said God was "His Father", the term "His" being *idion,* meaning God was His *own* Father (cf Rom 8:32, His *own* Son). ·

Despite their murderous intent towards Him and the charge of blasphemy, the Lord continued to declare His deity (vv.19-27). Having previously alluded to His divine sonship by referring to God as *His* Father, He then referred to Himself explicitly as the *Son* (of God the Father), reinforcing what the Jews had previously understood concerning His claims of divine sonship and His equality with God.

Verse 19 begins with a declaration of the divine "interdependence" between the Father and Son, the co-operative unity within the Godhead - "the Son can do nothing of [from] himself" (v.30; Jn 8:28; 12:49; 14:10).[11] This is a declaration of unity in divine *purpose*. The miracles performed by the Son were all done in co-operation with the Father. In the light of the Lord's previous and subsequent statements, this declaration cannot mean inferiority in His being. The Son is omniscient in that He is able to *know* and *see* the works of the Father, enabling Him to co-operate with Him in them. The Father's works and purposes are conceived in the heart and mind of His infinite being. Every divine work has its place in His eternal plan. The Son knows the divine works that conspire to fulfil the purposes of that plan. Finally, the Son claims omnipotence by declaring He can *do* "whatsoever" the Father does and do them in "like manner". How consistent with His previous claim and the understanding by the Jews that He placed Himself on equal footing with God in regard to the Sabbath and all divine works (v.17)! Being an equal participant in those divine works, he had to be equal in divine essence.

The Lord's disclosure of His deity does not end here. He puts forward three specific areas where His equality with God is to be apprehended, confirming His possession of the natural attributes and moral attributes of God.

1. *The Son's omnipotence*: His equality with God is affirmed through a specific example. The Son can not only raise the dead,

---

[11] Some say the Lord used this statement to correct the Jews, because they had mistakenly taken His words in verse 17 to mean He was declaring Himself equal with God. The clear meaning of the statement repudiates such a notion, quite apart from the context and the raft of expressions of equality that follow it. Why did He not immediately and emphatically declare they were horribly mistaken and even rebuke them for such a profanity? This would have immediately stemmed the tide of hatred against Him.

but *chooses* whom He will [raise], *as* the Father does (v.21). It is not here as the Father commands or delegates, but as the Father *does*. For the Son to do as the Father does, He must *know* and *work* according to the *manner* in which the Father performs His work. This cannot be anything less than according to the divine attributes, divine prerogative and divine glory.

2. *The Son's omniscience and divine morality.* The Father commits *all* judgement to the Son, the *Man* Christ Jesus (v.22). The Son's judgements are thus *universal* and *final*. The first truth means that there is no sphere of created existence, no created being that is not under His jurisdiction. To have the capacity to preside over this universal jurisdiction, the Son must be omniscient. The second truth means that the Son is the only Judge and His determinations are final. There being no appeals or abrogation in regard to His judgements, means that those judgements meet God's standard of absolute holiness. God "hath appointed a day, in the which he [God] will judge the world in righteousness by *that* Man whom He hath ordained" (Acts 17:31). As the righteous and final Judge of all, the Son must possess the moral attributes of God. He is "Jesus Christ the righteous" (1 Jn 2:1). But there is a further testimony to the Son as God in this matter. Scripture declares God Himself to be the universal and final Judge. He is the Judge of *all* the earth and He does all things right (Gen 18:25 cf 1 Sam 2:10; Heb 12:23). "The LORD [Jehovah] searcheth all hearts, and understandeth all the imaginations of the thoughts" (1 Chron 28:9; Jer 17:10). The "alls" and the jurisdiction - the hearts and thoughts, again reveal the needed divine capability – omniscience. This is emphatically declared to exist in Christ. "God shall judge the secrets of men by [the Man] Jesus Christ" (Rom 2:16). And, if we still believe that Christ plays a passive role in divine judgement, we stand corrected in that "all the churches shall know that I [the Son of God] am he [God] which searcheth the reins and hearts" (Rev 2:18, 23). Furthermore, God *Himself* presides over the Great White Throne of Judgment, before whom stand all the dead, small and great (Rev 20:12-13). If God has committed all judgement unto the Son, as the Son and the Spirit declare, then here is another incontrovertible testimony that the Father and the Son are one in purpose *because* they are one in essence!

3. *The Son is to receive equal honour with the Father.* The Son declares "all *men* should honour the Son, even as they honour the Father" (v.23). The Father must be honoured as God - exclusively and according to His infinite majesty. All this the Son claims in this section. It was so at His birth (Matt 2:1-2;11). The very angels of God are said to worship the Son (Heb 1:6). The Son is accorded universal praise and glory as God and as the Lamb (Rev 5:13). How jealously God guards His personal glory: "I *am* the LORD: that *is* my name: and my glory will I not give to another" (Isa 42:8). Here is "Another" who has no qualms about accepting the personal glory due to God, for He claims to be God and is God. And, here is one who, if created, is exhorting us unto blasphemy in that we are to give Him as a creature equal honour with God the Creator. In claiming equal tribute with the Father, the Son is teaching us the *distinctiveness* between the Son and the Father as well as of their *oneness.* They are Two yet One, each is worthy of honour and worship, equally, because they are One.

In these verses we have a clear and sustained revelation of the three marks of deity in Christ, and their witness to His undiminished and unceasing deity.

John 9

Jesus of Nazareth again claims equal honour with the Father in connection with yet another Sabbath healing. The compassionate eyes of the Great Physician fall upon the forlorn figure of a despised beggar blind from birth. In a moving display of divine sovereignty and grace, the Lord took that which was cursed - the dust of the earth, and used it to mark His gift of sight. The man's eyes were opened, not only to the beauty of the physical world, but to the divine glory of the Son of all righteousness unto eternal life.

However, blindness did prevail - in the hearts of the Pharisees. They cast out the cured man because he testified to the glory of God in Jesus of Nazareth. But the Good Shepherd sought him, and when he was found he was asked: "Dost thou believe on the Son of God?" Upon which the healed man declared, "Lord, I believe" (v.38). What was it that he believed? The truth that Jesus of Nazareth is the Son of God (vv.35-37)! Out of the abundance of his adoring heart, his mouth opened to render worship to this same Jesus. It was not, we observe, a case of "I understand", but "I believe on Him".

Jesus of Nazareth knew of God's jealousy and that the man's blindness was to manifest the works of God, yet He saw nothing amiss in being the object of faith and worship. Divine condemnation rests upon all who place their faith in men: "Thus saith the Lord [Jehovah]; Cursed *be* the man that trusteth in man, and maketh flesh his arm" (Jer 17:5). Divine commendation is upon all who put their trust in God: "Blessed *are* all they that put their trust in him [the Son]" (Ps 2:11-12).

6. Christ as the divine Sovereign over the Kingdom of God
Matthew 7:21-23
21. "Not every one that saith unto me, 'Lord, Lord', shall enter into the kingdom of heaven; but he that doeth the will of my Father which is in heaven.
22. Many will say to me in that day, 'Lord, Lord, have we not prophesied in thy name? and in thy name have cast out devils? and in thy name done many wonderful works?'
23. And then will I profess unto them, 'I never knew you: depart from me, ye that work iniquity'."
John 3:1-7
1. There was a man of the Pharisees, named Nicodemus, a ruler of the Jews:
2. The same came to Jesus by night, and said unto him, "Rabbi, we know that thou art a teacher come from God: for no man can do these miracles that thou doest, except God be with him."
3. Jesus answered and said unto him, "Verily, verily, I say unto thee, Except a man be born again, he cannot see the kingdom of God."
4. Nicodemus saith unto him, "How can a man be born when he is old? can he enter the second time into his mother's womb, and be born?"
5. Jesus answered, "Verily, verily, I say unto thee, Except a man be born of water and *of* the Spirit, he cannot enter into the kingdom of God.
6. That which is born of the flesh is flesh; and that which is born of the Spirit is spirit.
7. Marvel not that I said unto thee, Ye must be born again."

The Lord's ministry in regard to the kingdom of God reveals another insight into His deity. The terms "kingdom of heaven" and the "kingdom of God" apply to the one realm. The latter identifies God as the Creator and Sovereign in regard to His kingdom, the former refers to the character of God's kingdom and its seat of power. The term "kingdom of heaven" is peculiar to Matthew's Gospel, in keeping with its Jewish leaning. The Jews were familiar with the term "God of *heaven*" found in the OT. The title "God" was more familiar to the Gentiles, therefore the "kingdom of God" is predominant in the other Gospels.

As Sovereign over His kingdom, God has prerogative in regard to its *composition* - the subjects within it; its *course* - the destiny of it; and its *constitution* – its government. Because God is Sovereign He has the prerogative over who will be part of His kingdom. Christ exercises this divine prerogative in that He judges the confessions of men and so determines their place in the kingdom of God (Matt 7:21-23). He is God, the Omniscient Sovereign, who in absolute holiness searches the secrets of the hearts of men and tries the reins. Further, to be a subject of the kingdom, one must qualify to enter it (Jn 3:5). If Christ were less than God, then He, too, would need to qualify as a subject within God's kingdom. Such a thing is totally foreign to the Word of God!

Christ exercises divine prerogative in regard to the course of God's kingdom. The Jews rejected the kingdom of God in its Davidic covenant form, when they rejected the King who was to reign over it - Jesus of Nazareth. This brought a postponement of the kingdom of God in this aspect. Christ exercised the divine prerogatives of withdrawing and postponing it, heralding the coming of the kingdom of God in its present form (Matt 12-13). It was Christ through His personal sacrifice who brought the present aspect of the kingdom of God into existence! Therefore we have the Kingdom of God as the "kingdom of God's dear Son' (Col 1:13).[12] This is the present form of the kingdom of God. There can be no legitimate rival kingdoms to the kingdom of God.[13] So when Paul speaks of the kingdom of God's dear Son, he is referring to the kingdom over which God is Sovereign. The kingdom of God's dear Son speaks of the kingdom of God in regard to the Son as the Purchaser, Possessor and Preserver of the things that pertain to it. It is a matter relating to Christ's peculiar sonship and Him as the Reconciler of all things.

---

[12] Cf "The kingdom of Christ and of God", Eph 5:5.
[13] There is the illegitimate rival kingdom of Satan (Eph 6).

In Matthew 25:31-46, we have Christ as Sovereign. He is the Son of man, determining the constitution of the kingdom of God in its Davidic covenantal form, once postponed, then realised - the Millennial kingdom. He exercises on earth the divine imperial prerogatives within it.

7. Christ as Jehovah - the "I AM"

John 8:23-59

23. And he said unto them, "Ye are from beneath; I am from above: ye are of this world; I am not of this world.

24. I said therefore unto you, that ye shall die in your sins: for if ye believe not that I am *he*, ye shall die in your sins."

25. Then said they unto him, "Who art thou?" And Jesus saith unto them, "Even *the same* that I said unto you from the beginning.

26. I have many things to say and to judge of you: but he that sent me is true; and I speak to the world those things which I have heard of him."

27. They understood not that he spake to them of the Father.

28. Then said Jesus unto them, "When ye have lifted up the Son of man, then shall ye know that I am *he*, and *that* I do nothing of myself; but as my Father hath taught me, I speak these things.

29. And he that sent me is with me: the Father hath not left me alone; for I do always those things that please him."

30. As he spake these words, many believed on him.

31. Then said Jesus to those Jews which believed on him, "If ye continue in my word, *then* are ye my disciples indeed,

32. And ye shall know the truth, and the truth shall make you free."

33. They answered him, "We be Abraham's seed, and were never in bondage to any man: how sayest thou, Ye shall be made free?"

34. Jesus answered them, "Verily, verily, I say unto you, Whosoever committeth sin is the servant of sin.

35. And the servant abideth not in the house for ever: *but* the Son abideth ever.

36. If the Son therefore shall make you free, ye shall be free indeed.

37. I know that ye are Abraham's seed; but ye seek to kill me, because my word hath no place in you.

38. I speak that which I have seen with my Father: and ye do that which ye have seen with your father."

39. They answered and said unto him, "Abraham is our father." Jesus saith unto them, "If ye were Abraham's children, ye would do the works of Abraham.

40. But now ye seek to kill me, a man that hath told you the truth, which I have heard of God: this did not Abraham.

41. Ye do the deeds of your father." Then said they to him, "We be not

born of fornication; we have one Father, *even* God."

42. Jesus said unto them, "If God were your Father, ye would love me: for I proceeded forth and came from God; neither came I of myself, but he sent me.

43. Why do ye not understand my speech? *even* because ye cannot hear my word.

44. Ye are of *your* father the devil, and the lusts of your father ye will do. He was a murderer from the beginning, and abode not in the truth, because there is no truth in him. When he speaketh a lie, he speaketh of his own: for he is a liar, and the father of it.

45. And because I tell *you* the truth, ye believe me not.

46. Which of you convinceth me of sin? And if I say the truth, why do ye not believe me?

47. He that is of God heareth God's words: ye therefore hear *them* not, because ye are not of God."

48. Then answered the Jews, and said unto him, "Say we not well that thou art a Samaritan, and hast a devil?"

49. Jesus answered, "I have not a devil; but I honour my Father, and ye do dishonour me.

50. And I seek not mine own glory: there is one that seeketh and judgeth.

51. Verily, verily, I say unto you, If a man keep my saying, he shall never see death."

52. Then said the Jews unto him, "Now we know that thou hast a devil. Abraham is dead, and the prophets; and thou sayest, 'If a man keep my saying, he shall never taste of death.'

53. Art thou greater than our father Abraham, which is dead? and the prophets are dead: whom makest thou thyself?"

54. Jesus answered, "If I honour myself, my honour is nothing: it is my Father that honoureth me; of whom ye say, that he is your God:

55. Yet ye have not known him; but I know him: and if I should say, I know him not, I shall be a liar like unto you: but I know him, and keep his saying.

56. Your father Abraham rejoiced to see my day: and he saw *it*, and was glad."

57. Then said the Jews unto him, "Thou art not yet fifty years old, and hast thou seen Abraham?"

58. Jesus said unto them, "Verily, verily, I say unto you, Before Abraham was, I am."

59. Then took they up stones to cast at him: but Jesus hid himself, and went out of the temple, going through the midst of them, and so passed by.

This portion is full of pathos and rich in truth relating to the deity of Christ. There is much here to uplift the heart of the saint of God and at the same time extinguish all protests against the truth of the divine Man.

The Lord again challenges the benighted hearts of the Pharisees in regard to His deity, priming their conscience by declaring "I am from above" (v.23). He leaves no doubt over His prior existence and the location of it (heaven), so as to distinguish His Person from that of a mere man (cf 3:31). His next statement fanned the anger of the Jews. "If ye believe not that I am *he* [the One from above], ye shall die in your sins" (v.24). Two truths confront the Pharisees, both recurring in John's Gospel: Jesus of Nazareth is the *way* of salvation; and, *who* men believe Him to be is necessary *for* salvation (consistent with His prerogative over the forgiveness of sins and His divine holiness noted above). It is clear from these words alone, that a person cannot be saved if he/she rejects the truth of Jesus Christ as the *divine* Redeemer. Some may protest, "Is this not the very issue?" Indeed it is, but let us examine without prejudice the issue raised by the Lord. Can it be said in the light of the convergent biblical revelation already noted, that the Lord was asking the Pharisees to believe in Him as some specially created being in order that they be saved? The words, "if you do not believe I am *he*" speak of One who was sent - the divine Messiah, who is the "I am" of redemption, as the "I am" was the Redeemer of Israel in Exodus 3. It is not freedom here from the temporal bondage of Pharaoh, but from the eternal chains of sin, for "if the Son therefore shall make you free, ye shall be free indeed" (v.36).

Though the Pharisees were dull of hearing and slow to understand, the Lord graciously persists in dialogue with them, reaching a crescendo in that radiant expression of His deity - "Before Abraham was I am". Observe how He progresses to this point once He has declared His pre-existence and identified Himself as *the* way and the *Source* of salvation.

• He claims the divine title "Son of man", a title used for Jehovah (v.28; cf Dan 7).[14]
• He speaks of God as *my* Father (v.28), i.e., *His*.
• As the Son of man He chooses His disciples and claims their confession of *Him* on the basis of *His* word (v.30).
• Because He is the eternal Son [of God], the Person who abides

---

[14] We read here that the Son is "taught" by the Father. This expresses the subjection of the Son to the Father, and does not in any way teach inferiority of the Son to the Father.

forever, *He* can make men free "indeed". *He* is the Giver of eternal life (v.36).

• He claims innate knowledge of the Father, which speaks of His eternal being and His omniscient capacity to know the Infinite Father (v.38).
• He confirms and elaborates upon His pre-incarnate existence. He said earlier, "I am from above." Now He declares He is come "forth from God" (v.42), which reveals His pre-incarnate personality, Him being with God and coming from His very presence (cf Jn1:1, 14).
• He claims the love of the disciples knowing that God must be the sole object of man's affections (v.42; Deut 6:5).
• He asserts His sinless, perfect humanity, as would be expected of One who has the nature and holy character of God (v.46).
• His words are of absolute authority and reflect His divine prerogative. "If a man keep my sayings, he shall never see death" (v.51).

Through these judicious declarations Christ presents a sustained and harmonious revelation of His divine attributes and prerogatives, which testify to His undiminished and unceasing deity. Each statement added a highlight to the glowing portrait of His divine Person. His sublime claim recorded in verse 58 fired that radiance into its blazing glory. In answer to the question from the Jews, "whom makest thou thyself" (v.53), He avoided saying "before Abraham was, I was", which would be true of all creation prior to Abraham. He drew again from the revered theological framework of the OT, and with double assurance declared, "before Abraham was I am". On other occasions He used the term 'I am" *descriptively* - "I am the bread of life" (Jn 6:34 etc); and *prescriptively*, "I am the way" (Jn 14:6). Here "I am" is a title that expresses His timeless *identity*. It was used by God-Jehovah to refer to His own timeless existence. Christ claimed a like divine title earlier (v.24), but it appears that the Jews did not grasp its significance. Now the Lord identified Himself using a more potent expression having an unmistakable biblical context, which inflamed the anger of the sons of Abraham. His claim to be the "I am" was, to them, utterly blasphemous for at least three reasons.

1. *Historical*: Jesus of Nazareth claimed the name "I AM" which God-Jehovah had used to identify Himself to His people at the beginning of their history (Ex 3:13-18; 6:1-8). It was a name Jehovah employed to convict His doubting people of His divine authority and power in redemption. "Thus shalt thou say unto the children of Israel, 'I AM hath sent me unto you'." And God said moreover unto Moses, "Thus shalt thou say unto the children of Israel, 'The LORD [Jehovah] God of your fathers, the God of Abraham, the God of Isaac, and the God of Jacob, hath sent me unto you: this *is* my name for ever, and this *is* my memorial unto all generations'." (Ex 3:14-15). Not Moses now, but the divine Mediator who *is* the incarnate "I AM", stands before a recalcitrant generation of Abraham's sons.

2. *Covenantal*: The title "I AM" is associated with the hallowed covenant blessings Jehovah promised His earthly people. It is a name etched deep into the fabric of Israel's faith and hope, speaking of the Faithful One who holds the holy and glorious destiny of the nation. By referring to Himself as "I am", Jesus of Nazareth declares Himself to be that One who gave those promises to Israel and therefore the One who will fulfil them.

3. *Theological*: Most significant is the fact that "I AM" refers to God-Jehovah as the "Eternal One", a title the Jews held in the highest reverence. It spoke of the incomparable personal glory of Jehovah. "The words rendered 'I AM THAT I AM' are almost unapproachable". They denote "...a Personal, Continuous, Absolute, Self-determining Existence". The Hebrew term "I AM" marks "an eternal, unchanging Presence."[15]

---

[15] Girdlestone *Synonyms* p 37. Note the contrast in John 8:58 between *genesthai* - the coming into existence which is applied to Abraham and *eimi* - timeless being - "I am". "Undoubtedly here Jesus claims eternal existence with the absolute phrase used of God." A T Robertson *Word Pictures* Vol V p 158-159. *Ego eimi* (I am) is the formula for absolute, timeless existence. Vincent *Word Studies* Vol II p181.

If we reflect on the way Christ proclaims His deity in this passage, we note it is, in part, through a *revelation* of His divine natural and moral attributes. But in its greater part, it is proclaimed though *identification*. He declares Himself *to be* Jehovah and, through this, He claims all that the name Jehovah means to the Jews in terms of their history, covenants and theology. It is, therefore, as explicit a statement of His deity as if He had said "I am God-Jehovah". The Jews had no doubt He was claiming to *be* Jehovah when He spoke of Himself as "I am", clear evidence of which is seen in them immediately taking up stones to kill Him because of it (v.59). Did He know to do good yet did it not? The Lord's just claims in this portion are predicated on the truth declared in verse 18, "I am one that bear witness of myself, and the Father that sent me beareth witness of me".

"I am" - the absolute Being.

The term "absolute" means entire or complete, defining a case where no complement or equivalent exists. Jehovah is absolute in regard to His Person and His works. He is absolute in His Person because He alone is self-existent and uncreated, as expressed in His title "I am". He is absolute in regard to His works because He alone possesses the divine attributes to formulate and execute them.

Christ's undiminished and unceasing deity means that He, too, is absolute. He is the "I am". As the "I am" He is the absolute, uncreated eternal Word, who is equal to God and who was with God (Jn 1:1-2). As the "I am" Christ is the sole Reconciler of all things unto God. What else can be concluded from the Scriptures already noted and the emphatic personal pronoun in His declaration, "I am the way, *and* the truth, and the life (Jn 14:6)?" He means that He *alone* is the way, the truth and the life in all their integrated completeness. In all these divine matters He has no equal! If Christ were not God, then God would be excluded through such claims. His claims would indeed be blasphemous - if He were not God, for God is absolute truth and life (Ps 25:10; 91:4)! The enigma that both Christ and Jehovah are absolute, vanishes in the light of the biblical revelation of the plurality of Persons yet one Being of the Godhead.

8. Christ as the divine Son of God
John 10:22-39

22. And it was at Jerusalem the feast of the dedication, and it was winter.

23. And Jesus walked in the temple in Solomon's porch.

24. Then came the Jews round about him, and said unto him, "How long dost thou make us to doubt? If thou be THE CHRIST, tell us plainly."

25. Jesus answered them, "I told you, and ye believed not: the works that I do in my Father's name, they bear witness of me.

26. But ye believe not, because ye are not of my sheep, as I said unto you.

27. My sheep hear my voice, and I know them, and they follow me:

28. And I give unto them eternal life; and they shall never perish, neither shall any *man* pluck them out of my hand.

29. My Father, which gave *them* me, is greater than all; and no *man* is able to pluck *them* out of my Father's hand.

30. I and *my* Father are one."

31. Then the Jews took up stones again to stone him.

32. Jesus answered them, "Many good works have I shewed you from my Father; for which of those works do ye stone me?"

33. The Jews answered him, saying, "For a good work we stone thee not; but for blasphemy; and because that thou, being a man, makest thyself God."

34. Jesus answered them, "Is it not written in your law, I said, Ye are gods?

35. If he called them gods, unto whom the Word of God came, and the scripture cannot be broken;

36. Say ye of him, whom the Father hath sanctified, and sent into the world, 'Thou blasphemest,' because I said, 'I am the Son of God?'

37. If I do not the works of my Father, believe me not.

38. But if I do, though ye believe not me, believe the works: that ye may know, and believe, that the Father *is* in me, and I in him."

39. Therefore they sought again to take him: but he escaped out of their hand.

The Lord is in Jerusalem at the time of the Feast of Dedication. The predatory Jews spy Him among the crowd and encircle Him. Their purpose was to have Him declare *who* He is (v.24). He had done this before - so plainly that they had taken up stones against Him for blasphemy (alluded to in v.31). But again He declared His deity. "I and my Father are One" (v.30). Upon hearing these words the Jews accused Him of blasphemy and sought His death.

Some deny all this citing two arguments. In the first argument they go to chapter 17 where the Lord prays using similar expressions of unity in regard to believers and their relationship to the Father and the Son. Therefore, they say, the oneness of verse

30 is not exclusive to the Father and the Son. But what was the occasion and substance of this prayer that was made by the Lord just prior to His passion? He was soon to die on the cross, arise from among the dead and, shortly afterwards ascend to His Father. He prays therefore not only for those of His flock who are left behind at that time, but for all throughout the centuries "which shall believe on me through their word" (v.20). His prayer to the Father is that "they [all] may be as one, as we are [one]" (vv.11, 22), and, "that they may be one in us" (v.21).

Those who wrongly use this passage overlook vital aspects of the unity of which it speaks. First, the redeemed in Christ are the *subjects* of this unity. They belong to that one *spiritual* family of God. Second, the *substance* of this unity reflects that indissoluble unity that exists between the Father and the Son (v.11,22). Third, the *security* underlying this unity resides in the co-operative and co-equal Persons of the Father and the Son - "one in us" (v.21). "He that abideth in the doctrine of Christ, he hath both the Father and the Son" (2 Jn 9). Nothing here denies the equality between the Son and the Father. Rather, it declares it to be the basis of the unity spoken of in this passage - the unity of the redeemed in Christ.

In chapter 10 Christ identifies Himself as God before a disbelieving people. As is often the case, out of rebuke to the faithless flow words of blessing to the faithful. Again the eternal security of those in the Son is declared to reside in the oneness between the Father and the Son. There is a dilation of it here. Believers are held by One who is of the same substance as the Father, the Father's hand is, in essence, the Son's hand. The Father gives them into the Son's hand and, yet, they are in the Father's hand, for they one in their essential nature. What a blessed double clasp of salvation, security and shelter there is here for the sheep, in this, the sweetest of truths. What security is there if one hand is lesser than the other in power and nature - one belonging to some created being or to one whose deity can be diminished or halted? How Satan tries to shake the blessed assurance of those in Christ.

The second and more favoured opposing argument, asserts that the statement "I and my Father are one" refers to oneness in divine purpose, and not to divine essence. This Arian-inspired claim vaporises in the light of two observations. First, since when does unity in moral purpose between man and God lead to a charge of blasphemy? Surely the pious Jews would claim to be one with God in His moral purposes.[16] Second, the meaning of the statement, "I and my Father are one", has been clearly defined by the Lord's antagonists - the Jews, and by the Lord Himself. The Jews interpret these words to be about *identity*, and that Christ was claiming personal equality with God. The Lord does not attempt to alter their understanding. They admitted that their intention to stone the Lord was not because of His good works, which would be indicative of His moral purpose, against which the Jews had no quarrel (v.33). *They* had no doubt what Christ meant when He said, "I and my Father are one." The Jews were not inquiring about the Lord's moral purpose at all. Their question was "If thou be the Christ, tell us plainly" (v.24). The Lord gives them plain answers, I and my Father are one-and-the-same in essence (v.30). This was confirmed and complemented by His declaration, "the Father *is* in me, and I in him" (v.38). Observe the double force of this last expression. It is not simply "the Father is in me" or "I am in the Father", for either one by itself would not agree with oneness in essence declared in verse 30. The Lord's answers were so plain, that they prompted no demand for an explanation by the Jews who, certain of their meaning, sought to put Him to death. They judged Him, declaring, "thou, being a man, makest thyself God" (v.33).[17] The clearest of

---

[16] One (*hen*) - "one essence or nature", A T Robertson *Word Pictures* Vol V p 186. "The neuter *en* (one) denotes, according to the connection and for the purpose of the argument, unity of *will* and *power*, which rests on the unity of *essence* or *nature*: for power is one of the divine attributes, which are not outside of the divine essence, but constitute it. Even if we confine *en* to dynamic unity, we have here one of the strongest arguments for the strict divinity of Christ. It is implied even more in *esmen* (we are) than in *en*. No creature could possibly thus associate himself in one common plural with God Almighty without shocking blasphemy or downright madness. In this brief sentence we have, as Augustine Bengal observe, a refutation both of Arianism and Sabellianism: *En* refutes the former by asserting the dynamic (and, by implication, the essential) unity of the Father and the Son. 'I and the Father' and 'we are' refute the latter by asserting the personal distinction. Sabellianism would require the masculine *eis*, instead of the neuter; and this would be inconsistent with 'we are', and the self-conscious 'I'". (Schaff as given in the *The Numerical Bible* - The Gospels p 551). In John 10:30, by the use of the plural *sumus* (separate persons), the doctrine of Sabellius is dismissed, and by *unum*, the doctrine of Arius is refuted. See A T Robertson *Word Pictures* Vol V p 186.
[17] *Poieo* - to make. It means here as in Jn 8:53; 19:7,12, "To declare one or oneself anything". W E Vine *Expository Dictionary* p 30. Christ declared Himself God, possessing the divine natural and moral attributes!

statements from God are the ones that attract the greatest opposition from those who seek to deny Him.

The Lord's declaration in verse 15 provides conclusive revelation of the oneness in essence between the Son and the Father. "As the Father knoweth me, even so I know the Father". The Father's knowledge of the Person of His Son cannot be less than total knowledge. Neither then can the Son's knowledge of the Father be less than total knowledge, for as the Father knoweth me [i.e. totally], even so know I the Father [totally].[18] If the Son knows the Father in full measure, then the Son must be eternal, omniscient, omnipresent and omnipotent - very God.

Does Christ deny that He is Deity?

In vain persistence some argue the Lord's reply (vv.34-36) to the charge of blasphemy (v.31) is a disavowal of deity. If this is so, then it is belated and mischievous at the very least, for He had ample prior opportunity to correct any misconceptions regarding His deity. He quotes the OT passage where men were called gods (*elohim*) (Ps 82:1,6). The subject of this Psalm is the judgement of the unjust judges (elohim). Each of these men held the office of a judge, but they failed to judge on occasions when required and, when they did judge, they ruled in error. God, therefore, stands in their midst as their Judge (Elohim). The term elohim in the context of this Psalm is used to refer to men, men of Israel, who were judges sent by God, who were under His authority and responsible to Him. Jehovah who is the Supreme Judge in this court, is distinguished from these mortal judges by the use of Elohim (v.1).[19]

The purpose of this quotation by the Lord, as many have noted, is clear. If mortal magistrates under the authority of God can be called gods, why should the Jews object when Christ who came forth from God, who was one in essence with God and who was

---

[18] In John 8:55 the Lord uses *oida* - knowledge gained by intuition, to refer to His knowledge of the Father. It clearly reveals His deity. It is contrasted in this verse with the knowledge that the Jews should have of God through experience, *ginosko*! (W E Vine, *Collected Writings*, Vol 4 p 238). In all His wondrous dealings with them they still do not know Him. In John 10:15, knowledge is also *ginosko*. The *Father* knows the *Son* and the *Son* knows the *Father* on the basis of experience. No doubt this refers to the knowledge of each other through their eternal communion as the Father and the Son. "The Word was with God" (Jn 1:1); eternally in the bosom of the Father (Jn 1:18).

[19] See further W. Graham Scroggie D.D., *Know Your Bible - The Psalms* Vol II; London.

sent by Him, is called the Son of God - a divine title signifying He is God's *own* Son. Rather than negate His claim to deity, the Lord's application of this passage from the OT to Himself is in support of it, and it confirms the deity vested in the title "the Son of God". Besides, we need only observe the reaction of the Jews to know that the Lord did *not* use this quotation to deny His deity in any shape or form. His subsequent words, "the Father is in me and I in Him" (v.38) is as noted, a statement confirming His deity, for which they again sought to take (kill) Him (v.39), but His hour had not yet come.

9. Christ as the divine Son of the Blessed
Mark 14:55-64;

55. And the chief priests and all the council sought for witness against Jesus to put him to death; and found none.

56. For many bare false witness against him, but their witness agreed not together.

57. And there arose certain, and bare false witness against him, saying,

58. "We heard him say, 'I will destroy this temple that is made with hands, and within three days I will build another made without hands.'"

59. But neither so did their witness agree together.

60. And the high priest stood up in the midst, and asked Jesus, saying, "Answerest thou nothing? what *is it which* these witness against thee?"

61. But he held his peace, and answered nothing. Again the high priest asked him, and said unto him, "Art thou the Christ, the Son of the Blessed?"

62. And Jesus said, "I am: and ye shall see the Son of man sitting on the right hand of power, and coming in the clouds of heaven."

63. Then the high priest rent his clothes, and saith, "What need we any further witnesses?

64. Ye have heard the blasphemy: what think ye?" And they all condemned him to be guilty of death.

Matthew 26:57 & 62-66 (Lk.22)

57. And they that had laid hold on Jesus led *him* away to Caiaphas the high priest, where the scribes and the elders were assembled,.............

62. And the high priest arose, and said unto him, "Answerest thou nothing? what *is it which* these witness against thee?"

63. But Jesus held his peace. And the high priest answered and said unto him, "I adjure thee by the living God, that thou tell us whether thou be the Christ, the Son of God."

64. Jesus saith unto him, "Thou hast said: nevertheless I say unto you, Hereafter shall ye see the Son of man sitting on the right hand of power, and coming in the clouds of heaven."

65. Then the high priest rent his clothes, saying, "He hath spoken blasphemy; what further need have we of witnesses? Behold, now ye have heard his blasphemy.
66. What think ye?" They answered and said, "He is guilty of death."

On this occasion Jesus of Nazareth stands accused before Caiaphas the high priest. The answer He demands from the Lord is to take on the solemnity of an oath before God. "I adjure thee by the living God, that thou tell us whether thou be the Christ, the Son of God" (Matt 26:63). Once again the Lord's *identity* is the issue. "Art thou the Christ, the Son of the Blessed?" The Lord answers, "I am," Mark giving us the essence of the Lord's words, Matthew and Luke employing idiomatic expressions of agreement, "Thou hast said", and "Ye say that I am", respectively. To this affirmation the Lord adds a further avowal of His deity. They shall "see the Son of man [Jehovah's equal] sitting on the right hand of power, and coming in the clouds of heaven" (Matt 26:64, cf Dan 7). As noted, the "Son of man" is a divine title, which we take up in chapter 5. The ensuing charge of blasphemy and calls for His death, unequivocally support that fact the Lord had claimed equality with God. The High Priest rent His clothes, an act not permitted in times of mourning but allowed in instances of blasphemy. Was this another instance where the Lord acted contrary to what He believed to be true?

We should remark here on the Lord's reference to "the temple of His body" (misused by the Jews to bear false witness against Him (v.61)).[20] He is speaking here of His death and resurrection (Jn 2:18-21). His deity is expressed in His power and authority over life and death - "Destroy this Temple [my body], and in three days I will raise it up" (Jn 2:19). When His disciples witnessed His resurrection they remembered this statement (Jn 2:22) which, no doubt, moved Thomas to acknowledge His deity - "My Lord and my God!"

---

[20] This witness against the Lord was false because it charged Him with intending to destroy the temple (Matt 26:61; Mark 14:58), which He clearly did not say. He never said "I will destroy"; nor "I will build", but "I will raise" (Jn 2:19). Not only had the Jews failed to understand the Lord's words as referring to His body, but they altered them to take away their real meaning, which was that He was to be put to death by the Jews. He had the power to lay down His life and take it up again, as we note below.

10. Christ as the divine Son of the living God
John 6:66-71

66. From that *time* many of his disciples went back, and walked no more with him.

67. Then said Jesus unto the twelve, "Will ye also go away?"

68. Then Simon Peter answered him, "Lord, to whom shall we go? thou hast *the* words of eternal life.

69. And we believe and are sure that thou art that Christ, the Son of the living God."

Having been forsaken by others, the Lord is alone with the twelve, precious moments no doubt to Him and to His own. He asks them whether they, too, will leave Him. Peter answers - "Lord, to whom shall we go? thou hast *the* words of eternal life. And we believe and are sure that thou art that Christ, the Son of the living God."

Christ clearly was to the twelve disciples what Jehovah was to them and to their forefathers – the Giver of eternal life, the Eternal Life. John bears witness to this. "And this is the record, that God hath given to us eternal life, and this life is in his Son. He that hath the Son hath life; *and* he that hath not the Son of God hath not life" (1 Jn 5:11-12; 1:2). It is not, as emphasised throughout Scripture, simply that Christ can *give* eternal life. It is that *in* Him is eternal life. He said "I am...the Life", as the singular and veritable Source of it.[21] How priceless this is to our souls! He is the Source of eternal life because He is absolutely holy, for eternal life is secured on the ground of divine righteousness (that we might "become the righteousness of God in Him" and "accepted in the Beloved"). The Lord rebuked Peter on other occasions, but not here, for his words were true. Jesus of Nazareth is the "Christ, the Son of the living God" (cf Matt 16:16).[22]

11. Christ as the Resurrection and the Life
John 11:12-27

12. Then said his disciples, "Lord, if he sleep, he shall do well."

---

[21] In John 17:2 the Lord acknowledges that He was *given* the power to give eternal life by the Father. Note first that it is not "power" but authority. Secondly He speaks here as the dutiful Son under subjection to the Father, not as One who is inferior to Him.

[22] Note again the expression the "living God" and its use in the common judicial oath required before the Jewish religious hierarchy, "I adjure thee by the living God", mentioned earlier (Matt 26:63). The confession of Peter takes on the character and force of an oath before God!

13. Howbeit Jesus spake of his death: but they thought that he had spoken of taking of rest in sleep.
14. Then said Jesus unto them plainly, "Lazarus is dead.
15. And I am glad for your sakes that I was not there, to the intent ye may believe; nevertheless let us go unto him."
16. Then said Thomas, which is called Didymus, unto his fellow disciples, "Let us also go, that we may die with him."
17. Then when Jesus came, he found that he had *lain* in the grave four days already.
18. Now Bethany was nigh unto Jerusalem, about fifteen furlongs off:
19. And many of the Jews came to Martha and Mary, to comfort them concerning their brother.
20. Then Martha, as soon as she heard that Jesus was coming, went and met him: but Mary sat *still* in the house.
21. Then said Martha unto Jesus, "Lord, if thou hadst been here, my brother had not died.
22. But I know, that even now, whatsoever thou wilt ask of God, God will give *it* thee."
23. Jesus saith unto her, "Thy brother shall rise again."
24. Martha saith unto him, "I know that he shall rise again in the resurrection at the last day."
25. Jesus said unto her, "I am the resurrection, and the life: he that believeth in me, though he were dead, yet shall he live:
26. And whosoever liveth and believeth in me shall never die. Believest thou this?"
27. She saith unto him, "Yea, Lord: I believe that thou art the Christ, the Son of God, which should come into the world."

The miracle of life is demonstrated among the beloved of the Lord. Lazarus, the brother of Mary and Martha lay ill unto death. The sisters send for the Lord for they know of His power to heal the sick (v.3). But He delays His coming so that His mission of mercy is not one of healing Lazarus, but of raising him from death unto life. By doing this He points to the higher truth of His work as the divine Giver and Source of eternal life. He must confirm this truth through a miracle in which He raises the dead from the very grave itself.

Note the specific circumstances that are again consonant with the framework of the OT. Only Jehovah has the power and prerogative to kill and make alive; to bring "down to the grave" and bring up again (1 Sam 2:6). So Christ allows death and the *grave* to overtake Lazarus. In accordance with His divine power and prerogative, He chooses to raise whom He *will*, and manifest His divine glory - glory exclusive to Jehovah. He does this not only to glorify God, but to bring unqualified glory to Himself as the Son of God (v.4). This itself is an emphatic declaration of equality between the Son and the Father. Let the Jews come and minister their cold consolations. Let the body of Lazarus lie bound by death's icy grasp in the grave for four days. Then, and only then, will Jesus of Nazareth come. He comes not as the "Great Physician", but as the Son of God, the "Resurrection and the Life" (v.25). His command breaks the shackles of death and Lazarus comes forth bound in his grave clothes. "O death, where *is* thy sting? O grave, where *is* thy victory? The sting of death *is* sin; and the strength of sin *is* the law. But thanks *be* to God, which giveth us the victory through our Lord Jesus Christ" (1 Cor 15:55-57).

At Bethany the Lord again declared His divine natural and moral attributes. Exquisite humanity would have Him go to the sick-bed of Lazarus. However His deity takes Him to his grave, to proclaim His power over death, to manifest that He came that "they might have life, and that they might have *it* more abundantly" (Jn 10:10). Having manifested His deity, He declares the emancipating truth that only Deity can claim - "I am the resurrection, and the [eternal] life: he that believeth in me, though he were dead [spiritually], yet shall he live [life everlasting]: And whosoever liveth and believeth in me shall never die." Our hearts are directed to embrace this higher truth regarding His divine Person. He is the Source and Surety of eternal life.[23] To what end was this done? It was that God might be glorified and the "Son of God might be glorified" (Jn 11:4, 40).

Christ did what only God could do (vv.25,43)

CHRIST'S DEITY

| Christ chose to do what only God could choose to do (vv.5-14) | The glory of God was manifested in what Christ did (vv.4,40,45) |

---

[23] Only God is able to breathe into man "the breath of life" and create within him an eternal soul (Gen 2:7); only He can be asked for life and grant it, for our times are in His hand (Ps 21:4; 31:15); He only is the strength of life (Ps 27:1), who holds the prerogative over the life of our very souls (Ps 66:9).

12. Christ as Jehovah-Tsidkenu (my righteousness)
Luke 23:38-43

38. And a superscription also was written over him in letters of Greek, and Latin, and Hebrew, THIS IS THE KING OF THE JEWS.

39. And one of the malefactors which were hanged railed on him, saying, "If thou be Christ, save thyself and us."

40. But the other answering rebuked him, saying, "Dost not thou fear God, seeing thou art in the same condemnation?

41. And we indeed justly; for we receive the due reward of our deeds: but this *man* hath done nothing amiss."

42. And he said unto Jesus, "Lord, remember me when thou comest into thy kingdom."

43. And Jesus said unto him, "Verily I say unto thee, To day shalt thou be with me in paradise."

Calvary is the pivotal event in the work of divine grace. It was the sublime subject within the counsels of God in eternity past, and it became the focus of divine revelation, foreshadowed in Genesis 3:15, 22:7, Exodus 12, Leviticus 16 and many other OT passages. If we cannot see the divine glories of Christ here, we will not see them anywhere. The drama of the occasion invites our attention, its holiness demands reverent enquiry. Observe first the words of the penitent thief when he rebuked his libellous fellow: "Dost Thou not fear God?" These words and the grave circumstances in which they were spoken, betray his fear of God and impending eternity. He saw His dire need for salvation. But to whom does he turn to make his salvation sure? There is no appeal to Jehovah, to El Shaddai - the Almighty God or to Elohim - the God of creation. He sees the glory of God in the face of Jesus Christ, and entrusts His eternal soul to Him, for "He *is* my refuge and my fortress: my God; in him will I trust" (Ps 91:2-4).

Many disparage the claim that Christ is honoured as God because the Word of God enjoins and reveals men "honouring men". The objection fails when faith is brought into consideration. Hebrews 11 teaches that faith in God honours God, because when we place our faith in God, we admit to no help apart from God. Such honour is thus reserved for God - "cursed be the man that trusteth in man, and maketh flesh his arm". Scripture exhorts us in word and by example to place our faith in Christ (Js 2:1).[24] In so doing, it teaches us that Christ is to be honoured as God is honoured. Did not Christ say this very thing (Jn 5:23)? By placing his faith in Christ, the penitent thief (and the leper before him) honoured Christ as God. Further, the honour given to Christ is quite different to that rendered to men. This is because it is rendered in recognition of the fact that Christ did and claimed what only God could do, so evident within the Gospels.

The lesson from the penitent thief is clear. Faith must rest upon Christ, who is Jehovah Tsidkenu, Jehovah our righteousness. However, before the thief saw the all-sufficiency of Christ in salvation, he had to see Himself as a sinner under God's judgement (vv.40-41). Unless sin is confessed before God, Christ can never be confessed as Saviour. Many seek to follow Christ because of His righteousness. It is possible to do so but to have never partaken of the righteousness of God in Him. Many have adopted Christianity as a *cause* because of its inherent morality; pursued it as a *course* because of its charter of humanity; and even taken it up as a *commission* in view of its nobility. However they remain under divine condemnation never having experienced its true *confession*. The Gospel message is to "come and your sin confessing". Only then can conversion unto salvation take place. "God be merciful to me a sinner" (Lk 18:13). God was indeed merciful to this sin-confessing thief, for we hear the divine accents of eternal security from the divine Man: "Today shalt thou be with me in paradise." Surely this repentant heart saw Christ as "the resurrection and the life". To faith, a truth consummated in the future has a present reality.[25] Faith in God will always have its needed reward (Heb 11:6).

The total unqualified faith placed in Christ by this dying man testifies to the deity of Christ. But what of the words of Christ in this pre-eternal moment? They tell that He took entire responsibility for the dying man's eternal soul. He directed his soul to no other for salvation and invited his heart to rest exclusively on His

---

[24] "Faith in our Lord and Saviour Jesus Christ" A T Robertson *Word Pictures* Vol VI p27 cf Col 1:4; 2:5; 2 Tim 3:15.

[25] This is so in regard to consecration (for all who look for hasten, who look for His second appearance without sin unto salvation, Heb 9:28). There is a further radiant vision granted to this man and to all the penitent, the suffering Saviour and His glory which is to follow. "Lord, remember me when thou comest into thy kingdom." This man looked to the day of the future glory of the suffering Christ.

assurance of it. This would be absolute presumption if He was not the great God and Saviour. In this precious moment we have consummated all that Christ had declared regarding Himself as the absolute "I am": "I am the way the truth and the life"; "I am the Good Shepherd that giveth His life for the sheep"; "I am the bread of life", etc.

Calvary itself appears in history and on the Sacred Page *because* of the deity of Christ. It was necessary for God to become man, and as the divine Man put away sin for ever. This vital biblical truth is taken up at length in chapter 6.

13. Christ as Jehovah-Shalom, the Lord God
John 20:19-31

19. Then the same day at evening, *being* the first *day* of the week, when the doors were shut where the disciples were assembled for fear of the Jews, came Jesus and stood in the midst, and saith unto them, "Peace *be* unto you."

20. And when he had so said, he shewed unto them *his* hands and his side. Then were the disciples glad, when they saw the Lord.

21. Then said Jesus to them again, "Peace *be* unto you: as *my* Father hath sent me, even so send I you."

22. And when he had said this, he breathed on *them*, and saith unto them, "Receive ye the Holy Ghost:

23. Whosoever sins ye remit, they are remitted unto them; *and* whosoever *sins* ye retain, they are retained."

24. But Thomas, one of the twelve, called Didymus, was not with them when Jesus came.

25. The other disciples therefore said unto him, "We have seen the Lord." But he said unto them, "Except I shall see in his hands the print of the nails, and put my finger into the print of the nails, and thrust my hand into his side, I will not believe."

26. And after eight days again his disciples were within, and Thomas with them: *then* came Jesus, the doors being shut, and stood in the midst, and said, "Peace *be* unto you."

27. Then saith he to Thomas, "Reach hither thy finger, and behold my hands; and reach hither thy hand, and thrust *it* into my side: and be not faithless, but believing."

28. And Thomas answered and said unto him, "My Lord and my God."

29. Jesus saith unto him, "Thomas, because thou hast seen me, thou hast believed: blessed *are* they that have not seen, and *yet* have believed."

30. And many other signs truly did Jesus in the presence of his disciples, which are not written in this book:

31. But these are written, that ye might believe that Jesus is the Christ, the Son of God; and that believing ye might have life through his name.

This post-resurrection encounter has a special fragrance to redeemed hearts. It intimates that glorious promise, that "where two or three are gathered together in my name, there am I in the midst of them" (Matt 18:20). On both occasions the risen Lord utters words of comfort, but not before He takes up His rightful place among His own - in the midst!

Who uplifted the failing spirits and gladdened the hearts of the disciples after they fled in fear behind closed doors? Who breathed upon them, empowered them and imparted a holy commission? The risen *Lord!* But there was one who doubted – Thomas! However, when the Lord appeared to him in His radiant grace, his unbelief evaporated as the morning dew before the rising sun. Thomas confessed the One before him to be his *Lord* and *God.* Given its precision and context, this confession has the eminence to stand alone as an unequivocal witness to Christ's deity. But it does not stand alone. The Spirit of God has unreservedly placed it among a host of affirmations to the deity of Christ.

Yet, some desperate to deny the clear truth declared by Thomas' confession, tell us his words were an "exclamation", an impulsive outburst of amazement.[26] But note how the Spirit of God guards against such a falsehood and preserves its fragrant truth. Thomas' answer is recorded as a direct and considered response to the Lord's exhortation "be not faithless". His *answer* is prompted by his *belief,* as the Lord confirmed: "Thou hast believed" (vv.27-29). True faith and absolute conviction need no hesitation.

How did the other disciples respond to Thomas' confession? Being Jews, they held tenaciously to the command to worship the one God. Their fathers were exhorted to pay homage to the one and only God, Jehovah. God, who would have no other gods before Him (Ex 20:3), punished the nation when they lusted after other gods. They were not to worship any god beside Him (Ex 34:14). Furthermore, being Jews, they were very familiar with the title

---

[26] Eg. as found in the creed of the Socinians, a "Christian" cult that arose in the 17th century which denied the Trinity (and the deity of Christ), original sin and the Resurrection. It was the forerunner to the Unitarian movement.

"Lord God". It was used frequently in the OT to address Jehovah in a personal way. "I will praise thee, O Lord [Jehovah] my God, with all my heart: and I will glorify thy name for evermore" (Ps 86:12); "Art thou not from everlasting, O LORD [Jehovah] my God, mine Holy One?" (Hab 1:12).[27] In the NT, Jude speaks of "the only Lord God" (v.4). Christ Himself said that the first and great commandment is to love the Lord thy God with all thy heart, soul and mind (Matt 22:37).

It is against this background of strict Jewish monotheism, Christ's teaching in support of it, and the way Jehovah was addressed in the OT, that Thomas declared Jesus of Nazareth to be his Lord and his God. It is incontestable that he was confessing Him to be the sole Person to whom worship and homage is due, the One who is eternal, "from everlasting". What sacrilege if Christ were not God! How could the disciples refrain from objecting to such profanity from a "doubter" if they did not share Thomas' confession? How quickly and with what profound horror Paul and Barnabas responded when the people of Lycaonia regarded them as gods come "in the likeness of men". "*Which* when the apostles, Barnabas and Paul, heard *of*, they rent their clothes, and ran in among the people, crying out, And saying, Sirs, why do ye these things?" (Acts 14:14-15).[28] Peter, too, was quick to correct the ill-directed worship of Cornelius when he fell down and worshipped him, declaring, "Stand up; I myself also am a man" (Acts 10:26). Scripture records no gasp of amazement or recoil of horror from these disciples when Thomas claimed Jesus of Nazareth to be his God.[29]

---

[27] "Lord [Jehovah] my God": Gen 28:21 (Jacob); Deut 4:5 (Moses); Josh 14:8 (Caleb); 2 Sam 24:24 (David); 1 Kings 3:7 (Solomon), Ezra 7:28 (Ezra) etc. To these we can add the numerous references to Jehovah as "Lord God" in the OT. "In the Psalms and elsewhere there is found that significant title which the Apostle Thomas gave to the Lord Jesus when he had optical and sensible demonstration that He was risèn from the dead. Thus in Ps 35:23, the sacred writer uses the double title *Elohai* and *Adonai*, 'my God and my Lord;' and in Ps 38.15, we find *Adonai Elohai*, 'my Lord, my God'. See Girdlestone *Synonyms* pp 34-35. Since the latter part of the OT period, devout Jews fearful of being irreverent, refrained from pronouncing the name "Jehovah", as it was God's personal name. When they came across this name in the OT, they substituted the name *Adonai* (Lord). This meant they they could refer to Jehovah in a personal and intimate way without being irreverent, using the expression *my Adonai* - "my Lord".
[28] The apostles' horror was essentially because the people regarded them, who were mere mortal men, as gods. Note the two apostles "rent their clothes". For them to be regarded as deity was blasphemous!
[29] The Baptist, too, was forthright in denying that he was the Christ (Jn 1:20).

Of deeper interest is the Lord's response to Thomas' confession. He does not chastise Thomas for any ill-chosen words. This is significant for two reasons. First, Christ warned that "every idle word that men shall speak, they shall give account thereof in the day of judgement. For by thy words thou shalt be justified, and by thy words thou shalt be condemned" (Matt 12:36-37). Second, Christ Himself claimed there was only one God. "And the scribe said unto him, Well, Master, thou hast said the truth: for there is one God; and there is none other but he" (Mk 12:32). The Lord in His omniscience did not say to Thomas "Thou hast believed wrongly", but "Thou hast believed" (v.29). Does the Spirit of God intend that we regard the disciples as credulous idolaters and the Lord as a deceiver of men?

The Lord did rebuke Thomas because of the way in which he arrived at his confession - by sight. The reproof carries a blessing to others that confirms the truth of Thomas' confession: "Blessed *are* they that have not seen, and *yet* have believed." Believed what? The liberating truth Thomas confessed when his glowing heart acknowledged the risen Christ. Jesus of Nazareth is risen from among the dead according to His own prediction, prerogative and power and He is *therefore* both Lord *and* God. If Thomas' belief was merely in regard to Christ having risen, then why was his confession not limited to this fact and say nothing of the identity of Christ? A glorious day awaits those who believe, not one when doubt gives way to sight, but a day when hope gives way to sight, the day when the risen and ascended Lord comes for His own (1 Thess 4:15-16). Christ's resurrection manifested His deity to Thomas and caused him to declare that Jesus of Nazareth was his Lord and his *God.* Who else but God as man has the divine *right* to say - "I lay down my life, that I might take it again. No man taketh it from me, but I lay it down of myself. I have power [authority] to lay it down, and I have power [authority] to take it again" (Jn 10:17-18)? Observe the repeated emphasis on the personal pronoun "I", which is all of self. It is all of self, for it is all of God, since it is as God He speaks. It would be certain blasphemy otherwise. Who, save God, can utter words not only of divine right but of divine *might* - "destroy this temple (my body) and I will raise it up in three days" (Jn 2:19)? Men had seen the dead raised by Jesus of Nazareth, but here before them was this same One who had the power over His *own* life, for He is the divine Man. This prerogative possessed and executed by Christ, manifested His divine attributes and it entails the deepest of divine mysteries, indisputably revealing His deity.[30]

The doubting disciple was privileged in grace to have the Lord appear to him. But greater blessings are always the reward of faith, as we are informed in Hebrews 11 and by Peter: "Whom having not seen, ye love; in whom, though now ye see *him* not, yet believing, ye rejoice with joy unspeakable and full of glory: Receiving the end of your faith, *even* the salvation of *your* souls" (1 Pet 1:8-9).

Concluding remarks

To deny that the Gospels identify Jesus of Nazareth as God, is to rob them of their essential doctrine and drama, and reduce their inspired declarations to dreary uncertainties. Christ claimed and demonstrated that He was the divine Man. This was why many followed and worshipped Him, and also why many desired to kill Him. Time and again the Lord's claims of equality with God were met with bitter accusations of blasphemy and cries for His death (which refutes the view that Christ's deity was an invention of the post-apostolic fathers). In John 7 He is the man who "would not walk in Jewry [Judea], because the Jews sought to kill him" (v.1); "Is not this he, whom they seek to kill?" (v.25). He became known not just as a Sabbath-breaker, but as a persistent blasphemer deserving of death because He claimed to be equal with God. Yet, amidst the mounting maelstrom of hate, He never retreated from His claim to be "Lord of the Sabbath". He never sought to alter the clear and consistent belief among the Jews that He claimed to be "equal with God". Rather, He repeatedly declared His equality with God, perhaps none so absolutely as when He consoled His timorous disciples in that upper room. "Ye believe in

---

[30] As the divine Son in subjection Christ received the *commission* and *commandment* to lay down His life and take it up (Jn 10:18). This He did as the Son who was the obedient Servant of God, the Father. As a divine Person - God, He had the power *and* authority over His life. "I lay down my life, that I may take it up again." This He said and did as the divine Man, predicated upon His abiding natural and moral divine attributes! The Spirit of God presents both truths that we may apprehend that He who was very God was also the perfect Servant of God.

God, believe also in me" (Jn 14:1). What impious arrogance if He were not God! If we are to render to Christ all that we are required to do in this single command, let alone all else which is exhorted in the Gospels in terms of trust, honour, worship, love, and even our eternal soul, then God would be excluded if Christ were not God. It was not a matter of just believing what He said i.e., "believe me". It was a case of believing *in who He was*, and *what* He was. The value of what He said rested upon His divine Person. They were to believe *in* Him "also", meaning that they were to trust Christ for the same reason they trusted in God. If Christ were not God, there would be a fatal breach of that first and great commandment to love God with all our heart, soul and mind (Matt 22:37).

Are we to regard the words and deeds of the Man Jesus of Nazareth as the product of presumption and protracted fraud? Can we say of Him whom the Spirit endorses as "the faithful witness" (Rev 1:5), the One who dwells in the eternal sunshine of the countenance of God, that He knew to do good but conspired to do it not? "A faithful witness will not lie: but a false witness will utter lies" (Pr 14:5). Are we to suppose there was complicity by the Father in deception, for we are told "The Father that sent me beareth witness of me" (Jn 8:18)? It was the Father who expressed personal approbation of Jesus of Nazareth at His baptism. "This is my Beloved Son, in whom I am well pleased" (Matt 3:17). Despite the charges of blasphemy against the Son the Father's voice from the excellent glory repeated this ardent approbation, adding the commandment, "Hear ye Him" (Matt 17:5). If Christ is not very God, then a blasphemy was perniciously perpetuated by Him throughout His public ministry and condoned by the Father, who, in His omniscience, knows all the works of the Son.

In the light of the narratives in John 5 and 9, how can Jesus of Nazareth be a created being? A created being no matter how highly morally endued and noble, cannot possess the power and prerogative of the Almighty God. Therefore they can never deserve or claim the glory and honour due to God. A created being is but a "creature". Paul condemns those who change the truth of God into a lie, and worship and serve the creature *rather than* the Creator (Rom 1:25).[31]

---

[31] This verse (Rom 1:25) declares that Christ who is the Creator must be the object of worship and service.

How could Christ be an angel, for He unreservedly accepted worship from men and enjoined men to serve Him? John fell down before the angel in worship but was instantly reminded that angels are fellow-servants, and that he should worship God (Rev 19:9-10; cf Ps 148:2). Certain divine wrath awaits the angels who sought higher honour and left their appointed rank. "And *the* angels which kept not their first estate, but left their own habitation, he hath reserved in everlasting chains under darkness unto the judgement of the great day" (Jude 6). That MAN OF SIN, the son of perdition is marked as one who "opposeth and exalteth himself above all that is called God...shewing himself that he is God" (2 Thess 2:4). His end will be judgement at the hand of God. God is a "consuming fire" against all who seek honour above their divinely appointed place, as also witnessed in His destruction of Nadab, Abihu and the sons of Korah. Are we to accept that Jesus of Nazareth committed the sin of Lucifer, who sought to "ascend into heaven" and be "like the Most High", whose end shall be that he be "brought down to hell" (Isa 14:12-15; Rev 20:10)? According to God's divine rule, even an especially created being will be consumed with everlasting fire if it claims and accepts acclamations of equality with God. Yet, Christ, who consistently claimed equality with God received nothing but divine approbation. We, too, through divine precept and principle, are exhorted to exalt, worship and honour Him as God.

Note a clear example of this relating to the "Feasts of Jehovah".[32] Jehovah instituted these feasts for *His* honour and to *His* glory, to be observed by *His* people. In that OT economy He was the sole object of worship and honour. *His* works were the sole subject of commemoration and praise. In this church period, however, the feasts of Jehovah are no more. Christ annulled them all by instituting *the* new 'Feast' - the "Lord's Supper", which is to be observed by all who are the children of *God*. To what end? On these occasions we are to worship, praise and glorify *Christ*, in the remembrance of *Christ* – "this do in remembrance of me". We are to commemorate *His* work (Lk 22:19). When in obedient love we participate in His supper fixing our worship upon Him, we are not

---

[32] Such as the Passover, First Fruits and Feast of Weeks (Pentecost).

His accomplices in blasphemy, for He is God. He is Lord *also* of the Sabbath, Jehovah's equal!

It is notable that there are no warnings in Scripture against serving or worshipping Christ. The person most likely to be venerated as God among men would be Christ, given all that He did and claimed. And, the one most obligated to warn against worshipping Christ, if Christ is not God, is Christ Himself. But He issued no such warning. This is especially significant in the light of His moral perfection.

The Gospel narratives reveal with ineffable richness and certitude, that Christ claimed to be God and that He is God. This He did by claiming and manifesting all the marks of deity and the attributes of God, which He possessed entirely, equally, eternally and exclusively testifying to His undiminished and unceasing deity. He did all this knowing that among men it was creating both seething hatred and obedient faith towards Himself, while He walked in the unclouded sunshine of the Father's infinite delight. And, may we note again, that notwithstanding their extensive apologetic merit, the Athanasian and Nicene creeds did not initiate the doctrine of Christ's deity. They were but streams of affirmation, which could never rise above the Fountain-Head - Christ Himself, as recorded in the Gospels.

Accordingly, these inspired narratives issue a fearful warning to those who deny Christ's deity. May all who do this, heed the divine indictment against the disbelieving Jews, and, through obedient faith, accept the clear record of His deity revealed in the Gospels (Jn 8:44, 47). Only then will they come to know Him whom to know is life eternal. "And this is life eternal, that they might know thee the only true God, and Jesus Christ, whom thou hast sent" (Jn 17:3).

CHAPTER 4

Christ's Deity Seen in His Titles and Names

We have noted that during His life on earth, Jesus of Nazareth exhibited all the marks of deity. He did those things that only God could do. He exercised divine prerogative in what He did, and in so doing He revealed the glory of God. All this served to *manifest* Him as God, confirming the sacred truth that He was Emmanuel, God with us. Now we examine His titles and names, nine of them, which on the other hand serve essentially to *identify* Him as God, each one illuminating a majestic facet of His divine Person and work. His identification as God is revealed in His titles and names through:

- their *content* and *compass*;
- their *correspondence* with the names and titles borne by God;
- their *coincidence* with the marks of deity;
- the *confessions* and *challenges* associated with them.

We begin by considering two titles which refer to Christ's divine sonship, "the Son of God" and "the only begotten of the Father". Scripture is the record of God concerning His Son (1 Jn 5:10).

1. The Son of God
All four Gospels declare Jesus of Nazareth to be "the Son of God". They record this title upon the lips of - Satan (Matt 4:3), the men in the ship (Matt 14:33), the high priest (Matt 26:63), the Roman centurion (Matt 27:54), Mark (1:1), evil spirits (Mk 3:11), Gabriel (Lk 1:35), John the Baptist (Jn 1:34), Nathanael (Jn 1:49),

Martha (Jn 11:27) etc. Also the Lord in dialogue declared Himself to be the Son of God [the Blessed] (Mk 14:61-62; Jn 9:35-37; 10:36). This title is implicit each time He refers to Himself as "the Son", and God as "His" Father. The title, "the Son of God", is also given to Christ in Acts, the Epistles and in Revelation (Acts 8:37; 9:20; Rom 1:4; 2 Cor 1:19; Gal 2:20; Rev 2:18).

To serve the truth, it is vital yet not enough to show that Jesus of Nazareth bore the unique title "the Son of God". This is sufficiently plain from Scripture, as we shall note. We need to determine the divine status of this title. Does it express deity? Are the marks of deity associated with it? How did the Lord's contemporaries respond to it?

The term "sonship"

"Sonship" is a term that refers to the *position, possession, prospect* and the *prerogatives* that belong to a son.

The uniqueness of the title - "the Son of God"

Jesus of Nazareth owns this title exclusively, thereby identifying His unique sonship in regard to God.[1] We see this in the words of the angel to the virgin - that holy thing which shall be born of thee shall be called "the Son of God" (Lk 1:35). We see it, too, in the reason why John wrote his Gospel, that we "might believe that Jesus is the Christ, the Son of God (Jn 20:31). In Scripture Christ is never spoken of as "a son of God", being numbered among those referred to as the "sons of God". This is a term the Lord employed of others (Matt 5:9; Lk 20:36 [not "children" as in the AV]; Heb 1:5 cf Rom 8:14-17; Gal 4:7).[2] The fact that NT believers are the "sons of God" who are also the "children of God", and that Christ is never referred to as "a child of God", nor "the child of

---

[1] The reference to Adam by Luke as "the son of God" is not a title but an idiomatic expression to mark lineage (Lk 3:38).

[2] In the OT "sons of God" refer to angels (Job) and as some render it, to men/angels in Genesis 6. In Luke 1:32 Christ is "Son of *the* Highest" and in 6:35 we have men as "children [sons] sons of the Highest", the distinction between the particular and the general is again preserved. The Lord applies the latter title to those who exhibit the *moral* characteristics of God. Hebrews 1:5: "I will be to him a Father, and he shall be to me a Son." No title is stated here, only a relationship. This verse does not detract from the uniqueness of Christ as "the Son of God" despite the presence of the article. All that is being declared here is the existence of a particular relationship between Jesus of Nazareth and God, one of sonship (which brings into view the Fatherhood of God).

God", further establishes the uniqueness of Christ as "the Son of God".

The title "the Son of God" means that the sonship of the Creator-Redeemer in all aspects is wholly distinct from the sonship of the creature redeemed in Him. The position, possession, prospect and prerogatives of a believer in Christ as a son of God, are the consequences of *divine grace* and *adoption*, the latter because of the former. Those who are redeemed through divine grace are adopted into the family of God as sons through the Spirit of God sent by the Son of God (Rom 8:14-17; Gal 4: 3-7). We are *children* of God by (new) birth and *sons* of God by adoption. (How blessed when compared with our prior position, possession and prospect in the family of Adam.) Our birth and sonship is by the washing of regeneration and the renewing of the Holy Ghost (Tit 3:5), which brings us into a descendant spiritual relationship with the Father. We *became* sons of God and God *became* our Father at the time of our spiritual rebirth (Jn 1:12). Christ never became the Son of God. His sonship is not a consequential matter at all, for it abides on the unoriginated ground of *divine right*, which precludes adoption. If Christ is in any way a "created being", then to be a son of God, He, too, would have to be the subject of adoption. Nowhere in Scripture is Christ spoken of as being in any way "adopted" as a son by the Father (let alone being "regenerated" and "renewed" by the Holy Spirit).[3] In no sense is He "derived" from God, for He is the eternally co-existent Son, the Second Person of the Godhead.[4] Christ's sonship therefore entails uniqueness in position, possession, prospect and prerogative. "All things are delivered unto me of my Father: and no man knoweth the Son, but the Father; neither knoweth any man the Father, save the Son, and *he* to whomsoever the Son will reveal *him*" (Matt 11:27). It is as the Son of God that Christ reveals the Father, for they possess the same essential nature. Though we are sons of God, we can

---

[3] That Christ was 'adopted" by God to be His Son is referred to as the "Adoptionist" view of His sonship. It was held by the Ebionites (2nd century) and other heretical sects.
[4] Origen (c185-245) - the "eternal generation" of the Son. He preserved the divine nature but argued derivation. If using the term "generation" in regard to Christ as the Son of God, it is vital to bear in mind what Scripture insists upon - the Son was never "derived" from God nor adopted by Him!

never "declare" the Father, because unlike "the Son of God", we do not possess the divine attributes.

Scripture records further testimony to the uniqueness of Christ's sonship. In his temptation of Christ, Satan refers to Him as *the* Son of God (Matt 4:3,6).[5] Nathanael confesses Jesus of Nazareth to be "the Son of God" and "the King of Israel" (Jn 1:49). The title the Son of God expresses Christ's divine *sonship* in regard to His eternal kingdom. He is the Son of God who is appointed Heir of all things (Heb 1:2). The latter title speaks of His divine *sovereignty* in relation to the earthly Messianic kingdom. Both titles mark two convergent themes in biblical prophecy concerning the coming divine One. Upon his confession a blessing was conferred upon Nathanael by the Lord - I say unto you henceforth you shall "see heaven open, and the angels of God ascending and descending upon the Son of man" (Jn 1:51). Peter confesses Jesus of Nazareth to be "the Christ, the Son of the living God". Here the church is in view and fittingly the Son of God is the Son of the *living* God, identifying the Son as the *foundation* of the Church which is His Body (Matt 16:16-18). This confession marks the theme of NT revelation and a blessing upon Peter. "Blessed art thou, Simon Barjona: for flesh and blood hath not revealed *it* unto thee, but my Father which is in heaven"(v.17). There is here, too, something of the unique possession and prerogative of the Son of God. He declares the Church to be "My Church", which He alone will build! In John 6:69 Peter again declares Christ to be "the Son of the living God". The title on this occasion expressing the essential *faith* of those who comprise His Body, the Church.

"My" Father and "Your" Father

In His references to God as His Father, the Lord chose words that assiduously guarded His distinctive sonship as "the Son of God". He spoke of Himself as "the Son", never as "a Son". He never used the term *our Father* which would convey the idea that God bears the same paternal relationship to the redeemed creature as He does to "the Son", the Redeemer. As believers we are encouraged to call God "our Father", but when we do so we can

---

[5] "If thou be the Son of God": Satan knew the truth of it. His attack was designed to bring into disrepute the work of the Son as the perfect Servant of God, One who seeks to do only the will of Him who sent Him (see also Lk 4:41).

never include Christ. With the Lord it is always, "your Father" and "my Father", as illustrated in that post-resurrection scene when He declared to Mary, "Touch me not; for I am not yet ascended to my Father: but go to my brethren, and say unto them, I ascend unto my Father, and your Father; and *to* my God, and your God" (Jn 20:17).[6] He did not say, "I go to *our* Father," for He desired to communicate and preserve the distinctive relationship He has with God as "the Son of God".[7]

This distinction is preserved in the disciples' prayer: "When ye pray, say, our Father...", not, when *we* pray, *we* say "our Father" (Lk 11:2). It is preserved, too, in regard to the coming kingdom. "Come, ye blessed of my Father, inherit the kingdom prepared for you from the foundation of the world (Matt 25:34). And again, He will not drink of the fruit of the vine until "I drink it new with you in my Father's kingdom" (Matt 26:29). When the Jews sought the more to kill the Lord (Jn 5:18), we noted it was not because He said that God was "our Father", but that He said God was "His" Father, which expressed His unique sonship as the eternal Son of God. The Jews had no doubt that when Jesus of Nazareth claimed to be the Son of God, He was claiming to be God - the unique Son of God! To His disciples in that deeply moving final week of His private ministry, where we might expect it otherwise, the Lord does not speak of the many mansions in "our Father's house", but of the many mansions "in *my* Father's house" (Jn 14:2). God declares His Son to be His beloved Son, not one of His beloved sons. Neither is Christ one of the begotten sons of God, but the only begotten Son of God

"The Son of God" who is "the Son of the Most High" and "the Son of the Highest"

The uniqueness of the title "the Son of God" is also seen in its

---

[6] The term "my brethren" is merely an expression of kinship employed to identify the disciples as sharing a common purpose with Him in His earthly mission - to do the will of God. "For whosoever shall do the will of my Father which is in heaven, the same is my brother, and sister, and mother" (Matt 12:50 & Mk 3:35). Note also it is "my brethren" not "our brethren", again assiduously preserving the uniqueness of His Person and His divine glories, even where it involves kinship in purpose. In other instances the term brethren is used to identify Jesus of Nazareth as of the stock of Israel (Acts 7:37); and as part of a family (Lk 8:19).

[7] The distinction in His manhood is also preserved through His use of "my God" and "your God", quoted above!

exclusive association with two titles used for Jehovah. In the OT Jehovah is called "the Most High" (Gen 14:18; Ps 46:4; Isa 14:13; Dan 3:26 cf 25, etc) and "the Highest" (Ps 18:13; Lk 1:35). In the NT we have Christ uniquely as "the Son of God" who is also exclusively "the Son of the Most High" (Mk 5:7), essentially, the Son of Jehovah![8] As the "Son of God" He is also uniquely "the Son of the Highest [Jehovah]" (Lk 1:32). Both associations mark His eternal being and unique sonship as One who is of the same essential nature of Jehovah. It was through the power of the Highest [Jehovah] that the divine eternal Son became man (Lk 1:35).

Not just uniqueness in sonship but deity in sonship!

It is clear that the title "the Son of God" marks the unique sonship of Jesus of Nazareth. But does it reveal deity? From what we have observed so far it most surely does, but let us gather further revelation of it.

The view of heaven

In Luke 1:35 we have the moral glory associated with the title "the Son of God". "That holy thing which shall be born of thee shall be called the Son of God" and His name shall be Emmanuel. This moral glory is distinguished in that it is the *divine* moral glory, for it is the holiness that belongs to One who is very God, Emmanuel, God with us (Matt 1:23; Isa 7:14). Emmanuel is one of the titles of God in the OT.

The view of Christ and His opponents

Of all the titles claimed by Jesus of Nazareth, none it appears consistently outraged the Jews more than His claim to the title "the Son of God". They correctly took this title to be an expression of deity, and Christ was therefore guilty of blasphemy when He claimed it. This is clearly evident in their petition before Pilate. "We have a law [the law relating to blasphemy], and by our law he ought to die, because he made himself the Son of God" (Jn 19:7).[9] Their jibes, too, showed they believed this title to declare deity. If He really was God's Son, He could, through His inherent divine

---

[8] Cf "sons of the Highest" in the moral sense, noted above (Lk 6:35).
[9] We note here and in Mark 1:1 the variation "Son of God".

power come down from the cross (Matt 27:40); if He was in fact the Son of God - God's *own* Son, God would in divine love deliver Him from it (Matt 27:43).

Returning to the dialogue between the Lord and the Jews in John 10, we recall a particular aspect of it in regard to the title "the Son of God". The dialogue begins in verse 24 with the Jews demanding that the Lord declare if He is the Christ. It ends in verse 39 with their desire to stone Him. What had transpired? The Lord said something they regarded as blasphemous for they state quite clearly, "thou, being a man, makest thyself God" (v.33). What He had said was, "I and my Father are one" (v.30). Instead of answering their initial demand directly, He put before the Jews a declaration of His deity. This was His prime intention in that encounter with them. Note what He did next. He linked His declaration of His deity and their perception of it directly with the title "the Son of God" *and* to His ownership of it (v.36). This is not all, for He then confirmed the deity vested in this title by declaring "the Father is in me, and I in him" (v.38), indicating His eternal sonship as "Son of God". Because of this the Jews again sought to take Him. In all this we have deity proclaimed, claimed and perceived in the title "the Son of God".

There is perhaps no better example of this than when Jesus of Nazareth was arraigned before the high priest: "I adjure thee by the living God, that thou tell us whether thou be the Christ, the Son of God" (Matt 26:63). The Lord first confirms that He is the Son of God with the expression "Thou hast said", an expression of affirmation that He had also used when identifying Judas as His betrayer: "Master, is it I?" He said to him, "Thou hast said." (Matt 26:25).[10] He then confirms the deity vested in the title "the Son of God", by linking it to a divine title revealed in the OT - "the Son of man". "Jesus saith unto him, Thou hast said: nevertheless I say unto you, Hereafter shall ye see the Son of man sitting on the right hand of power, and coming in the clouds of heaven." The reaction of the high priest confirms the deity revealed through the association. He rent his clothes, saying, "He hath spoken

---

[10] Note the similar expression of affirmation "Thou sayest it" was used by the Lord when Pilate asked if He were the King of the Jews. (Mk 15:2, cf Jn 18:37). He is indeed the King of the Jews, as He is indeed the Son of God.

blasphemy; what further need have we of witnesses? behold, now ye have heard his blasphemy. What think ye? They answered and said, He is guilty of death" (Matt 26:63-66). How very different to Nathanael's acceptance of the Lord's claim to this title (Jn 1:51)! These events provide a clear testimony from Christ and His opponents, that whoever bore the title "the Son of God" was deemed to be in possession of the natural and moral attributes of God. No further evidence on Christ's claim to be deity was required by the Jews. He had answered plainly!

The view of Christ and His followers
    The One bearing the title "the Son of God" is the object of faith, worship and honour, the sole right of God. "Then they that were in the ship came and worshipped him, saying, Of a truth thou art the Son of God" (Matt. 14:33); "Jesus heard that they had cast him [the cured blind man] out, and when He had found him, He said unto him, 'Dost thou believe on the Son of God?' He answered and said, 'Who is he, Lord, that I might believe on him?' And Jesus said unto him, 'Thou hast both seen him, and it is he that talketh with thee.' And he said, 'Lord, I believe.' And he worshipped him" (Jn 9:35-38). As the Son of God, Jesus of Nazareth accepts faith, worship and honour from men, tributes that are reserved solely for God!

"The Son of God" and salvation unto eternal life
    Salvation belongs to the Lord [Jehovah] and it is solely of Him (Ps 3:8; Jonah 2:9), because only He is holy and righteous and can forgive sins. Jesus of Nazareth as "the Son of God", possesses this same divine prerogative for He, too, possesses absolute holiness and righteousness, the constant theme of the Gospels. Scripture reveals that the Person who is called "the Son of God" has the divine prerogative of salvation. This is evident in that this title is associated with the following:
• The *condition for* salvation - "Whosoever shall confess that Jesus is the Son of God, God dwelleth in him, and he in God" (1 Jn 4:15); "...that believing ye might have life through his name [Jesus, the Son of God]" (Jn 20:31). "...he that hath not the Son of God hath not [eternal] life" (1 Jn 5:12).
• The *confession of* salvation - *Outwardly*: Before the eunuch could

102

be baptised he had to confess, "I believe that Jesus Christ is the Son of God" (Acts 8:36-37). We have it too in the testimony of Paul. "And straightway he [Paul] preached Christ in the synagogues, that he is the Son of God" (Acts 9:20). *Inwardly*: "He that believeth on the Son of God hath the witness [of eternal life] in himself" (1 Jn 5:10).

• The *confidence in* salvation: "These things I have written unto you that believe on the name of the Son of God; that ye may know that ye have eternal life" (1 Jn 5:13).

The title "the Son of God" is a divine title because of its indisputable association with the divine prerogative of salvation. The Son of God is plainly and confidently confessed as the Giver and Source of salvation unto eternal life, a prerogative and a power that can never be possessed or exercised by a created being whose life depends upon the One who created him! "And whosoever liveth and believeth in me shall never die. Believest thou this? She [Martha] saith unto him, Yea, Lord: I believe that thou art the Christ, the Son of God, which should come into the world" (Jn 11:26-27). Peter declares, "Lord, to whom shall we go? thou hast the words of eternal life. And we believe and are sure that thou art that Christ, the Son of the living God" (Jn 6:68-69).

"The Son of God" and the Church

It is the Son of God who has the divine prerogative to "baptize with the Holy Ghost" (Jn 1:33-34). Who but God has the authority to co-operate with the Spirit of God in a matter that involves the formation of the church of God, the union of its members with each other and with their risen and glorified Head? Who but One who is omniscient can fulfil the promise to the local churches, that "where two or three are gathered together in my name, there am I in the midst of them" (Matt 18:20)? It is Jesus of Nazareth, the Son of the living God, who is the very Foundation of the church (Matt 16:16-18).

Though few among many, the above examples are sufficient to demonstrate that the title "the Son of God" is invested with deity. The contemporary understanding of what this title meant, its association with the marks of deity, the teaching of Scripture in regard to its uniqueness, together with the explicit divine approbation it received, reveal this to be indisputably so. Given that the title "the Son of God" is a divine title, it identifies Christ as the *eternal* Son of God, and marks His *eternal* sonship, which we now take up.

The eternal sonship of Christ - its vital importance
Some professing Christians deny that Christ, the Son of God, was the pre-incarnate and eternal Son of God, preferring to believe that He became the Son of God at His resurrection. They cite Romans 1:4 as proof. Christ was "declared *to be* the Son of God, according to the spirit of holiness, by the resurrection from the dead". The word "declared" (*horizo*), they assert, means to "appoint". Christ was appointed the Son of God upon His resurrection and thus He was not the *pre-incarnate* neither the *eternal* Son of God!

There are two vital points to note before we examine this errant teaching and the scriptures cited in support of it. Firstly, if Christ *became* God's Son, then He falls into the category of all others who also became sons of God. He is therefore one of a number, "a son of God". Such a title and position given to Him contradicts the Spirit's revelation of Him as "the Son of God". Christ's sonship is unoriginated, eternal! Secondly, Scripture clearly refers to Christ being God's Son before His incarnation.

Christ the pre-incarnate Son
Paul declares clearly in his Roman epistle that the *Son* pre-existed His *incarnation*. The *Son* was *sent* in the likeness of sinful flesh (8:3, cf 1 Jn 4:10;14), indicative of the complete coincidence between Pauline and Johannine Christology. The *fact* of Christ's sonship is not the subject of Romans 1:4. It is the *character* of it. It is His sonship *in power* - its character which is marked (or "appointed") by His resurrection. His resurrection was evidence of the divine power that He possessed as the *existing* divine Son of God. The "greatness" of this power is seen in that He should lay down His life that He may take it up again. God, too, is said to raise Him up to display the greatness of *God's* power (Eph 1:19-20), revealing the unity of purpose and power within the Godhead. What compelling revelation we have here not only for the Son's

pre-incarnate sonship, but also for His eternal sonship! It is never a case of Christ's sonship resting upon His resurrection. It is, rather, the Son's resurrection that rests upon His divine sonship. The power displayed in Him as the Son through His resurrection, also brings into view His holiness. He was the sinless accepted sacrifice for sin. In Romans 1:4 we have therefore a declaration *of* Christ's divine sonship that was revealed *through* His "greatness" *in resurrection*. This greatness is indicative of His deity in that death had no dominion over Him![11]

Christ's pre-incarnate sonship is seen also in His *communion* with His Father. The glory the *Son* had with the Father "before the world was", declares that the relationship between the Father and the Son existed before time (Jn 17:5). These words intimate precious recollections by the Son on earth of the communion He had with His Father in heaven. It intimates, too, the distinct personality of the Son and the Father. His pre-incarnate sonship is further revealed in the pre-incarnate *commission* He had from the Father. The Father *sent* the *Son* who came *forth* from the *Father*, to be Saviour of the world (1 Jn 4:14; cf Jn 8:23). If the Father existed before the Son's incarnation then the Son must also have existed before His incarnation.

In His answer to Pilate the Lord refered to the purpose of His *birth* - "To this end was I born" (Jn 18:37). He reiterated His answer but altered it and said, "for this cause came I into the world". The first answer is essentially historical and governmental, associating His cause with His physical birth pointing to Him as the future King of kings on earth (Rev 19). The second is in essence eternal and moral. It tells us that He who was with God *came* and refers to His incarnation, intimating His pre-existence in eternity past.[12] It points to Calvary and His work of reconciling all things unto God. The Lord said He was born and that He came, but never does He or Scripture say to this end or for this cause He was created!

---

[11] Four other occasions come to mind where Christ's divine sonship is particularly declared or "marked out" (although the word *horizo* is not employed) - Matt 3:16-17, the Son's Godhood in *sanctification*; Matt 16:16-18, the Son's Government in *preservation*; Matt 17:1-8, the Son's Glory in *transfiguration*; Matt 27:40, the Son's Grace in *salvation*.

[12] We take up the Incarnation in chapter 8, but note here that it was not simply a virgin giving birth miraculously through divine conception. It was a virgin giving birth by divine conception to One who pre-existed!

Scripture speaks of Christ being sent *as* God's Son. It never states He was sent *to become* God's Son; it never speaks of a beginning to Christ's sonship at all, for His sonship always was and will ever be! He was, however, sent to become a *Servant* (Phil 2:7)!

The Spirit of God carefully preserves the pre-incarnate sonship of Christ in biblical prophecy. Referring to the Incarnation, Isaiah declared a son is *given* - not born. This statement itself speaks of the Son's pre-incarnate existence. The context of the passage confirms this, for the statement stands in striking contrast to a child *born* (Isa 9:6). The former marks His pre-incarnate sonship, the latter His manhood taken on at His incarnation. God, the Father, gave the One who was with Him in eternity past, His Son (Jn 1:1). Christ declares He is the Son whom the Father "sanctified and sent into the world" (Jn 10:36). This order intimates the Son's pre-incarnate existence. He who pre-existed was sanctified - set apart, and *then* sent by His Father! The Holy Spirit was also "sent". Is not the Spirit of God the divine Spirit, the "Eternal Spirit" (Heb 9:14), who existed prior to being given and sent by God to be our Comforter and Spirit of Adoption (Jn 14:16; Gal 4:6)?

Christ - not simply the pre-incarnate Son, but also the eternal Son
Here again Scripture brings two convergent lines of truth before us:
• The Son's *deity* is revealed. This in turn intimates the eternal relationship between the eternal Father and His eternal Son.
• The Son's eternal *relationship* with the Father is revealed. In turn, this intimates the Son's deity – His eternal being.

In John 1:1-2, the Spirit announces the deity of the Son: "The Word [who is the Son] was God". Being God, the Son is eternal, the eternal Son. If the Persons are eternal, then the relationship between them must be eternal. In this same chapter the eternal relationship between the Word and God is revealed. The Word who is the *Son* was *eternally* in the *Father's* bosom (Jn 1:18). The expression "which is in the bosom of the Father", refers to "a timeless state, an eternal condition and relation...and implies the unbroken continuation of it in the days of His flesh."[13] We have here the eternal relationship between the

---

[13] W E Vine *Collected Writings* Vol 1 p 218.

Father and the Son. If the relationship between the Persons is eternal, then the Persons involved in the relationship must be eternal. We will observe more concerning this later.

To deny the eternal sonship of Christ is to cast a shadow over the infinite love of God because it asserts that He did not give His *own* Son for sin. A created being, however especially and splendidly fashioned above all other creation, can never comport with the sublime love of God, for He *so loved* the world, that He sent *His* Son to be a sacrifice for sin. "Herein is love, not that we loved God, but that he loved us, and sent his Son *to be* the propitiation for our sins" (1 Jn 4:10). What unrestrained and unrequited divine love flows from the truth that God *sent* His *Son*, "the only begotten Son, which is in the bosom of the Father"; the "Son of His love" (Col 1:13, "His dear Son").

If Christ became God's Son at any point in time then the integrity of the eternal Triune Godhead is diminished. The Second Person of the Godhead, the Son, cannot be co-eternal and co-equal with the Father and the Holy Spirit! It would mean, too, that prior to creation God was without affection, and that He is not the eternal Father revealed in the Word of God. When Scripture speaks of the infinite love of God the Father, it invites us to consider more than just His infinite possession of it, but also to acknowledge His infinite *expression* of it. Upon whom then did His eternal love repose in eternity prior to time and all creation if not on the eternal Son? "For thou lovedst me [the Son, as the Son] before the foundation of the world" (Jn 17:24). If there is no eternal Son there can be no eternal Father!

The unique relationship between the Son and the Spirit

The unique relationship between the Son of God and the Spirit of God is a further revelation of the deity of the Son. The deity and personality of the Holy Spirit are clearly taught in Scripture.[14] The

---

[14] The distinct Person of the Holy Spirit is seen clearly in the promise given by Christ, "I will send you another [*allon*] Comforter" (Jn 14:16). *Allon* (allos) refers to a numerical difference not a qualitative one. W E Vine *Expository Dictionary* p 60. Thus the Comforter (the Spirit of God) is "another Person" who is a comforter like Christ. The deity of the Holy Spirit is plain in that He is the "Spirit of God" possessing the divine natural attributes of God: *omnipotence* - the works of creation and salvation (Gen 1:1-2; Tit 3:5); *omnipresence* - (Ps 139:7); *omniscience* - (1 Cor 2:10). He is the "Eternal Spirit" (Heb 9:14) as Christ is the Eternal Son! The Spirit of God has the moral attributes of God - He is the "Holy" Spirit of God; the Spirit of truth (Jn 14:17). He has a "personality" in that He can be grieved (Eph 4:30); vexed (Isa 63:10). He has divine prerogative (1 Cor 12:11).

same attributes of deity and distinction of Person that apply to the Son and the Father, apply to the Spirit of God. The rule relating to the possession of the attributes of God and the three marks of deity can be used to discern the deity of the Spirit of God from Scripture.[15]

The Son of God is absolute truth, and so, too, is the Spirit of God absolute truth (Jn 14:6, 17; 1 Jn 5:6). Which created being has such an equality with the Spirit of God? The Holy Spirit is a divine Person, and His equality with God the Father and the Son is also seen in title. The Holy Spirit is the "Spirit of God" who is also "the Spirit of Christ" (Rom 8:9; 1 Pet 1:11, cf the "Spirit of Jesus Christ", Phil 1:19 and the "Spirit of his Son", Gal 4:5-7). These divine titles reveal the divine co-operation between the Spirit of God and the Son of God in the believer's salvation, sanctification and sonship. Who is it that "dwells" in the believer (Rom 8:9-11)? It is the Spirit of God, who is also the Spirit of Christ and the Spirit of the Son! In John 15:26 and 16:7, the Spirit of God like the Son of God is said to have proceeded from God (cf Jn 8:42).

2. The only Begotten Son

The term "only begotten" - *monogenes*, is used to describe the "only son" of the widow of Nain, the "one only daughter" of Jarius and the "only child" of the man in Luke 9 (Lk 7:12; 8:42; 9:38). In each case *monogenes* refers to the one-and-only person within a particular category of persons. That there was no other son, daughter or child, also means that the relationship between the parent and child was an exclusive one. *Monogenes* is used in regard to Christ. As "the Son of God", He is "the *Only Begotten*" (Jn 1:18; 3:18).[16] He stands alone as "the Son of God", and, therefore, He enjoys an unshared relationship with God as *His own* Father. How preciously consistent this is with what we saw earlier revealed in Scripture in regard to His unique and eternal sonship - His own declaration of it and the Jews' understanding of it! There is, too, intimation of His singular sonship in the parable of the vineyard (Mk 12). In this parable

---

[15] For instance, observe the Spirit's exercise of divine prerogative in 1 Corinthians 12:11, which means He possesses the attributes of God, and possesses them entirely, equally, eternally and exclusively!

[16] In John 1:14 the article is absent, stressing the character of the Son's being as that of the Father.

with a dispensational lesson, we identify Him as the "one" son who is the "well-beloved" of the father (vv. 6-8), the son who is of the same nature of the father (who is certainly not an adopted son).

There is, however, another aspect to the term "monogenes" when it is applied to Christ in Scripture, seen in the unique sonship of Isaac. Abraham had many sons, the firstborn in time was by Hagar the bondwoman, followed by Isaac his son by his wife Sarah, and then his sons by his concubine Keturah. Yet Isaac is referred to as the "only begotten" of Abraham (Gen 22.2). The expression cannot mean that he is the only son of Abraham or even his son born first in time. It refers to the unique *nature* of the relationship between Isaac and his father, irrespective of time and order of generation. He was the son of the union between Abraham and Sarah, the free-woman, the wife of Abraham. Isaac was the only begotten son in that he was Abraham's sole legal heir. He was, too, the son of divine promise, the *only one of His kind*, in that he was the *lone* object of his father's *love*, and his entire hope in *lineage* (Gen 17:15-16).[17] As the "only begotten", Christ is *only one of His kind*. He possesses a unique, divine sonship, possessing the title deeds to all the Father's possessions.[18] Being the Son of promise, all divine pledges are consummated in Him, and God through Him will bring many sons into glory.[19]

As noted earlier, to assert as some do that Christ's sonship had a beginning is contrary to Scripture. *Genos* speaks of birth and it does imply the existence of a paternal relationship as well as a point in time when that relationship began. However, as we have seen, when used in the context of biblical revelation concerning Christ, in no sense can it mean that He came into being after the Father, i.e., He was "derived" from the Father.[20]

---

[17] The relationship between Abraham and Isaac reveals blessed intimations of Christ as the only begotten of the Father. For instance, to Isaac was given "all that he [the father] hath" (Gen 24:36). In regard to the Son, "The Father", we are told, "hath given all things into his hand" (Jn 3:35). "All the things that the Father hath are mine" (Jn 16:15).

[18] Being 'the only one of a kind', Christ cannot be, as some assert, Michael the archangel in Daniel 10 and 12. Michael is 'one of a kind' – "one of the chief princes" (guardians of the Jews) (Dan 10:13).

[19] "The begetting is not an event of time, however remote, but a fact irrespective of time. Christ did not *become*, but necessarily and eternally *is* the Son. He, a Person, possesses every attribute of pure Godhood. This necessitates eternity, absolute being; in this respect He is not "after" the Father" (Moule). W E Vine *Expository Dictionary* p140.

[20] "The best old Greek manuscripts (Aleph B C L) read *monogenes theos* (God only begotten) which is undoubtedly the true text." A T Robertson-*Word Pictures*, Vol 5 p 17; also W E Vine *Expository Dictionary* p 140.

The only begotten Son - His ministry and deity

When Scripture refers to Christ as the only Begotten Son, fragrant aspects of His work in sonship are brought before us, revealing His possession of the divine attributes, prerogatives and glory. It was, we recall, as the only Begotten Son that He declared God (Jn 1:18). In regard to the nature of the Godhead, the *only begotten Son*:

declared the Father	Jn 1:14
declared God	Jn 1:18

In regard to the ministry of the Godhead, the *only begotten Son*:

declared divine love	Jn 3:16 - God is Love
declared divine judgment (light)	Jn 3:18 - God is Light
declared divine life	1 Jn 4:9 - God is Life

When the Lord uttered the words of John 14:6, He spoke as the only Begotten Son of God, revealing His deity. "I am the way [divine love], [and] the truth [divine light], and the life [divine life]. No man cometh unto the Father but by me."

"This day I have begotten thee"

How are we to interpret God's prophetic words in Psalm 2:7 concerning the Messiah, "Thou art my Son, this day have I begotten thee", found in Acts 13:33, Hebrews 1:5 and 5:5, which were fulfilled in Christ? Given the truth of Christ's eternal sonship, this expression cannot mean that He *became* the Son at a point in time. This is supported by the precedent declaration in each case - "Thou art my Son" - the Son who existed at the time. It was not, "This day have I begotten thee, Thou art now my Son". Scripture does not say here or anywhere else, "Thou hast *become* my Son"! The pre-existing Son as the firstborn is brought into the *world* - not brought into *existence* as the Son (Heb 1:6).

What then does this expression mean? We will use Acts 13 as our reference since it furnishes us with the first-mentioned instance of the case in the NT. Note first that the word "begotten" is coupled with the expression "this day", giving it a clear dimension in time. There is therefore a conspicuous difference between the present and the previous context of the use of the term "begotten".

Second, the portion emphasises a particular *work* of the Son rather than the relationship between the Son and the Father. The passage deals with works unto God. David is referred to as having been "raised unto" a particular work, to rule as king over Israel (v.22). In verse 23, Christ is "raised" unto the work saving Israel. In verses 32-33, Paul speaks of God raising up Jesus of Nazareth in order to fulfil the promises made unto the fathers of Israel. In each case the person concerned is brought to a point in time, a time of readiness to begin a work or to fulfil a promise (David to rule Israel; Christ to be the Saviour of Israel; Christ to fulfil the divine promises made to Israel).

This is the context in which the term "begotten" is used in regard to Christ in the three passages before us.[21] In Acts 13, it is the Son being raised - begotten or brought to readiness at a certain day/time to perform the work of salvation. This has nothing at all to do with Jesus of Nazareth *becoming* God's Son. In Acts 13 and Hebrews 1:5, that day was the day of His *Incarnation*, as confirmed in the Galatian Epistle. "But when the fulness of the time had come, God sent forth His Son, made [come] of a woman, made [come] under the law, to redeem those who were under the law, [and note again in regard to *our* sonship] that we might receive the adoption as sons" (Gal 4:4-5).[22] Observe once more that God *sent forth His Son*, One who was set apart, teaching that the Son existed prior to His incarnation.

In Hebrews 5:5 the day of the Son being begotten is the day of His *ascension*. After His life and sacrificial work on earth had ended, He was raised up unto a High Priest, the subject of Hebrews 5. The three applications are summarised as follows:

Scripture	"This Day"	Explanation	The Son - His Work
Acts 13:33 Heb 1:5	Incarnation	The Son come down in *condescension* to do the work of salvation	The Son as our Saviour
Heb 5:5	Ascension	The Son gone up in *glorification* to do the work of intercession	The Son as our Great High Priest

[21] A farmer may declare when surveying his ripened crop ready for harvest, "This day I have begotten it", having raised it up to this day. His "relationship" with his crop pre-existed this point in time.
[22] The day of His resurrection is mentioned in verse 34 to have us acknowledge the resurrection as part of the work of salvation for which Christ was raised up (begotten). This truth is dilated in the writing of the Roman Epistle. "[Christ] who was delivered for our offences, and was raised again for our justification" (Rom 4:25).

3. The Son of man

"Whom do men say that I the Son of man am?" (Matt 16:13).[23] The Lord used this title of Himself. In the NT, it is used predominantly within the Gospels because it expresses His humanity and humility evident during the days of His rejection. But it is also associated with His glorification, for He is the Son of man at God's right hand, to whom all power and judgement is given (Matt 24:30-31 etc). The first and last use of this title in the Gospels is noteworthy, indicative of Christ's condescension and His glorification respectively, as Jesus the Man (Matt 8:20; Jn. 13:31). The title "the Son of God" identifies *God* as the Man Christ Jesus, and that all things are *unto* Him. The title "Son of man" identifies Christ as the *man* who is God and that all things are *under* Him. He was always the Son of God, but it was not until His incarnation – His manhood, that He became the Son of man.[24]

This title is first mentioned in the OT where it generally refers to men. There is however in prophecy, application of it to the Godhead. In Daniel 7:9 the description of the One called the Ancient of Days (God), is applied without qualification to the One referred to as the Son of man in Revelation 1:13-14. This is an important connection, since the Son of man in Revelation is none other than Jesus Christ - who then is also the Ancient of Days. The Lord corroborates this link by identifying Himself as the Son of man given in Daniel 7:13 (Mark 14:62 cf Matt 24:30). "And Jesus said, I am: and ye shall see the Son of man sitting on the right hand of power, and coming in the clouds of heaven." Observe again the telling reaction of the High Priest to the Lord's words. He rent his clothes, an act which we have noted, is in response to blasphemy. What blasphemy lay here in the eyes of the priest? It was that Christ took unto Himself a divine title, and in so doing He identified Himself with the personality, position and posture of deity. We have then, the incontestable revelation that the Son of man and the Ancient of Days in Daniel 7 are of the Godhead, the Son of man being a distinct Person within the Godhead.

---

[23] Christ was never "a son of a man" nor "a son of man".

[24] Cf Vincent - "Messianic Lordship could not pertain to his preincarnate state: it is a matter of function, not of inherernt power and majesty. He was *essentially* Son of God; he must *become* Son of man." Vincent *Word Studies* Vol IV p 380.

There are, too, divine prerogatives associated with the title "Son of man". One we noted was in regard to the Sabbath. But the Son of man is not just Lord of the Sabbath, for He said He was Lord *also* of the Sabbath (Mk 2:28). As God, the Son of man is "Lord of all" (Acts 10:36 cf Jehovah, Josh 3:11,13; Zech 6:5).

A particular divine prerogative of the Son of man is in regard to judgement, revealing His divine judicial glory. He has been given authority to execute judgement "because he is the Son of man" (Jn 5:27). As the Son of man He judges the churches of God (Rev 1-3) and the works of all men (Matt 16:27), which can only be done if He possesses the natural and moral attributes of God.[25]

Then there are further wondrous glimpses of the deity of the Son of man conveyed by His own words that sparkle like everlasting stars. During a conversation with His disciples in the synagogue at Capernaum, the Lord asked, "*What* and if ye shall see the Son of man ascend up where he was before?" (Jn 6:62).[26] If they had difficulty in believing He was to rise from the among dead, then how would they react if they saw Him ascend to the Father, from whose presence He as the Son of God came to earth (cf Jn 1:1 etc)? We have here another revelation of His pre-incarnate personality (cf Jn 3:13; 17:5). It was not, we might add, merely a case of Him going up to heaven, but ascending to the right hand of God, the place of dignity and deity (Heb 10:12).

His deity as the Son of man is also seen in the connection between this title with the title "the Son of God". Both come together in the divine Man. As the Son of man who is also the Son of God, He is the Source of eternal life, a mark of deity, Jn 3:15-16; cf Jn 6:53. In the next section we note that the Son of man is also the divine Messiah.

4. The Messiah

The title Messiah is from the Hebrew "Mashiah" meaning "anointed". It was a given to those who were anointed or "set apart" for God's purposes. Among them were: the Messiah Prince of Daniel (Dan 9:25);

---

[25] The absence of the article in Revelation 1:13, "Son of Man", serves to stress the moral character of Him as the Son of Man, as "the One who is qualified to act as the Judge of all men." "The term 'like unto' serves to distinguish Him as there seen in His glory and majesty in contrast to the days of His humiliation." W E Vine *Expository Dictionary* p 50. He is qualified to judge men because He possesses the moral character of a holy and righteous God.
[26] Where He was before as the Son of God.

a king of Israel (I Sam 2:10); Israel's priests; and even Cyrus the goodly king (Isa 45:1). Jesus of Nazareth however, was *the* anointed of God, set apart as *the* Messiah. On earth He singularly owned and accepted this title (Jn 4:25-26). He is explicitly called "the Messiah" in John 1:41 and by intimation in John 4:25. In other passages He is "the Christ", corresponding to the Hebrew *Mashiah*. We noted earlier that Scripture reveals Christ as God, man and a servant of God. These three identities converge in Him as "the Messiah". Wisdom personifying the pre-incarnate Messiah declared "I was set up [anointed] from everlasting" (Prov 8:23).

Our twofold purpose

The promised Messiah of the OT was unquestionably a man. It is His deity that has been disputed. Our first task therefore is to determine if the Messiah promised to Israel is Deity; our second to establish if that same Messiah was Christ Jesus – the Anointed Man.[27] If Scripture reveals the Messiah of the OT to be divine and identifies Him as Jesus of Nazareth, then we have further revelation of Christ's deity and the plurality of Persons within the Godhead.

There are many OT passages that tell of the coming Messiah. Our focus is on two of the better known, which are of special help in the matter before us.

Psalm 110

1. The LORD [Jehovah] said unto my Lord [Adonai], "Sit thou at my right hand, until I make thine enemies thy footstool."
2. The LORD shall send the rod of thy strength out of Zion: rule thou in the midst of thine enemies.
3. Thy people *shall be* willing in the day of thy power, in the beauties of holiness from the womb of the morning: thou hast the dew of thy youth.
4. The LORD hath sworn, and will not repent, "Thou *art* a priest for ever after the order of Melchizedek."
5. The Lord at thy right hand shall strike through kings in the day of his wrath.
6. He shall judge among the heathen, he shall fill *the places* with the dead bodies; he shall wound the heads over many countries.
7. He shall drink of the brook in the way: therefore shall he lift up the head.

This Psalm is one of many "Messianic" Psalms, Psalms that foretell the Person and work of the Messiah (Lk 24:44). It is the

---

[27] Our consideration of Acts 13:33, Hebrews 1:5 and 5:5 in regard to Psalm 2, already shows this to be the case.

most frequently quoted Psalm in the NT, revealing the Messiah as the Everlasting Priest and King exalted and glorified (v.1). The promised Messiah of Israel will, in Himself, unite the offices of Priest and King. As Priest, His priesthood is eternal and according to the Melchizedek order (v.4). As King, the Messiah will conquer the nation's foes, establish and reign over His kingdom on earth - the Millennial kingdom (vv.1-3; vv. 5-7 cf Ps 45, Heb 1:8).

Jehovah is the Messiah of Psalm 110

Is the Messiah of Psalm 110 Deity? Is the Messiah of Psalm 110 Jesus Christ? If we permit Scripture to interpret itself, we receive a clear affirmative answer to both questions.

The opening statement identifies three persons:

- the *Speaker* - Jehovah, "the Lord said..."
- the *Subject* - David's Lord (Adonai), "unto my Lord..."
- the *Scribe* - David, receiving the revelation from the Spirit of God.

The first Person mentioned "Lord" (v.1) has the title *Jehovah*, the Eternal God. The second Person, the One David calls "my Lord" who is the subject of the Psalm and has the title *Adonai*, is the divine Messiah. Adonai is a Hebrew divine title, evidence of which is seen in the total subjection David is willing to give to Him.[28]

The NT reveals that David's Lord of Psalm 110 is Deity. The Lord questioned the Pharisees - "What think ye of Christ [the Messiah]? whose son is he?" (Matt 22:42). He did not ask "What think ye of Christ?" or "Who is the Messiah of the OT?" He desired a deeper work in their hearts drawn from the theological framework of the OT. He wanted them to acknowledge the *divine sonship* of the Messiah revealed in Scripture, and confess Him as the One who was the embodiment of it. His question therefore was "whose *son* is he [the Messiah]"? The Pharisees replied, "David's son".[29] The course of His conversation with them can be paraphrased as follows.

---

[28] Some suggest David is the second mentioned "Lord" in the first line. This is manifestly incorrect, for David is the writer of this Psalm, as declared by Christ Himself. "David himself said by the Holy Ghost" (Mk 12:36). Further, David can never be the priest "forever after the order of Melchizedek" (Ps 110:4).
[29] The title "Son of David" is used in reference to Jesus of Nazareth chiefly in Matthew's Gospel in keeping with its Messianic theme. Its use in regard to Him was never questioned (Matt 12:23; 15:22; 20:30 etc). His Messiahship was rejected by the Jews because He identified it with deity. It was not, if thou be the Messiah come down from the cross, but if thou be "the Son of God" come down (Matt 27:40!

The Lord asks: Whose son is the Messiah [the Christ]?

The Pharisees reply: David's son.

The Lord then asks: If the Messiah is the son of David - a mere descendant of his, then why in Psalm 110 did David refer to Him as Lord?

And further,

If the Messiah of Psalm 110 is Lord, then how can he be David's son, a mere descendant of David?

If the Pharisees said that the Messiah of Psalm 110 is David's son, a mere human descendant of David, then why did *David* call Him "my Lord", to whom he must render honour, glory and obedience? On the other hand, if the Messiah is Deity, then how can *they* call the Messiah David's son, a mere human descendant of David, and thus deny the Lordship David gave to Him - His deity? Both questions required the Pharisees to admit that the Messiah was more than David's mere descendant. He was God! [30]

Consider also that if the Messiah in Psalm 110 is a mere descendant of David and not Deity, there would be no point to the conversation at all. The Jews correctly believed the OT Scriptures that the Messiah would come from the royal line of David, a man who would deliver them and make them a great nation. They well knew that Christ was of that line (Matt 1:20; 9:27; 12:23 etc).

Clearly, the Messiah is God and the One to whom Jehovah said "Sit thou on my right hand till I make thine enemies thy footstool" is God's Son – Adonai, Jesus of Nazareth. This is the confession the Lord desired from the Pharisees in reply to His questions "What think ye of Christ? Whose son is he?" He speaks of Himself as the Messiah - the Incarnate Son of God, Emmanuel, God with us. And this is what Christ meant when He exhorted "Search the scriptures ...they are they which testify of me" (Jn 5:39). To all this the Pharisees were ignorant and, when enlightened, they refused to believe - "no man was able to answer him a word, neither durst any *man* from that day forth ask him any more *questions*"(Matt 22:46). [31] They were indeed

---

[30] The Lord's use of Psalm 110 to point to His deity and divine sonship means that Psalm 110 intimates the First and Second Persons of the Trinity in the expression "My Lord said unto my Lord"!

[31] Christ is depicted in this Psalm at the right hand of God - as their risen and glorified Messiah. This is another truth unseen by the Jews concerning the One standing before them, which was also the subject of their prophets.

a stiff-necked and rebellious people, whose heart "is waxed gross, and their ears are dull of hearing, and their eyes have they closed; lest they should see with *their* eyes, and hear with *their* ears, and understand with *their* heart, and should be converted" (Acts 28:26-27).

Jehovah, the Messiah of Psalm 110, is Jesus of Nazareth

Is the divine Messiah of Psalm 110 Jesus of Nazareth? The use of this Psalm by the Lord to challenge the Pharisees in regard to His own identity is, itself, sufficient proof that it is. But there is additional evidence.

Firstly, aspects of the person and work of the Messiah of the OT are applied indisputably to Jesus of Nazareth in the NT. This is particularly brought out in the prophetic portions of Scripture, especially Psalm 110, noted below. These examples, though few among many, amply testify that Christ is the divine Messiah of the OT in regard to His Person and redemptive work.

Psalm	OT Text - Jehovah	Theme/Work	NT - to Christ
2:7	The Lord said unto me, Thou *art* my son; This day have I begotten thee.	The Messiah as the Son of God, was raised to the purposes of God.	Heb 1:5; 5:5
8:4-6	What is man that thou art mindful of him? And the son of man, that thou visiteth him. For thou hast made him a little lower than the angels, And has crowned him with glory and honour…Thou hast put all *things* under his feet.	The Messiah as the Son of man, as the glorified second Man and last Adam.	Heb 2:6-8
22:1	My God, my God, why hast Thou forsaken me?	The Suffering Messiah/Saviour	Matt 27:46 etc
22:18	They part my garments among them, And cast lots upon my vesture	The Suffering Messiah/Saviour	John 19:24
110:1	The Lord said unto my Lord, sit thou at my right hand, until I make thine enemies thy footstool.	The Messiah as the Everlasting King.	Heb 1:13
110:4	Thou art a priest forever after *the* order of Melchizedek.	The Messiah as the Everlasting Priest.	Heb 5:6
118:26	Blessed *be* he that cometh in the name of the Lord.	The Messiah as the son of David.	Matt 21:9

Secondly, in his address to the Jews after Pentecost, Peter uses Psalm 110 to identify Jesus of Nazareth as the Messiah. "For David is not ascended into the heavens: but he saith himself, The LORD [Jehovah] said unto my Lord, Sit thou on my right hand, until I make thy foes thy footstool" (Acts 2:34-35). He underpins this with his next statement. "Let all the house of Israel know assuredly, that God hath made that same Jesus, whom ye have crucified, both Lord and Christ [Messiah]" (Acts 2:36).

There is in Psalm 110, a wondrous revelation that the Messiah of the OT is not only Deity, but the divine Son of God, who is David's Lord, who is none other than Jesus of Nazareth, the Christ of the NT. This being the case, note again the oneness yet distinction in the Persons within the Godhead revealed in Scripture.

Isaiah 53:1-12

1. Who hath believed our report? and to whom is the arm of the LORD revealed?

2. For he shall grow up before him as a tender plant, and as a root out of a dry ground: he hath no form nor comeliness; and when we shall see him, *there is* no beauty that we should desire him.

3. He is despised and rejected of men; a man of sorrows, and acquainted with grief: and we hid as it were *our* faces from him; he was despised, and we esteemed him not.

4. Surely he hath borne our griefs, and carried our sorrows: yet we did esteem him stricken, smitten of God, and afflicted.

5. But he *was* wounded for our transgressions, *he was* bruised for our iniquities: the chastisement of our peace *was* upon him; and with his stripes we are healed.

6. All we like sheep have gone astray; we have turned every one to his own way; and the LORD hath laid on him the iniquity of us all.

7. He was oppressed, and he was afflicted, yet he opened not his mouth: he is brought as a lamb to the slaughter, and as a sheep before her shearers is dumb, so he openeth not his mouth.

8. He was taken from prison and from judgment: and who shall declare his generation? for he was cut off out of the land of the living: for the transgression of my people was he stricken.

9. And he made his grave *with the* wicked, and *with the* rich in his death; because he had done no violence, neither *was any* deceit in his mouth.

10. Yet it pleased the LORD to bruise him; he hath put *him* to grief: when thou shalt make his soul an offering for sin, he shall see *his* seed, he shall prolong *his* days, and the pleasure of the LORD shall prosper in his hand.

11. He shall see of the travail of his soul, *and* shall be satisfied: by his

knowledge shall my righteous servant justify many; for he shall bear their iniquities.
12. Therefore will I divide him *a portion* with the great, and he shall divide the spoil *with the* strong; because he hath poured out his soul unto death: and he was numbered with the transgressors; and he bare the sin of many, and made intercession for the transgressors.

Isaiah's prophecy centres on the coming *Messiah-Servant* - "the Servant of Jehovah", notwithstanding specific references to Israel, David and Isaiah himself as servants of God (20:3; 37:35; 41:8; 44:21; 48:20; 49:3). Chapter 53, which unquestionably refers to the Messiah, is in its application a crescendo in the credal witness of Christianity, and in its correct prophetic interpretation, an emphatic testimony to the sovereign grace of God in relation to Israel.

Now what do we have here concerning the deity of the Messiah? Consider chapters 52, 53 and 54. The prophet speaks of Israel's redemption and of their Redeemer who is the Messiah-Servant. The chapters may be outlined as follows. In chapter 52 we have the sure *promise* of Israel's redemption. "Therefore the redeemed of the LORD shall return, and come with singing unto Zion; and everlasting joy *shall be* upon their head: they shall obtain gladness and joy; *and* sorrow and mourning shall flee away" (51:11; 52:2 etc). In chapter 53 we are given the sacrificial *purchase* of Israel's redemption, which fulfills the promise of redemption. "Surely he hath borne our griefs, and carried our sorrows: yet we did esteem him stricken, smitten of God, and afflicted. But he *was* wounded for our transgressions, *he was* bruised for our iniquities: the chastisement of our peace *was* upon him; and with his stripes we are healed" (vv. 4-5). In chapter 54 there is the sequel, the *prosperity* that springs from Israel's redemption. "Enlarge the place of thy tent, and let them stretch forth the curtains of thine habitations: spare not, lengthen thy cords, and strengthen thy stakes; For thou shalt break forth on the right hand and on the left; and thy seed shall inherit the Gentiles, and make the desolate cities to be inhabited" (54:2-3; etc). Viewed sequentially, these three portions give a blessed insight into the design of divine redemption and its covenant character, enabling us to have a greater appreciation of the One upon whom it rests.

It is in the realm of prosperity wrought by *redemption* that the identity of the Messiah-Servant as the Redeemer of Israel is revealed in all His uncreated glory. We have here prophetically what is given in song historically in Exodus 15. In chapter 54, the Messiah is not the suffering Servant of chapter 53, but the Servant who is the Sovereign (v.5). As Sovereign, the Messiah is heralded as Israel's *Maker, Lord of Hosts, Redeemer, Holy One* and *God* (of the whole earth). These titles mark the unmistakable deity of the Messiah. Moreover, in verse 8, the Messiah-Redeemer is explicitly declared to be "Jehovah thy Redeemer".[32]

There is another facet of the personal glory of the Messiah-Servant given to us in these chapters which anticipates the second of our two initial questions - His perfect manhood in the Person of Christ. He is the *man* of sorrows, the Son of God who came in fashion as a man to be "numbered with the transgressors", to pour out His soul unto death and to "bear the sin of many" (53:12). A divine declaration in chapter 54 reveals His identity, deity and perfect humanity: "The Lord [Jehovah] of hosts *is* his name; And thy Redeemer". He is a *Kinsman* Redeemer - *goel* (vv.5,8). How fitting that a prophetic portrait of our heavenly Boaz – Jesus of Nazareth, is given to us in these chapters relating to redemption and the prosperity flowing from it to the redeemed.

The kinsman Redeemer of Israel given in Isaiah 53 identified Himself in chapter 44 as Jehovah, using the transcendent title - "I *am* the FIRST and I *am* the LAST" (Isa 44:6). The title "First and Last" expresses the eternal being of Jehovah, which is associated here with a declaration of His deity, "beside me *there is* no God". In Revelation, Jesus Christ is twice referred to as the First and the Last (Rev 1:17; 22:13), a matter we take up later.

Isaiah's Messiah is Deity. Is He also Jesus of Nazareth? He is indeed, because the character and work of the Messiah-Servant foretold by Isaiah, is unquestionably applied to Christ in the NT.

---

[32] The glory of the Messiah-Redeemer is pathetically revealed in the Psalms. He is there the Sin-Offering of Psalm 22; the King of glory and "the Lord [Jehovah] of Hosts", the Victor in Ps 24. We have, too, His identity and glory heralded in the victory song of Moses. "Jehovah" is first praised as Redeemer, "He [Jehovah] is become my salvation." He is triumphant, "glorious in power" and "glorious in holiness" (Ex 15:1-11). The Redeemer, who promises salvation to Israel in a day to come, who purchases it through His suffering, and through whose mighty arm prosperity flows to the nation in abundant measure, is none other than Jehovah - the "Lord of Hosts", the "Holy-One of Israel", the "God of all the earth" - Jesus the Messiah, the Christ of God.

Philip identified the Messiah-Servant of Isaiah 53 as Jesus of Nazareth to the Ethiopian (Acts 8:32-33). His Christ-centered ministry drawn from this very portion, provoked a Spirit-led confession from the eunuch identifying Christ as the Messiah - He is "Jesus Christ [Messias] the Son of God" (v.37). In Matthew's Gospel, which is especially Messianic, the Spirit of God applies the words of Isaiah to Christ. "That it might be fulfilled which was spoken by Esaias the prophet, saying, 'Behold my servant, whom I have chosen; my beloved, in whom my soul is well pleased: I will put my spirit upon him, and he shall shew judgment to the Gentiles. He shall not strive, nor cry; neither shall any man hear his voice in the streets. A bruised reed shall he not break, and smoking flax shall he not quench, till he send forth judgment unto victory. And in his name shall the Gentiles trust" (Matt 12:17-21; cf 1:22-23). The Messiah-Servant, the Redeemer of Israel is truly man - Jesus of Nazareth, and very God.

Jeremiah 23
A King is promised to Israel. He is identified as One who is raised "unto David a righteous BRANCH" (v.5).[33] This indisputably refers to Jesus of Nazareth, here as the coming *Messiah-King* of the Davidic legal line. There are explicit references in both Testaments to this grand truth (Jer 33:14-17; Eze 37:21-28; Matt 1:20; Lk 1:31,33; Rev 22:16). What is particularly blessed however, is the divine title the inspired prophet applies to the Messiah-King in verse 6. He is to be called "The Lord [Jehovah] our Righteousness". Again we have a revelation of the deity of the Messiah. In this prophetic portion, Jeremiah gives us the Messiah-King who is very God, whom the NT declares to be none other than Jesus of Nazareth. He brings into view His divine moral glory as well as His uncreated Person as Jehovah our Righteousness, who is Jesus Christ *the* Righteous (1 Jn 2:1).

Jeremiah 17:5-7 and Psalm 2:12
We conclude this section by linking the words of Jehovah in Jeremiah 17 with Psalm 2, another Messianic Psalm. Jehovah

---

[33] We remember here the "raising" of the Son of God in the sense of Him being "begotten" to do a work. Here we have a further reference to it.

pronounces a judgement, noted earlier - "cursed be the man that trusteth in man, and maketh flesh his arm". It is not simply that a man is unwise to trust in man, but that he is accursed for it – even to his eternal peril. God is the sole object of faith. "Trust in Him [Jehovah-God] at all times" (Ps 62:8); and "with all thine heart" (Pr 3:5); and "forever: for in the Lord Jehovah is everlasting strength" (Isa 26:4). Yet, in Psalm 2:12 the Spirit of God inspires the psalmist to proclaim blessing on "all they that put their trust in Him" [the Messiah]. If the Messiah is not God, then Jehovah's curse abides on all who put their trust in Him, and a contradiction confronts us. If Christ is not God, then the penitent thief on the cross is eternally lost because he placed his absolute trust in a mere man. It means, too, that Christ who claimed his absolute trust perpetrated a fateful deception. Such notions, of course, cannot be sustained in the light of Christ's moral perfection and His present glorified place at the right hand of God. Christ is indeed God!

From the few portions of Scripture raised in this section, it is evident that the Messiah of the OT is God and He is none other than the Man Jesus of Nazareth. Paul sorrowed over the stubborn unbelief of Israel in the light of the manifold blessings they have received from God (Rom 9). The blessed promise made to them was that the Messiah would come through the seed of Abraham after the flesh. He is Christ Jesus, who is over all, God blessed forever (9:5).[34]

5. Saviour

The God of the Bible is "the Saviour". What ineffable grace and blessed assurance abides in this imperative truth! The title *Saviour* speaks of a Holy God whose infinite love and mercy moved Him to meet the need of sin-cursed man. The title *Saviour* is a divine title. God Himself claims it and the glory associated with it exclusively. "I, *even* I, *am* the LORD [Jehovah]; and beside me *there is* no saviour" (Isa 43:11). This alone is sufficient warrant to accept Christ as God, for He is by God's Spirit explicitly given the title and glory as *Saviour*, as we now observe.

---

[34] This portion reads: Christ, as according to the flesh, the One who is over all, God blessed forever. See A T Robertson *Word Pictures* p 381 Vol IV; W E Vine *Collected Writings* Vol 1 p 472-473.

God is the one and only Saviour
This is true *nationally* in regard to Israel: "Yet I *am* the LORD thy God from the land of Egypt, and thou shalt know no god but me: for *there is* no saviour beside me" (Hos 13:4; Isa 43:3,10; 45:15 etc). It is also true *universally*: "And *there is* no God else beside me; a just God and a Saviour; *there is* none beside me. Look unto me, and be ye saved, all the ends of the earth: for I *am* God, and *there is* none else" (Isa 45: 21-23). This truth is declared in the NT. Referring to Jews and Gentiles, Paul declares, "For this *is* good and acceptable in the sight of God our Saviour" (1 Tim 2:3; Jude 25 etc). In Titus, Paul refers to the love of God our Saviour appearing to man (Tit 3:4-6). It is true *personally*: speaking of God, Job declared "For I know *that* my redeemer liveth" (19:25 cf Ps 19:14). Mary was inspired by the Spirit to exclaim the truth that God was her personal Redeemer. "My soul doth magnify the Lord, and my spirit hath rejoiced in God my Saviour" (Lk 1:46-47).

Christ, too, is the one and only Saviour
All that uniquely belongs to God as the Saviour is ascribed to Christ. How can this be except that Christ is God - the Second Person of the Trinity? Christ is the Saviour of Israel, for He is, as we have observed, the Messiah-King, the kinsman Redeemer of Israel who is none other than Jehovah. The NT confirms this explicitly. "For unto you [Israel] is born this day in the city of David a Saviour, which is Christ the Lord" (Lk 2:11). The name "Jesus" as noted earlier, actually means "Jehovah-Saviour".[35] Jesus will "save His people [Israel] from their sins" (Matt 1:21). Jesus will "reign over the house of Jacob" and He will have an eternal kingdom (Lk 1:33). Christ, the Son of man, is the Saviour of Israel nationally and spiritually, for as the son of David according to the legal and royal line, He will deliver them from Gentile bondage and rule over them. In Him, the Son of Abraham, Israel will partake of the covenant blessings promised by Jehovah.

God is the universal Saviour and so too is Christ. "This is indeed the Christ, the Saviour of the world" (Jn 4:42). Corroboration comes

---

[35] Cf Girdlestone: "It is as Jehovah that God became the Saviour of Israel, and as Jehovah He saves the world; and this is the truth embodied in the name of Jesus, which is literally Jehovah-Saviour." Girdlestone *Synonyms* p 38.

from Christ Himself. He is the Spring of everlasting life to any who thirst (Jn 4:7-14); the Bread of Life to any who hunger (Jn 6:35); the Door, open to any who seek salvation and sustenance (Jn 10:9). "Whosoever" believes in Him shall not perish but shall have everlasting life (Jn 3:16). Paul identifies God as "*God our Saviour*". Yet, in the next breath, without qualification and mindful of the sacred OT truth that God is the sole Saviour, he speaks of Christ as "*The Lord Jesus Christ our Saviour*" (Tit 1:3-4). In these verses He reminds us of the hope of eternal life, which rests on and in "the Saviour". God is the Saviour for He is the Source of eternal life. Christ, too, is the Saviour, the Source of eternal life. This foundation truth is declared in the Gospels and corroborated in the Epistles.

The same correspondence in these titles is found in Titus 2:13, supported by the context and a rule of grammar. The two titles are fused into one, giving "the great God and our Saviour, Jesus Christ", which is an explicit declaration of Christ's deity.[36] The context agrees with this in three ways.

1. Both titles converge and unite in an event - an "appearing". This can only be the second-coming of *Christ.* So we have 'that blessed hope and the glorious appearing [the appearing of the glory] of our great God and Saviour, Jesus Christ'. He who appears is declared to be both God and Christ. God will appear then as he did in His first Advent in the Person of His Son (v.11).

2. Paul contrasts the popular saviour of the world - the great god of the Roman empire, Caesar, with the greatness of Jesus

---

[36] "Our great God and Saviour Jesus Christ". According to the grammarians, the rules of grammar require that where two nouns that have the same case, are linked by *kai* - "and", then if the first noun has the article but the second does not, the second noun refers to the same thing as the first noun does and is a further description of the first noun. "Both expressions refer to the same individual. The deity of the Lord Jesus is brought out here by a rule of Greek syntax." Wuest *Word Studies*, Pastoral Epistles Vol II p 195. "Our God and Saviour Jesus Christ" RV., where the pronoun "our" coming immediately in connection with "God", involves the inclusion of both titles as referring to Christ, just as in the parallel in ver. 11, "our Lord and Saviour Jesus Christ" (AV and RV); these passages are therefore a testimony to His Deity". W E Vine *Expository Dictionary* p 322. The grammar gives us three analogous expressions from the Second Epistle of Peter, each expressing Christ's deity. For the grammatical basis see A T Robertson (even Schmiedal, Winer-Schmiedal, *Grammatik* p 158) *Word Pictures* Vol VI p147; W E Vine, *Expository Dictionary* p 322; Wuest *Word Studies* Vol II p 17). 2 Peter 1:1 "our God and Saviour Jesus Christ"; 1:11 "our Lord and Saviour Jesus Christ"; 3:18 "our Lord and Saviour Jesus Christ".

Christ.[37] The term "our" is polemic, because as far as Christians are concerned, Jesus Christ is the *great God* and Saviour of the world. This blessed title is borne by Jehovah. He is the "great God" (Deut 10:17; Ezr 5:8; Ps 95:3; Pr 26:10 etc). His greatness in salvation is given in that "beside me [Jehovah] *there* is no saviour" (Isa 43:11). And why? It is because of His exclusive divine natural and moral attributes. Jehovah's saving greatness was witnessed among men, as indeed was that of the great God and Saviour Jesus Christ. "God was manifest in the flesh, justified in the Spirit, seen of angels, preached unto the Gentiles, believed on in the world, received up into glory" (1 Tim 3:16).

3. The word "who" in verse 14 is singular, which is consistent with only one Person being referred to in verse 13. It must follow then that *God* is the One who gave *Himself* for us (v.14). This is the foundation truth of divine salvation, and we focus on it in chapter 6 (cf Acts 20:28; Rev 1:18). (The divine title "God our Saviour" in 3:4 is corroborative).

Romans 1 testifies to the personal equality between God and Christ in salvation. In verse 1 it is the *gospel of God*, which promises salvation in God's Son Jesus Christ, as intimated by the prophets of old. In verse 16 it is the same gospel, but now owned and sourced as the "gospel of Christ", which is the "power of God unto salvation". What God promises in His infinite grace, He provides through His infinite power. The expression the *gospel of Christ* brings out the aspect of grace, "that while we were yet sinners, Christ died for us" (Rom 5:8). There cannot be two Saviours, any more than there can be two Messiahs or two Masters, "for either he [man] will hate the one, and love the other; or else he will hold to the one, and despise the other" (Matt 6:24). Neither can there be two 'gospels', having two different Authors, for man will choose one gospel and reject the other. The very notion of two "Gospels" is contradictory. The connection between the above portions of Titus and Romans in regard to the deity of Christ can be illustrated as follows:

God our Saviour (Tit 1:3) – The Gospel of God (Rom 1:1)
Christ our Saviour (Tit 1:4) – The Gospel of Christ (Rom 1:16)

---

[37] The citizens of Syrian Antioch called the followers of Christ "Christians", and by this they meant that Christ was their Deity cf Caesar among the Romans.

All this is wondrously consistent with the divine title "the Son of God" and the divine prerogative of salvation associated with it.

6. Emmanuel - the Mighty God

The Philistines took captive the Ark of the Covenant, the vessel indispensable to the presence of God among His people, during the days of Phinehas. The Shekinah glory was no longer in the midst of Israel.[38] What dark and forlorn days they were, moving the brooding heart of Phinehas' wife to name her child *Ichabod* - "Where is the glory?". "The glory is departed from Israel: for the ark of God is taken" (1 Sam 4:21-22). But it is not Ichabod now, it is Emmanuel! In unbridled joy the angelic host proclaimed glory to God in the highest, on earth peace, goodwill toward all men, for the angel of the Lord declared, "Behold, a virgin shall be with child, and shall bring forth a son, and they shall call his name Emmanuel, which being interpreted is, God with us" (Matt 1:23; Isa 7:14). The Spirit of God declares the name, the divine identity and the divine intention of the One who bears the name. God was to come among His people in person, even into the world, a Light to the Gentiles, in the likeness of men and in fashion as a man,

The relevant OT and NT portions clearly reveal that the Child promised, the Son given and He who is Emmanuel, is none other than Jesus Christ. "Now all this was done, that it might be fulfilled which was spoken of the Lord by the prophet" (Matt 1:22).[39] Emmanuel is spoken of in Scripture as:

- the Child and Son of promise - Isa 7:14
- the Child and Son as Sovereign in prospect - Isa 9:6
- the Child and Son in person - Matt 1:22-23.

There is no doubt that Emmanuel is Jesus Christ who is God, but let us see more of His deity revealed here. The name Emmanuel, thrice mentioned in Scripture (Isa 7:14; 8:8, Matt 1:23), speaks of deity for it means "God with us". It is a compound name containing

---

[38] The Shekinah glory refers to the shining forth of the glory of God, indicative of His presence, His dwelling among men from within the inner sanctuary of the Tabernacle (Ex. 40:34 cf Jn. 1:14).
[39] Surely this voids all speculation that this prophecy was fulfilled in the time of Ahaz. The sign referred to was given to the "house of David" (Isa 7:13)!

the name of God - *El*, He who is "strong". Many persons in Scripture have compound names that are based on the divine name - Isaiah, 'the salvation of Jehovah'; Jeremiah, 'God will raise up'; Elisha, 'salvation of Jehovah'. It is vital then to trace the *correspondence* of the name Emmanuel with the names of God, and note the *coincidence* of this name with the marks of deity.

The One called Emmanuel, the Messiah, is also called "the mighty God - *el-gibbohr*" (Isa 9:6). Some incorrectly take this title to refer to a mere man who is a mighty-deliverer of Israel.[40] He is indeed a man, but He is also Jehovah. The title "the mighty God" belongs to Jehovah. Isaiah foretells that the remnant of Israel will forsake Gentile power and rely on Jehovah their Mighty God. "The remnant shall return, *even* the remnant of Jacob, unto the mighty God" (Isa 10:21-22 cf Deut 7:21; 10:17; Jer 32:18).[41] If Scripture refers to the Messiah and Jehovah as *the* Mighty God, then which of the two can possibly be a lesser god?[42]

The Spirit of God inspired the prophet to identify that Babe in Bethlehem's manger as *the mighty God!* We have seen the might of His arm laid bare in the Gospel narratives, quite apart from all the potent judgments that will be wrought by Him when He comes in glory and in power (Matt 26:64). His infinite might and divine glory are evident through His divine attributes and prerogative. He can heal the leper; He has power to lay down His life and take it up again; to raise Lazarus; to forgive sins. His Gospel is the power of God unto salvation. He is Christ, the power of God (1 Cor 1:24). "The exceeding greatness of his [God's] power to us-ward who believe, according to the working of his mighty power, which he wrought in Christ" (Eph 1:19-20).

Let us bring together two instructive prophecies concerning Israel's future Messianic Ruler, the Mighty God. First, He is the child born and Son given and He has the divine name Emmanuel (Isa 9). Second, He comes out of Judah and His "goings forth

---

[40] Some suggest this passage refers to Hezekiah's birth and rule. However, as noted by others, this is inconsistent with the chronology of his birth and is incompatible with the language used.
[41] This interpretation is supported by the Targum.
[42] Scripture speaks of "the land" as belonging to Israel. Though covenanted to Israel as a *possession*, it is Jehovah who owns the land (Isa 14:25; Jer 2:7; 16:18; Eze 38:16; Joel 1:6 etc). Yet, the land is said to be owned by Emmanuel (Isa 8:8). Emmanuel has co-equal prerogative of ownership.

have been from of old, from everlasting" (Mic 5:2).[43] What we have here is the Incarnation. The Ruler must be a real man because He was born into humanity. He must be a Jew since He is from the line of Judah. And He must be deity, for His goings forth are from the days of eternity. He was the Son *given* – the pre-incarnate Son. Without doubt, He is the Word who in the beginning was with God and who was God, the Eternal Life who was with the Father (Jn 1:1-2; 1 Jn 1:2).

7. Emmanuel - the Everlasting Father

Clearly, Christ, the Son of God who is the Messiah, is not the Father. The term "Everlasting Father" is properly rendered "the Father of eternity", which is an idiomatic expression referring to the One to whom the eternal ages belong. As such, it conveys the eternal being of the Messiah, Christ Jesus.[44]

8. Jesus – Jehovah the Saviour

The name Jehovah we have noted, commands a unique place and reverence among the Hebrews because it is God's personal name. "They shall call on my name, and I will hear them: I will say, It *is* my people: and they shall say, The LORD [Jehovah] *is* my God" (Zech 13:9). Hebrew literature may refer to "the Elohim" (the God) or "my Elohim" (my God), but never "the Jehovah" or "my Jehovah". When a Hebrew says "my God", what he is in fact saying is "my Jehovah".[45] Three periods of existence - past, present and future are embraced in the name Jehovah, speaking of Him who always was, is and will ever be. This divine name is represented by its four consonants - "YHVH".[46]

We have observed a great deal that identifies Jehovah as Jesus of Nazareth, and now add a further account of it, looking first at some passages of Scripture that *identify* Him as Jehovah, *personally, prophetically* and *practically.*

---

[43] Jehovah, too, is "from everlasting" (Hab 1:12).

[44] "The Messiah was to be the Father, the Spring, or Source of everlasting life to all the world" Girdlestone *Synonyms* p32.

[45] See Girdlestone *Synonyms* p 36.

[46] YHVH is referred to as the Tetragrammaton of "Jehovah" (A Tetragrammaton is a sacred word represented by four letters). This name was not to be spoken among the Jews and when they came across the Tetragrammaton, they would use a substitute name.

Personally - through their shared names:

Shared Name	OT	Text - (God) Jehovah	NT	Text - Christ
The Holy One	Isa 1:4; 43:3	"they have forsaken the LORD [Jehovah] they have provoked the Holy One of Israel"	Acts 3:14	"But ye denied the Holy One and the Just, and desired a murderer to be granted unto you"
The First and the Last / Beginning and ending	Isa 44:6	"I [Jehovah] am the First and I am the Last"	Rev 1:8,17; 2:8; 22:13	"I am Alpha and Omega, the beginning and the ending, saith the Lord, which is, and which was, and which is to come..." "I am the First and the Last" (Rev 1:17).
"I AM"	Ex 3:13-15	"I am that I am"	Jn 8:58	"Before Abraham was I am"

Prophetically: Prophecy relating to Jehovah, which at first sight may appear contradictory and fragmented, is wondrously harmonised when the NT applies them unequivocally to Jesus of Nazareth. This not only reveals His deity, but it confirms the divine inspiration of the prophetic Scriptures. The following table presents some examples of this:

Jehovah	OT Text	Jesus Christ	NT Text	Fulfilment in Jesus Christ
"The Lord [Jehovah] is my Shepherd"	Psa 23:1	"I am the Good Shepherd"	Jn 10:11	The Shepherd
"Sanctify [Jehovah] the LORD of hosts himself; ...And he [Jehovah] shall be for a sanctuary; but for a stone of stumbling and for a rock of offence to both the houses of Israel"	Isa 8:13-14	"And a stone of stumbling, and a rock of offence, *even to them* which stumble at the word, being disobedient: whereunto also they were appointed"	1 Pet 2:6-8	The Messiah
"Prepare ye the way of [Jehovah] the Lord"	Isa 40:3	"Prepare ye the way of the Lord"	Matt 3:3	The Messiah/ Servant

Jehovah	OT Text	Jesus Christ	NT Text	Fulfilment in Jesus Christ
"That unto me every knee shall bow, every tongue shall swear"	Isa 45:23	"At the name of Jesus every knee should bow"	Phil 2:10	King and Judge
"He shall be called the Lord [Jehovah] our righteousness"	Jer 23:6	"Jesus Christ the Righteous"	1 Jn 2:1	Righteous Redeemer
"Whosoever shall call on the name of the Lord [Jehovah] shall be delivered"	Joel 2:32	"Whosoever shall call on the name of the Lord shall be saved"	Rom 10:12-14	Saviour
"And the Lord [Jehovah] said unto me, 'Cast it into the potter; a goodly price [thirty pieces of silver] I was prized at of them'."	Zech 11:13-14	"And said unto them, What will ye give me, and I [Judas] will deliver him unto you? And they covenanted with him for thirty pieces of silver"	Matt 26:15	the prophesied Redeemer

Practically: Jesus Christ is to Israel and to us, all that Jehovah is to Israel and to us as God, as seen in the compound titles associated with Jehovah.

Compound Name: Jehovah -	OT Text	Occasion	Meaning	Correspondence to Jesus Christ
Jehovah-Jireh	Gen 22:14	Offering of Isaac	"Jehovah will provide" - the Provider	Christ the Provider - Abundant life (Jn 10:10); All spiritual blessings (Eph 1:3)
Jehovah-Ropheca	Ex 15:26	The bitter waters of Marah made sweet	"Jehovah thine healer"	Christ the Great Physician. - Physically (Mk 1:40-45 etc) - Spiritually (Jn 3:16 etc)

Compound Name: Jehovah -	OT Text	Occasion	Meaning	Correspondence to Jesus Christ
Jehovah-Nissi	Ex 17:15	Victory over the Amalekites	"Jehovah my banner" - the Source of strength and victory	Christ the Source of strength - He will be the strength of Israel (Jer 23 etc); He is the One in whom we have strength against the flesh (Phil 4:13)
Jehovah-Mekaddeshcem	Ex 31:13	Sanctifying of the Sabbath day	"Jehovah who sanctifies"	Christ who sanctifies (1 Cor 1:30; Heb 10:10)
Jehovah-Shalom	Judg 6:24	Visitation by Jehovah to Gideon during Midianite oppression	"Jehovah is peace"	Christ is peace: - to Israel (Isa 9:6) - to us, our Peace (Jn 20:19,26; Rom 5:1)
Jehovah-Tsebahoth	1 Sam 1:3-11; (1 Kings 18:15 etc)	Hannah's petition for a son	"Jehovah is the Lord of Hosts"	Christ the Lord of Hosts (Ps 24:9-10)
Jehovah-Rohi	Ps 23:1	David's Psalm of dependence on Jehovah	"Jehovah my Shepherd"	Christ my Shepherd (Jn 10)
Jehovah-Heleyon	Ps 7:17	Psalm of praise unto Jehovah	"Jehovah Most High"	Christ the Son of God Most High (Mk 5:7 see also Dan 7:27; Acts 16:17)
Jehovah-Tsidkenu	Jer 23:6	The future deliverance of Israel by their Righteous King	"Jehovah our Righteousness"	Jesus Christ the righteous Deliverer: - to Israel (Jer 23); to us (1 Jn 2:1; 2 Cor 5:21)
Jehovah-Shahmmah	Eze 48:35	The future Millennial city of Jerusalem	"Jehovah is there" - the abiding presence of Jehovah among His people	Christ in the midst of His redeemed people; - for Israel (Ps 47:8-9; 48 etc) - for us (Matt 18:20)

Jehovah's messenger

There is an instance where Jehovah is identified as Jesus of Nazareth in prophecy which is particularly instructive. In Malachi 3:1 Jehovah makes a prophecy about His coming. Prior to His coming He will send His messenger to prepare the way before Him. "Behold, I [Jehovah] will send my messenger, and he shall prepare the way before me." In Isaiah 40:3, the words that this messenger will speak when he comes are given - "The voice of him that crieth in the wilderness, Prepare ye the way of the LORD [Jehovah], make straight in the desert a highway for our God."[47]

Three questions arise. Has this prophecy been fulfilled? If it has been fulfilled, then who was this messenger of Jehovah? And, before whom did He go? All three questions have been clearly answered in the person of John the Baptist. The Baptist, it is written, was "the man sent from God" (Jn 1:6). He is explicitly declared to have been the one spoken of by the OT prophets. "Thou [John the Baptist] shalt be called the prophet of the Highest [Jehovah]: for thou shall go before the face of the Lord [Jehovah]" (Lk 1:76; Matt 3:3; Mk 1:1-3; Lk 1:17; Jn 1:23).[48] He was without doubt Jehovah's ordained messenger. Before whom did John the Baptist go and prepare the way? The OT declares Him to be Jehovah. The NT reveals Him to be Jesus of Nazareth, the Incarnate Jehovah. If there is any truth to be had in Scripture at all, then it rests on the indisputable and glorious fact that Jesus Christ is Jehovah-God! We will see more of this blessed truth in section 4 of chapter 5.

9. Lord

Christ claimed this title and it is frequently applied to Him in the NT, especially by the apostle Paul. What did Paul and his contemporaries perceive this title to represent? The Septuagint (LXX), gives a good understanding of the matter. The Septuagint is a Greek translation of the OT, undertaken by seventy eminent scholars for the benefit of Greek-speaking Jews (c.250 BC). The

---

[47] Note again, not "our Jehovah" but "our God".

[48] Mark employs the second person, "Behold I send my messenger before *thy* face", to prepare *thy* way, whereas Malachi uses the first person in regard to Jehovah, "*my* messenger" and "before *me*". Mark's Gospel presents the Incarnate Servant, and his use of the second person declares and preserves the relationship between Jehovah, and Jehovah as the Incarnate Servant in the Person of Christ, the Son of God.

text was well known within the early Christian churches comprising Jews and Gentiles. Portions of it are quoted in the NT.

The first point to note is that the seventy translators used *Kurios*, the Greek equivalent of *Adonai* (Lord), to translate the divine name *Yahweh* and *Elohim*.[49] Second, given that the NT writers were strict monotheists, it is significant that they did not qualify the use of *Kurios* when they applied it to Christ. Rather, when the title is associated with Christ in the NT, it is explicitly connected with the attributes of God, other divine titles, and with Him as the object of universal worship and praise (Phil 2:11). He is everywhere in Scripture what God is as Lord - the Lord in *Person, the* Lord; and to us, *the* Lord in *pledge*, in *plea,* and *the* One in whom we have our blessed and certain *prospect - my* Lord, *our* Lord. Are we to charge the Spirit of God with indiscriminate inspiration? Undoubtedly the title "Lord" when applied to Christ in the NT, has the explicit intention of declaring His deity. It is His *deity* confessed in the title ''Lord' in Philippians 2:11, that glorifies God the Father. He was once Deity in humility, now Deity in exaltation - "Wherefore God *also* hath highly exalted Him".

The title "despotes"

The Greek word *despotes* refers to one who possesses "supreme authority".[50] The Greeks would only use it in reference to deity. In the NT it is used with reference to Christ (2 Tim 2:21; 2 Pet 2:1; Jude 4) and God (Lk 2:29; Acts 4:24), giving a clear intimation of Christ's equality with God, consistent with all that we have noted concerning it.[51]

The unfolding of divine titles and names - what it reveals

The names and titles of Christ compose a blessed portrait of His deity and His perfect humanity. In concluding this chapter, we note

---

[49] A T Robertson *Word Pictures* Vol VI p 10. The Romans used *kurios* to refer to their emperors when worshipping them – they were deity to them. "Most important of all is the early establishment of a polemical parallelism between the cult of Christ and the cult of Caesar in the application of the term *Kurios*, 'lord.' (Deissmann, *Light from the Ancient East*, p 349); A T Robertson *Word Pictures* Vol IV p 168. Both Jewish and Roman use indicate that the title represented deity.
[50] W E Vine *Expository Dictionary* p 18.
[51] See A T Robertson *Word Pictures* Vol VI p 160; p 187. Jude 4, "Our only Master and Lord" – Jesus Christ.

briefly what the progressive unfolding of these divine titles and names signifies.[52]

The unfolding relationship between God and man

Before God chose Israel, He was known as **Elohim**, a divine name that essentially identified Him as the *Creator* of heaven and earth. As Elohim He is the One Being yet a plurality of Persons (Gen 1:1). He was to be worshipped as the Giver and Sustainer of life.[53]

However, with the divine choosing and calling of an *earthly* people, new divine titles and names come into view. These epithets reflect the particular relationship between God and Israel, His covenant people. After God's unconditional promise to Abraham and his seed (Gen 12), He revealed Himself as the **Most High** (Gen 14:18) - the All-Supreme One, who is to the assured *position* of an earthly people, the *Possessor* of heaven and earth. Then in Genesis 17:1 we have God revealed as **El-Shaddai** - the Almighty God. He will bless Abraham's seed and make him a mighty nation, bringing kings out of his posterity. As El-Shaddai He is Israel's *Provider*, the God who covenants with His chosen nation, mighty in grace and blessing assuring their earthly *prospect*.

A further dimension of this covenant relationship is revealed in Exodus 6:3, in that God revealed Himself as **Jehovah**. Though God was known as Jehovah among the patriarchs prior to this time, the essence of His name was not fully revealed. As Jehovah, He is the unchangeable *Redeemer* of His earthly people, bringing into view their *purchase* (v.6; cf Isa 53-54). Jehovah is God's special name to Israel - "Jehovah thou *art* our God" (2 Chron 14:11; Lev 19:2; Zech 13:9). This name also reveals the eternal nature of Israel's God, as does the name **I am that I am** (Ex 3:13-14). There are, too, the various compound variations of the name Jehovah (see p.130-131). As they unfold, they articulate unique historical, prophetical and spiritual relationships between Israel and

---

[52] There is also a parallel progressive revelation of God in regard to His Being in Scripture. In the beginning He is revealed essentially as the Almighty Creator, and we are invited to apprehend His natural attributes - His divine power and wisdom. When sin enters His creation, His moral attributes are unfolded - His divine righteousness, love, grace and mercy, first through God as Jehovah, then through God as the Son (Heb 1:1-2).

[53] "In the beginning God [*Elohim* - plural] created [singular] the heaven and the earth." The term *Elohim* is plural and it is consistent with the doctrine of the plurality of the Persons of the Godhead. See Girdlestone *Synonyms* p 22.

their eternal God. The divine title **Messiah** reveals Jehovah as the Sovereign-Deliverer of Israel. All these names refer to the *one* God.

The divine titles in regard to the church itself

The unique choosing and calling of the church – God's *heavenly people*, created a very different relationship between God and man, evident in the church's purchase, position and prospect.[54] This different relationship is reflected in the new divine titles and names. In the OT where Israel was the focus of God's purpose among men, God was predominantly known as Jehovah and Messiah. But when the church becomes the object of God's purpose and pleasure, we have revealed for the first time on the Sacred Page, the divine titles **God the Father** (Jn 6:27; Gal 1:1; 2 Cor 6:17-18; 1 Pet 1:2), and the **Only Begotten of the Father** (Jn 1:14 cf 1:18; 3:18). In the NT God is still the one God, but now necessarily revealed as the Father, and the Son and the Holy Spirit. This Triunity is vital to the appreciation of the relationship between God and His redeemed heavenly people, corporately and individually.[55] The divine names Elohim, El Shaddai and Jehovah, for all their glory, we say most reverently, are not appropriate.

We note this firstly in regard to the *constitution* of the church – the Body of Christ, which is based on the distinction yet equality and co-operation of the Persons of the Triune Godhead. The church's centre is God, for the church is the church of *God* (1 Cor 15:9; Gal 1:13). It is not the church of Jehovah, for the church is not Israel, but a holy people, one new man comprising both Jew *and* Gentile (Eph 2:14-16). The church's foundation is the *Son* - His Person and His work of redemption (Eph 2:16-20; 1 Pet 2:6-7). Its unity is of the *Holy Spirit* (Eph 2:22; 4:3-4). The *commencement* of the church is also associated with the distinction, co-operation yet equality between the Persons of the Godhead. The Father sends the Holy Spirit in response to the prayer of the Son. The Holy Spirit indwells each believer and by virtue of the

---

[54] Though this relationship is different, it too is grounded upon the inviolable standard of divine righteousness and it brings into view the necessity of the divine man as the perfect Sacrifice.

[55] We see here again the error and scriptural unintelligence of those today who call themselves "Jehovah's witnesses". They have never understood dispensational truth nor partaken of the common ground upon which Jew and Gentile now stand in Christ, for they are sadly themselves not in Christ, having denied His deity.

baptism of the Spirit, they are of the Body of Christ, the church (Jn 14:17; Rom 8:9; 1 Cor 12:13; Gal 4:6). To His chosen earthly people God is the God of Abraham, Isaac and Jacob (1 Kings 18:36; Acts 3:13); but to the church, His heavenly people, He is "the God and Father of our Lord Jesus Christ" (Eph 1:3; 2 Cor 1:3).

The local church too, in its constitution reflects the distinction, divine partnership and essential unity within the Godhead. The local churches are the "churches of God", the "churches of Christ" and "the churches of the saints" (1 Cor 11:16; Rom 16:16; 1 Cor 14:33 respectively). The first term speaks of their origin - they are *of* God, His very habitation, the second of their ownership - they are *in* Christ, and the third tells of their unity *through* the Spirit.

The unfolding titles in regard to those comprising the church

For those within the church the purposes of God are not revealed as the prerogative of Jehovah, but of the Triune God. Each Person of the Godhead is identified in His co-operative, conjoint, yet specific role. God the Father has chosen us (Eph 1:3-4), the Son of God has redeemed us (vv.5-7) and the Spirit has sealed us (vv.13-14). What rich, distinguished *positional* truths are here for those in the Body of Christ! In his Second Epistle John speaks of the *security* of the believer. He declares that those who do not abide in the doctrine of Christ "have not God" (v.9). But when he speaks contrastingly of those who *do* abide in the doctrine of Christ, he reflects on the new relationship and unique blessings intimated in the titles "the Father" and "the Son" - a dilation of the general title "God" in verse 9. This highlights our peculiar blessing, not from God or Jehovah (which would speak to an Israelite), but from the Father, as His *children*, and in the Son of God as *sons* of God. In Hebrews 1:1 we are reminded that God has again spoken, not as Elohim through divine fiat that brought creation into being, but as Son, through divine filiation, through which He brought redemption unto man. Believers as sons are not brought into the land by the divine Messiah, but into glory through the divine Son (Heb 2:10). Our *sonship* rests on the divine Son who is eternal, giving us the surety of our choosing in Him before the foundation of the world (Eph 1:3-4). It is the divine Son who became man through the Spirit of God, and it is by that same Spirit that we are sons of God (Lk 1:35; Tit 3:5-7 etc).

In regard to individual believers in Christ and their walk, not Jehovah but the Trinity is in view, revealing peculiar *practical* truths. Peter reminds us in regard to our *service*, that we are "Elect according to the foreknowledge of God *the* Father, through the sanctification of the Spirit, unto the sprinkling of the blood of Jesus Christ [the divine Man]" (1 Pet 1:2). As the First Testament gives way to the New, God is revealed to His children as "God the Father". This unfolds a particular preciousness to each child of God in Christ "the Son of God". The Father gave them to the Son and none shall pluck them out of the Father's hand - "I and my Father are one" (Jn 10:29-30). Our eternal security is seen not only in God, but also in the *divine Father*, and in the *divine Son*, held in the double-clasp of John 10. We have both the Father and the Son (2 Jn 9). God is the benevolent Father brooding over His individual children redeemed by His beloved Son, attending to their temporal and spiritual needs. God revealed as the Father brings into view sonship and heirship - the unique sonship of Christ and our relationship to God as sons of God, heirs of God and joint heirs with Christ. Our righteousness is of God, but it strikes a particular note of blessing in that we are the righteousness of God in Him [Christ, the divine Son, 2 Cor 5:21]; Israel's righteousness is of Jehovah (Isa 54:17). Our supplications, too, take on a supremely sacred note knowing that our praises and prayers ascend to the Father, and do so through the Son, as enabled by the Holy Spirit. We also know the Spirit of God as the Spirit of Adoption. He places and seals us as sons of God in the family of God, whereby we cry "Abba Father", and possess an inheritance as sons (Rom 8:14-15). All these blessing in our sonship are of God, who is now revealed as the Father, the Son and the Holy Spirit.[56]

The unfolding titles in regard to the nature and the glory of the Godhead
    A plurality of the Godhead was intimated in the OT but brought into greater light in the NT. The unveiling of the Trinity reveals the

---

[56] It is not only in regard to the Church and Israel that we have particular divine titles revealed. God's dispensational program is characterised by certain divine titles. His divine title as the Son of man for instance, is especially associated with God in His personal administration in the Millennial kingdom. The title brings before us God's glory restored on earth through the divine Second Man and Last Adam, Jesus Christ (so, too, the titles King of kings and Lord of lords)! Christ is never "King" reigning over the Church. He is the "Head" of the Church which is His Body.

glory of the Godhead - one Being comprising three co-existent, co-equal and co-operative Persons. Each Person possesses the divine attributes entirely, equally, eternally and exclusively, and they each possess the three marks of deity.

The miracles that were done by Christ were done in His own power, speaking of His distinct divine personality, yet they were also done by the power of the Father in Him (Jn 14:10) and by the power of the Holy Spirit (Matt 12:28). The Son's resurrection was accomplished through His own power (Jn 2:19-21), but it was also accomplished by the Father and by the Holy Spirit (Eph 1:17-20; 1 Pet 1:31; 3:18). Our adoption as sons of God is to do with God who is the Father, with Jesus Christ and with the Spirit of Adoption (Eph 1; Rom 8:14-15). The Lord declared

"my Father worketh" - that divine work on earth of the Father which was past;

"hitherto I work" - that divine work by the Son which then was on earth;

and the Holy Spirit will lead into all truth - the divine work that is presently performed on earth.

The deity and work of the Servant-Messiah was foretold in the OT. But not until the divine titles are unfolded in the NT, do we know Him as the Servant-Son, the Only Begotten of the Father full of grace and truth.

The following diagram may assist the reader in a further study of these vital and blessed truths concerning the progressive revelation of God through His divine titles in His Word.

The ONE TRIUNE GOD - His titles and names revealed progressively in regard to:			
MAN (Universal)	ISRAEL (National and Covenantal)	THE CHURCH (Corporal)	THE BELIEVER (Personal)
Elohim Spirit of God	The Most High El Shaddai Jehovah Messiah	God the Father The Son of God The only begotten Son Jesus [Jehovah- Saviour] The Holy Spirit Spirit of Christ Spirit of Adoption	

CHAPTER 5

A Fourfold Revelation
of Christ's Deity

So far we have noted Christ's deity revealed in the Gospel narratives and proclaimed in His names and titles. In this chapter, we examine certain passages of Scripture which bring before the saints of God sublime truths pertaining to Christ – His deity and humanity, and at the same time meet contemporary challenges to them. The principal portions studied are the first chapters of the following books, John's Gospel, Colossians, Hebrews and Revelation. Each presents a convergent yet particular truth concerning the deity of Christ.

- John   - His *Eternal* glory   - the Son of the Father
- Colossians   - His *Pre-eminent* glory - God's "dear Son"
                                           - the Christ of God
- Hebrews   - His *Personal* glory   - God as Son
- Revelation   - His *Judicial* glory   - the Son of man

All these books present what Christ has done - His work and its blessed provision. But they only do so once we have been given a clear revelation of *who* and *what* Christ is. We will also consider other passages within these same books which corroborate the revelation of Christ's deity and perfect humanity.

John 1:1-14

1. In the beginning was the Word, and the Word was with God, and the Word was God.
2. The same was in the beginning with God.
3. All things were made by him; and without him was not any thing made that was made.
4. In him was life; and the life was the light of men.

5. And the light shineth in darkness; and the darkness comprehended it not.

6. There was a man sent from God, whose name *was* John.

7. The same came for a witness, to bear witness of the Light, that all *men* through him might believe.

8. He was not that Light, but *was sent* to bear witness of that Light.

9. *That* was the true Light, which lighteth every man *that* cometh into the world.

10. He was in the world, and the world was made by him, and the world knew him not.

11. He came unto his own, and his own received him not.

12. But as many as received him, to them gave he power to become the sons of God, *even* to them that believe on his name:

13. Which were born, not of blood, nor of *the* will of *the* flesh, nor of *the* will of man, but of God.

14. And the Word was made flesh, and dwelt among us, (and we beheld his glory, *the* glory as of *the* only begotten of *the* Father,) full of grace and truth.

Before John unfolds the eternal redemptive truths in his Gospel, He declares the ineffable majesty of the Person upon whom they rest. The deity and perfect humanity of the Redeemer impart eternal value to His work in redemption and confer absolute authority to His declaration of the Father. John therefore begins his account with a divine portrait of the Good Shepherd, the One who declared Himself to be "the way", and "the truth" and "the life". He composes and presents this portrait dogmatically, leaving no room for capricious imagination or vain speculation. He records what the Spirit of God has been pleased to reveal - *facts*, which we are to accept by faith according to their plain meaning.

The term "logos"

The "logos" or "Word" is central to John's presentation of the Son of God. In essence, logos means a thought expressed through speech. In John's day it was a common term with an uncommon application.[1] We need then to determine what John, under the Spirit's guidance, meant this word to represent. This can only be determined within the context of Scripture. The Gospel of John presents three indisputable truths concerning the Word:

---

[1] Appendix 2 presents some further remarks on the term logos.

- The Word existed in eternity past - before the incarnation.
- The Word became flesh - the incarnation.
- The Word incarnate is Jesus Christ.

In what form did the Word exist before the incarnation? Some believe the Word was a "thought" abiding within the mind and heart of the eternal God. Others take the Word to refer to a pre-incarnate creation, a specially created being. The first view denies the personality of the Word, the latter denies His deity and slights His perfect humanity.

The pre-incarnate personality of the Word

The Lord Himself declares His pre-incarnate personality as the Word. In John 17:5 He speaks of the glory He ("I") had with the Father before the world was, revealing that He, the Word, was a *Person* before His Incarnation.

- The personal pronoun "I" refers to a Person, and the term "with" indicates a Person existing alongside another Person. The Son was therefore a Person distinct from the Father (cf 6:33, 51; 8:23, 42).
- The *Father* abode with the One who was His *Son*. This speaks of a relationship and communion between two *distinct* Persons.
- Before the world was, the Son had an awareness of the glory He possessed with the Father. Only a person can have such awareness.

In the same chapter the Son declares He was *loved* by the Father before the foundation of the world. The giving, receiving, awareness and acknowledgment of affection can only take place between distinct Persons (17:24). There is, too, a certain premeditation in the words of the Lord, which speak not just of His pre-existence, but of His personality as well. Declarations such as, "For I came down from heaven, not to do My own will, but the will of Him that sent Me", surely convey the truth that His divine mission was a matter that preoccupied the heart of a living Person prior to His incarnation (Jn 6:38; 8:23,42; 10:10; Mk 10:45; Lk 5:32;19:10 etc). As noted earlier, the Father "set apart" and *then* sent the Son (Jn 10:36), which cannot refer to the Word as anything other than a Person. There is in all this alone, ample revelation from Scripture that the Word existed before the incarnation and did so as a Person.

The deity of the Word in John's Gospel

What then of the *deity* of this pre-incarnate Person, the Word?

Let us note the deity of Christ given in verse 1, being attentive to what has been *revealed* rather than to any inferences that may be drawn. John does not begin by declaring "the Word was God", thereby giving us in the first instance the oneness *between* God and the Word. His opening line is "In the beginning was the Word", because the reader is to focus on the timeless being of the Word *Himself.* His abode is the realm of eternity. He is in Himself eternal – Jehovah-God, a fact that would be plain to John's contemporary readership. The Word is Jehovah - the Eternal One and He is Jesus, Jehovah-Saviour. He possesses the undiminished and unceasing glory of the Eternal God. This is in keeping with the theme of the Son's eternal glory in this Gospel. It is in this Gospel that we have the inimitable expressions of His eternal Being - "I am"; "I and my Father are one".

The expression "in the beginning" does not have the same meaning as in Genesis 1:1, where it refers to the beginning of time and creation. The truth that in the beginning God *created* is not the same as in the beginning God *existed.* The former is temporal and it is associated with a divine act in time. The latter is eternal and indicative of divine existence apart from time.[2] Here the matter is of *being,* and not one of *bringing into* being. Both truths converge in verse 3, which is consistent with the Word being the Creator. He can only be the Creator if He is Himself uncreated and 'underived', eternal.

Besides declaring the eternal existence of the Word, John reveals the Word's distinct personality, reminiscent of his declaration of it in chapter 17 and in his First Epistle. The Word did not abide alone. The Word and God coexisted in that the Word was *with* God – face to face with Him, as recounted by the Lord (Jn 17:5). To be "with" indicates a distinction in personality.[3]

To these two revelations concerning the Word, the apostle adds

---

[2] "But John elevates the phrase from its reference to a point in time, the beginning of creation, to the time of absolute pre-existence, before any creation, which is not mentioned until verse 3. This beginning had no beginning." Vincent *Word Studies* Vol 2 p 24.

[3] This is corroborated by the grammar. With God (*pros ton theon*). "*Pros* with the accusative presents a plane of equality and intimacy, face to face with each other." Similarly we have an Advocate *with* the Father (1 Jn 2:1). A T Robertson-*Word Pictures* Vol V p 4. Dods remarks, the term *pros* here "means more than *meta* or *para,* [near or beside] and is regularly employed in expressing the presence of one person with another.... This preposition implies intercourse and therefore separate personality." M Dods, "The Gospel of St. John" - *Expositors* Vol 1 p 684. "Not in God but with God, as person with

that "the Word was God", revealing that the Word and God possess the same essential nature.[4] This is an explicit declaration of the deity and the personality of the Word. In revealing the deity of the Word, Scripture establishes His personality.

It is not here or anywhere else we must add, that the Word was *a god* as some spuriously assert. Apart from the grammatical objections to such a base notion, John bowed to the strict monotheism demanded by Jehovah.[5] He was opposed to the pagan polytheism of his day and, furthermore, his pen was guided by the Spirit to anticipate the error of Gnosticism. It is therefore inconceivable that John would allow the slightest suggestion that the Word was one of many gods. His statement that the "Word was God", refutes the notion that the Word was *another* god. The charge of blasphemy against Christ by the Jews was not because He made Himself *another* god, but because He made Himself equal with the one true God. "Before me there was no God formed, neither shall there be after me" (Isa 43:10).

Everything that is ascribed here to the Word by John is corroborated by the claims of Jesus of Nazareth. He was with the Father before the world began; He was sent by the Father; He was

---

person eternally" Chrysostom. "Living union and communion.....i.e., in social relations with us (Mark 6:3; Matthew 13:56) ...."To be present with the Lord", 2 Corinthians 5:8). "Abide and winter with you" (1 Corinthians16:6). "The eternal life which was with the Father" (1John 1:2). Thus John's statement is that the divine Word not only abode with the Father from all eternity, but was in the living, active relation of communion with Him." Vincent *Word Studies* Vol II pp 33-34. Besides the grammar, the pre-existence and distinct Person of the Word is given by the Word Himself in this very Gospel, as noted above: "I (the personal pronoun) am the living bread which came down from heaven" (6:33,51); It was as the pre-existing Living Bread that He descended from heaven. As the Living Bread He must possess the divine attributes – entirely, equally, eternally and exclusively.

[4] The grammar is instructive here also. The Spirit of God avoids declaring "and the God was the Word" (*ho theos en ho logos*), which would mean all that is of the Godhead is manifested in the Word - the doctrine of Sabellianism, which denies the distinct divine personality of the Word (See A T Robertson *Word Pictures* Vol 5 p 4-5; Vincent *Word Studies*, Vol II p 34). Further, according to the rules of grammar, the *Word* carries the article and is therefore the subject of the sentence; the term God, is the predicate, giving "and the Word was God". As the subject, the Word is the Person spoken of, and God, as the predicate, describes the nature of the subject - the Word's divine nature! "The word *God*, used attributively, maintains the personal distinction between God and the Word, but makes the unity of essence and nature to follow the distinction of person, and ascribes to the Word all the attributes of the divine essence" (Vincent *Word Studies*, Vol II p 34-35).

[5] "The effort to weaken the force of the word of God here by the absence of the article is perfectly futile; except in reciprocal propositions the predicate never has the article." J N Darby. The NT often uses the term "theos" [God] without the article, allowing the context to determine that God - not some lesser god is intended (Matt 5:9; Jn 1:6; Rom 1:17 etc.). The spurious rule invented by some to interpret the second "theos" in John 1:1 as "a god", if applied to other passages having the same construction would give an absurd and heretical rendering. Matthew 5:9 would be "sons of a god" and John 1:18, "No man hath seen a god". (See Vincent *Word Studies* Vol II p 34).

that Bread of Life which came down from heaven; He was from above; He and His Father are one; He that hath seen me hath seen the Father, etc.

John's triads of Deity concerning the Word
The three revelations concerning the Word in verse 1 can be outlined as follows:
- "In the beginning was the Word" - the *timeless existence* of the Word;
- "the Word was with God" - the *distinct personality* of the Word;
- "the Word was God" - the *divine identity* of the Word.

Note again, these statements are *not* inferences but plainly revealed facts concerning the Word. This is not to say that it is improper to use them to identify correlative truths through inference, given that those truths are corroborated from Scripture. Take for instance the Word being "with" God and the fact that the Word "was" God (the distinct personality and deity of the "Word"). Together they identify the eternal *coexistence, coequality* and *co-operation* between the Word and God, and intimate the plurality within the Godhead. These truths are revealed in creation, redemption and that which pertains to the church. The Word, being eternal and the Son of God, also means the Son is eternal, and that He was not derived from God.

We have then in verse 1, doctrine in the form of a triad, each part itself a decisive principle of truth. Together they compose an unassailable testimony to the deity of the Word, which anticipates the further unveiling of His divine Person and work in this Gospel. Discard or diminish any one of these truths and we will open the floodgates to a tide of erroneous doctrine. The eternal existence of the Word is a noble truth for it dismisses the Arian idea that the Word is a created being. By itself however, it may do little to defeat the false notion that the Word is an "eternal thought" in the mind of the eternal God. This is denied by the personality of the Word which is declared in the truth that the Word was "with" God, "face to face". Any further objection to the Word's deity is dealt a fatal blow by the third statement that the Word was God. When we view this verse as the Spirit of God intends, with a mind unspoiled by philosophy and carnal intellect, we will see the complete declaration for what it is, a simple and straightforward statement of Christ's deity.

A further examination of verse 1 reveals another triad of truth concerning the Word. The former underlines the Word's "being", this one His "existence":

• the sphere of His existence - *eternity*;
• the substantive nature of His existence in eternity - *personality*,
• the supernal sovereignty of His existence in eternity - *deity*.

The same truths are revealed in verse 2, but here *both* the Word and God are declared to have existed "in the beginning". It places *God* where the Word Himself was – in the beginning. This confirms the distinct personality of the Word and His eternal coexistence and equality with God. Any notion that the Word is derived from God is again refuted.[6]

A quartet of truth - Verses 1 & 14

A marked contrast is brought before us when we immediately consider verse 14. Timelessness gives way to time. We are to acknowledge that the Word who was *with* God in the beginning came *among* men. What condescension! Note how assiduously the Spirit of God protects the divine Person of the Word in this change of realm, and how He anticipates the diabolical detractions in the light of it. The Word *became* flesh yet He possessed the glory as of the only begotten of the Father, full of grace and truth. When the Son stepped into time, His deity remained undiminished and unceasing, evident in His absolute declaration of the divine *Father*. How important this truth is to our eternal hope! He is presented here as One who rose from the eternal counsels of God, who stepped into time to do that which the Father had sent Him to do. ("Thou art my Son, this day have I begotten thee", Acts 13:33; Heb 1:5; 5:5). We can expand the triadic theme as follows:

• "In the beginning was the Word" - the *timeless existence* of the Word
• "the Word was with God" - the *distinct personality* of the Word
• "the Word was God" - the *divine identity* of the Word

---

[6] The Spirit inspires John to declare that in the beginning the Word was with *God*, rather than the Word was with the *Father*! Though true enough, the latter statement would not be a natural association with the truth that the Word was God! And, neither would it have the most appropriate coincidence with Genesis 1:1 - in the beginning God created!

- "the Word became flesh" - *the perfect humanity* of the Word
  It is noteworthy, that John does not explicitly mention the fact of the Word stepping into *time*. He states the Word became flesh and dwelt among men, directing our attention to the incarnation and to the nature of the divine Man. The Word's subjection as a servant of God is not mentioned here either (although we see His gracious condescension in that the Word became "flesh"). John's purpose is to emphasize the eternal nature and glory of the Word who became flesh. An appreciation of all that relates to His sonship, service, sacrifice and subjection, can only occur after the undiminished and unceasing divine glories of the Word as God, the Creator, the Life and the Light, are brought before the heart and mind of the reader. The things of Christ peculiar to John's Gospel - the Word as the sacrificial Lamb of God who takes away the sin of the world, the Good Shepherd, and the presentation of Christ as the Servant in chapter 13, claim a deeper affection from us once we know that it was the *divine* Son, who was the Lamb that was slain, the Good Shepherd who gave His life for His sheep, the One who stooped to wash the feet of His disciples. John's preamble is not a protracted Theophany or Christophany. It declares Jesus Christ as God manifest in flesh, walking among men in His undiminished and uncreated divine glory. To what end? That we should believe that Jesus is the Christ, *the Son of God*, and thereby have life through His name (Jn 20:31).[7]

The Word as the Creator
John affirms the deity of the Word by identifying Him as the Creator (v.3). He does this through two reciprocal truths. Firstly he declares the *plenitude* of the Word's creation – "all things were created by Him". The totality claimed here must not be compromised. Everything that is created is the work of the Word. This excludes the notion that the Word was Himself created. Some resort to an outrageous interpolation insisting that "all things" means "all *other* things" (v.3). That is, Christ created everything except Himself, who they say was created by God. But the Holy

---

[7] There is here an instructive comparison with John's First Epistle. When speaking to those who believe in the deity of the Word, it is not the *prospect* of eternal life but the *possession* of it. "These things I have written unto you that believe on the name of the Son of God; that ye may know that ye have eternal life" (1 Jn 5:13).

A Fourfold Revelation of Christ's Deity

Spirit anticipated this error by inspiring the second truth - "without him was not any thing made that was made." The expression "not anything", literally "not even one thing", is absolute.[8] Here the Word is the *prerequisite* to *all* creation. This second truth complements and reinforces the first. All creation was through the power and prerogative of the Word. If the Word was indispensable to *all* creation, then how could He be created?

There is more in regard to the eternal being of the Word in verse 3. In association with verse 1, we are invited in the first part of verse 3 to consider the Word as He Himself is - eternal, and therefore acknowledge Him as the Creator of *all* things (all things were made by Him). The second part of verse 3 invites us to consider *all* things in creation, and acknowledge the Word as their Creator (cf Ps 19:1; Rom 1:20).

Every truth John has revealed here concerning the Word as the eternal Creator, is the exalted theme of adoring hearts bowed before Jehovah the Creator. "Thou art worthy, O Lord [Jehovah], to receive glory and honour and power: for thou hast created all things" (Rev 4:11). What a resounding dismissal of the forlorn notion that Christ is some created being! What an emphatic censure against liberal theologians who press for Christ's "divinity" rather than His deity!

Deity and creation

Let us dwell a little more on why the Spirit of God identifies the Word as the Creator in this Prologue. First of all, it is because Deity is *preoccupied* with and *proven* by the prerogative and power of creation. All three marks of deity are manifested by the work of creation. Whoever is accredited with it must be God. God Himself says so and we dare not deprecate it. Who is God's equal? "To whom then will ye liken me, or shall I be equal? saith the Holy One" (Isa 40:25). God supplies the answer. The One who created all things is His equal. "Lift up your eyes on high, and behold who hath created these *things* [the things Christ is revealed to have created], that bringeth out their host by number: he calleth them all by names by the greatness of his might, for that *he is* strong in

---

[8] We will refer to this error again in regard to Colossians 1:16-17. Note however the absurdity if this same exegesis was applied to Revelation 4:11, where Jehovah is said to be the Creator of "all things". The cults must then say if they are at all consistent (which of course they are not) - Jehovah is the Creator of "all *other* things".

147

power; not one faileth" (v.26). God anticipated the attack on the deity of the Word and He provided the defence to it. His answer expresses the very thing that John through the Spirit has required us to do regarding the Word in verse 3. At Mars' Hill, Paul informed the philosophers that it was God who "made the world and all things" (Acts 17:24).[9] The Word who created all things is God's equal. This is why the Spirit of truth presents the Word as the Creator without any qualification in John's Prologue and elsewhere, as we shall note.

But there is another equally vital reason why John presents the Word as the Creator of *all* things. The object of his Prologue is to unveil the divine credentials of the *Saviour* of men, who cannot be anyone but God Himself. ("I, *even* I, *am* the LORD [Jehovah]; and beside me *there is* no saviour", Isa 43:11.) This is a vital doctrine that we take up in the next chapter. The truth that Christ is the Creator-God must be established as a critical prelude to the Spirit's emancipating message in this Gospel and its appeal to our faith. The saving work of the Good Shepherd and the reconciling work of the Lamb depend on His deity.

John's Gospel - The divine Word - the Saviour

John does not give us an earthly genealogy of the Word because as the eternal God the Word has no earthly genealogy.[10] Prominence is given to the Word's deity because His deity is vital to the efficacy of His work as the divine Saviour. The "temptation" too, is omitted, because the One John particularly presents is the divine Son. Christ was tempted in the vain effort to spoil His testimony as the perfect Man, the obedient Servant of God.[11] The Spirit of God selects and arranges the content of John's Gospel to amplify the truth of the deity of the Saviour. Immediately after the Prologue and John's

---

[9] Not all "other" things.

[10] Mark, too, does not furnish a genealogy of Christ, since he presents Christ as the lowly servant among men. As Sovereign, Christ has a genealogy (Matthew's Gospel presenting His "legal" lineage in regard to Joseph's line). As the Son of man Christ has a genealogy (Luke's Gospel, presenting His lineage in regard to Mary's line).

[11] The Transfiguration – the outward sovereign glory of Christ, is omitted by John in his Gospel because his Gospel begins with an emphatic declaration of the divine Person of Christ, and Christ's deity is continually revealed in it as the *Son of God*. Matthew includes the Transfiguration because it intimates the Exalted Sovereign glorified in the Kingdom of God; Mark, the Exalted Servant, and Luke the Exalted Son of man. John presents the Son - Jesus of Nazareth, as very God - the Eternal One!

witness, we have the Word as the divine Lamb, who takes away the sin of the world. His omniscience is seen in the calling of Nathanael. All three marks of deity are revealed in the Word's miracle of turning water into wine at Cana. In this He "manifested forth His glory; and His disciples believed on Him" (Jn 2:11). This is followed by His cleansing of the temple and the declaration of His deity in that *He* will raise up His body in three days (Jn 2:19).

What wondrous grace that God should come down to dwell amongst men. The word "dwell" is "tabernacle". It reminds us of the sanctuary in the OT in which God was pleased to dwell among His people. The sublime blessing here of course, is that the glory of God the Father is unveiled for all to behold in the Person of His beloved Son, One who is greater than the temple (Matt 12:6).

The Word as the Life and Light

In verse 4 the glory of the Word as Creator is associated with His personal glory. We are to behold the Word as LIFE and LIGHT, and acknowledge the divine essence abiding in Christ. "God is Light" (1 Jn 1:5). Jehovah, too, in His personal glory is Light (Isa 60:19). Jesus Christ was from the beginning the Word of Life (1 Jn 1:1).[12] This last title brings together the titles of the Lord as "the Word" and "the eternal Life" (Jn 1:4; 11:25; 14:6; 1 Jn 1:2), presenting Him as the Creator, the Giver and Sustainer of all life.

The deity of the Word - John's First Epistle

Jesus of Nazareth is the "Word of Life", and He was "that eternal life, which was with the Father" - before the Incarnation (1:1-2).[13]
• The Word of *life*: to impart life, the Word must be a divine Person, The Word who is *the* Life (Jn 1:4).
• That *eternal* life: being eternal, John's Word is undeniably Deity.
• That eternal life which was *with* the Father: we have here

---

[12] In John 1 it is *in* the beginning. Here it is *from* the beginning, which speaks of the coming of the Word into the world as Man, His condescension and grace in taking on humanity, as the apostles attest in verse 1.
[13] John's words here are essentially in regard to the *Person*, rather than the blessing that flows from faith in the Person. This is clear from the tactile and optical experiences of the apostles referred to in verse 1, and in that the Word of life was *with* the Father. It is also evident from the theme of the Epistle. Eternal life in Christ is to be seen as vitally connected with the One who is in Himself the eternal life - the Son of God!

again the Word's distinct divine personality and eternal sonship.

Proverbs 8:22-31 - the Word
"The LORD [Jehovah] possessed me in the beginning of his way, before his works of old. I was set up from everlasting, from the beginning, or ever the earth was...When he prepared the heavens, I *was* there: when he set a compass upon the face of the depth:.. Then I was by him, *as* one brought up *with him*: and I was daily *his* delight, rejoicing always before him; Rejoicing in the habitable part of his earth; and my delights *were* with the sons of men."

May we take in the wondrous intimations given by the Spirit of God here which announce the Word as John has revealed Him. Wisdom personifying the Word was *in* Jehovah but also *with* Him, intimating His deity yet distinct personality (Jn 1:1-2). Wisdom was set up [anointed] from everlasting. He cannot therefore be a created being and He existed in the beginning (Jn 1:1). This same One was "brought forth" (vv.24,25). He was a participant in the past counsels of the Triune God, from where He was brought forth to undertake His ordained divine works (cf Ps 2:7; Acts 3:13; Heb 1:5; 5:5). He was with Jehovah, enjoying communion and fellowship with Him in eternity and in the work of creation (Jn 1:3). He was Jehovah's delight – His Beloved Son, sharing the glory He had with Him before the worlds were (Jn 17:5). His delights, too, were with the sons of men, a sure intimation of the incarnation and all that it entails - the Word became flesh and dwelt among men (Jn 1:14).

Colossians 1:12-20; 2:8-9
Chapter 1:12-20:
12. Giving thanks unto the Father, which hath made us meet to be partakers of the inheritance of the saints in light:
13. Who *hath* delivered us from the power of darkness, and *hath* translated *us* into the kingdom of his dear Son:
14. In whom we have redemption through his blood, *even* the forgiveness of sins:
15. Who is *the* image of the invisible God, *the* firstborn of every creature:
16. For by him were all things created, that are in heaven, and that are in earth, visible and invisible, whether *they be* thrones, or dominions, or principalities, or powers: all things were created by him, and for him:

17. And he is before all things, and by him all things consist.

18. And he is the head of the body, the church: who is *the* beginning, the firstborn from the dead; that in all *things* he might have the preeminence.

19. For *it* pleased *the Father* that in him should all fulness dwell;

20. And, having made peace through the blood of his cross, by him to reconcile all things unto himself; by him, *I say*, whether *they be* things in earth, or things in heaven.

Chapter 2:8-9

8. Beware lest any *man* spoil you through philosophy and vain deceit, after the tradition of men, after the rudiments of the world, and not after Christ.

9. For in him [Christ] dwelleth all the fulness of the Godhead bodily. And ye are complete in him, which is the head of all principality and power.

What valiant glories of the Son adorn this first chapter of Colossians. Their noble purpose was to revive the hearts and hope of the saints at Colossae by repudiating Gnosticism which denied the Son's deity and His real humanity.

The Son as the image of the invisible God

The Son is "the image of the invisible God" (Col 1:15). By itself, image - *eikon*, has the connotation of likeness. In Scripture it takes on the meaning of *representation*.[14] The Word of God, as noted, never refers to the Son being "like" God, because He is God.

The word *eikon* is used in the sense of representation in regard to Christ in 2 Corinthians 4:4. It was also used by the Lord to refer to the imprint of the head of the Roman Emperor on contemporary coinage. Caesar's image represented his imperial authority and so the Lord declares "render to Caesar the things that are Caesar's and to God the things that are God's" (Mk 12:16-17). In Romans 8:29 the term refers to the moral conformity of the sons of God. Their lives are to reflect and represent the moral character of the Son of God. The generations of the first man Adam, bear his "image", and being of him they represent him. This is in contrast

---

[14] W E Vine-*Expository Dictionary* notes: "...in Col 1:15, "the image of the invisible God" gives the additional thought suggested by the word "invisible", that Christ is the visible representation and manifestation of God to created beings; the likeness expressed in this manifestation is involved in the essential relations in the Godhead, and is therefore unique and perfect; "he that hath seen the Son hath seen the Father", John 14:9" p 247. See, too, Daniel 2, 3, telling us that the "image" in the dream was a representation. Cf the image errected by Nebuchadnezzar in the plain of Dura.

to the heavenly representation of the generation belonging to the second man, Christ (1 Cor 15:49).[15]

In the passage before us, the Son is the representation of the *invisible* God. The contrast and context brings into view the Son who is seen, who is the visible representation of God who is unseen. The Son is "essentially and absolutely the perfect expression and representation of the Archetype, God the Father."[16] He is both the *manifestation* as well as the *representation* of God, not in regard to God's appearance, but in regard to His divine *nature*. Verse 19 clarifies the context - all the fulness of the Godhead dwells in the Son. That the divine nature is in view is substantiated by the divine glories which are attributed to the Son, His glory in creation, redemption etc. Given the Son and the Father are distinct Persons, what is seen of the Father in the Son cannot reflect their common personality, but their common entity - the divine essence.[17]

The pre-eminence of the Son

The divine Son became flesh, and as man among men He represents the invisible God. He must therefore be acknowledged as pre-eminent in all things, the One who 'holds the first place'.[18] He is the *logos* of John, but here it is His pre-eminent glory rather than His eternal glory.

Paul's triad of deity concerning the Son - in creation

A little reflection upon Colossian 1:16-17 puts us on familiar ground. Paul like John, presents facts that invite faith not conjecture, and he too rests the deity of the Son on His creatorial glory. In verse 16 we have a triad of truth in regard to the Son. *All things* were created -
- by (in) Him — - the Son's *power* in creation,
- through Him[19] — - the Son's *prerogative* in creation,
- for (unto) Him — - the Son's *pleasure* in creation.

Note the coincidence between the three interdependent marks

[15] Adam, too, is declared to be the image of God and he was, in a fashion, God's visible representation. He was given dominion over living things etc. Adam, in his representation was but a figure of Him who was to come - the Last Adam, the Second man.
[16] W E Vine *Expository Dictionary* p 247
[17] In Hebrews 1:3 therefore, it is not the Son as the express image of the "Person" of the Father, but of *God* - His divine "substance".
[18] A T Robertson *Word Pictures* Vol IV p 480
[19] Not "by" Him as in the AV.

of deity and the threefold anatomy of deity in this verse. It will serve to elucidate the deity of the Son in what follows and remind us of the thematic consistency of Scripture.

By Him - the Son's divine attributes, enabling creation

DEITY OF THE SON

Through Him - the Son's divine *prerogative* in creation

For (unto) Him - the glory, the Son's divine *pleasure from creation*

The Spirit inspired Paul as He inspired John to declare that *all* things were created by the Son, again revealing the plenitude and the exclusive power and prerogative of the Son in creation. Here, too, the totality declared must not be mitigated. *Everything* that is created is the work of the Son, which again repudiates the notion that the Son was Himself created. How resolutely the Holy Spirit guards this truth.[20]

In this Epistle, Paul refutes the view that Christ is a "lesser deity" who is ranked among the angels. This is why he speaks specifically of the Son's *power, prerogative* and *pleasure* in creation, and why he delineates the universal realm over which the Son reigns and receives honour as the Creator - thrones, dominions, principalities and powers.[21]

Each strand in Paul's triad presents a particular truth concerning the Son's pre-eminence. The Son's creatorial glory is given clear expression in that *in* Him were all things created. He had the inherent power to create all things, therefore He possesses the

---

[20] And how persistent are the cultists in their vain efforts to deny it. Here, too (vv.16-17), they fallaciously insert the word "other", one after each of the four" alls" (cf Jn 1:3). This is in spite of the fact that no such word appears in the original Greek text and, that the word "other" is totally opposed to the context, which relates to Paul's fight against the Gnostics, who sought to limit Christ's deity. Appeals to other verses such as Luke 13:2 illustrate the contrivance behind the fallacy. There "all" is used in a relative context - "these sinners" relative to "all *other* Galilaeans".
[21] Some, who are confounded by the clear truth of this passage, such as the Unitarians, resort to spiritualising Paul's reference to creation. Paul, they say, is not referring to the literal creation of Genesis, but to the creation of the kingdom of God on earth or to the Body of Christ. These are spurious arguments employed to avoid the clear teaching of the deity of Christ in this passage. For one thing, in view of the Gnostic heresy it would be inconceivable that the Spirit of God would refer to anything other than creation as given in Genesis 1 (and of course the moral dimensions pertaining to it mentioned below). The realms of habitation are given - things in heaven and earth visible and invisible. Thrones, principalities etc. refer to the holy angels, fallen angels, demons (Eph 6:12) as well as the province of man.

divine attributes of God entirely, equally, eternally and exclusively. Creation displays the eternal power of *God* (Rom 1:20). We noted earlier how emphatically creation is ascribed to God Himself in Genesis and in Isaiah. God *Himself* – actively, created the heavens and the earth (Isa 45:18; cf Amos 4:13; Acts 4:24 etc). Is there a contradiction in Scripture when it reveals that both God and the Son created all things? Indeed not! There is no inconsistency whatsoever, given that we accept the clear teaching of Scripture that Christ is God. In this portion we have another instance of the recurring revelation of the distinct personality of the Son and the plurality of Persons within the Godhead.[22]

Observe now the link between the first and second strands in the triad. Divine prerogative cannot be exercised apart from the divine attributes. In the first strand we have the Son in His creatorial *might*, in the second His creatorial *right*. In Genesis we are informed that God exercised creatorial prerogative in that He ordained the days and the order of creation within them. Colossians informs us that the Son exercised this same prerogative, for creation was *through* Him. That is, it was dependent upon the Son's power and *will* (Jn 1:3). Paul employs a tense here that takes us back to a completed event in the past - Genesis 1.[23]

We note also, that apart from the material universe, creation involved a moral dimension. The declaration "Let us make man in our own image" (Gen 1:26), not only expresses the divine co-operation within the Persons of the Godhead, it also reveals the moral dignity and responsibility God intended for man in regard to creation. Adam was divinely appointed the racial head of man and he was given moral responsibility over God's handiwork. There was, too, the divinely installed moral relationship between Adam and Eve as man and wife, and of the moral setting and testing of man in the garden. Creation set in place the moral principle that man should look upon it and worship the incorruptible and invisible God, not corruptible images made by men which denied God's

---

[22] The plurality of the Godhead is seen also in the Hebrew of Ecclesiastes 12:1 - "Remember now thy Creators in the days of thy youth" (Girdlestone p 23). Only one God, as emphatically declared in the OT, yet a plurality of Creators: cf Gen 1:1.

[23] "The all things" – "The article gives a collective sense – *the* all, the whole universe of things. 'Were created' is *ektisthe*, the aorist tense, denoting a definite historical event." Vincent *Word Studies* Vol III p 469.

eternal power and Godhead. All these matters are integral to God's moral dealings with man and could only be derived from His divine moral nature.[24] Since the Son created all things, it was His divine moral prerogative that established these moral principles in creation.

The Son created all things *unto* Him. In this third strand we have the Son's creatorial *delight*, bringing into view His divine glory. All creation, both moral and material has in its origin and design to bring pleasure to the righteous heart of the Creator and glory to His name. It is the divine pleasure experienced in the beginning when God created the heaven and the earth. It is also the divine pleasure and glory experienced when all creation will be restored to God through the Son in *righteousness* (v. 20). "Whom the heaven must receive [the imperative reception because of righteousness] until the times of restitution of all things, which God hath spoken by the mouth of all his holy prophets since the world began" (Acts 3:21).[25] Only One who is absolutely holy can fix, consummate and derive pleasure from such a righteous purpose in regard to creation. God was in Christ, reconciling the world unto Himself. We should not think of the Son of God passively deriving pleasure from creation, but *contriving* it.[26] This extracts a particular divine fragrance from the triad in verse 16.

These strands inspire the rhapsody of everlasting praise before the throne, "Holy, holy, holy, Lord God Almighty". The worthy object is Jehovah, who is indeed Christ. He is worthy to receive glory and honour and power. Why? Because He has created all things, and for His pleasure they are and were created (Rev 4:8-11).

---

[24] In this very chapter we see the important distinction between the headship of Adam and of Christ, the headship of Christ in redemption, and of Adam in condemnation - moral and spiritual truths declared in Genesis chapters 1-3, which underwrite precept and principle in the NT in regard to the church (i.e. 1 Tim 2:11-13).

[25] "All things" in this verse and in Colossians 1:20 does not speak of the impenitent unrighteous being reconciled. They are eternally lost, their very judgment is a mark of God (in Christ) reconciling matters on the ground of divine righteousness! We see here again the divine prerogative of Christ in judgment and reconciliation on the ground of His reconciling blood as the Lamb of God. "And there shall in no wise enter into it any thing that defileth, neither *whatsoever* worketh abomination, or *maketh* a lie: but they which are written in the Lamb's book of life" (Rev 21:27, cf Rev 20:11-15).

[26] For Him: '*unto* Him'. "All things, as they had their beginning in Him, tend *to* Him as their consummation, to depend on and serve Him". Vincent *Word Studies* Vol III p 468 - 470.

Creation delegated to an angel?

Was the Son a created being, an angel whom God empowered and delegated to do the work of creation? It is abundantly evident from what we have already noted in Scripture, that this is at the very least a fallacious fantasy. Let us make two further observations. First, the Son as the Creator of all things created the angels (Col 1:16). Second, this act of creation is attributed to Jehovah (Ps 148:2,5). Thus another fatal blow is delivered to the Gnostic practice of angel worship, and to all denials of the deity of the Son predicated on the notion that He was a created angel delegated by God to create.

Christ as the Agent in creation

Christ is revealed as the *Agent* of God in creation. This expression comes from the preposition *dia* in Colossians 1:16, signifying "by means of". Never forget however, that creation, as in the case of all divine work, is predicated on the sublime co-operation and co-equality between the Persons of the Godhead: creation (Gen 1:1; 1:26); salvation and sanctification (Eph 1); and in matters relating to the Church (Matt 28).[27] In Romans 11:36, which we consider next, *God-Jehovah* is revealed as the Agent of creation. He is the Source - *ex*, the Agent - *di* and the object of it - *eis*. What an enigma except for the biblical revelation of the Triune God!

A complementary triad of deity in Romans

"For who hath known the mind of the Lord [Jehovah]? or who hath been his counselor? Or who hath first given to him, and it shall be recompensed unto him again? For of him [the Lord, Jehovah], and through him, and to him, *are* all things: to whom *be* glory for ever. Amen" (Rom 11:34-36; cf Isa 40:13-14). Paul notes three aspects of Jehovah's glory which he has through the Spirit of God attributed to Christ in Colossians 1:16:

• of Him — all things are according to Jehovah's *power;*
• through Him — all things are by Jehovah's *prerogative;*
• for [unto] Him — all things are for Jehovah's *pleasure.*

---

[27] Christ – "as the Designer, the Creator and the Object of creation. He is the goal as well as the cause". All is carried out by the Son in ineffable, infinite and indissoluble fellowship with the Father. W E Vine *Collected Writings* Vol 2 p 532.

In this dispensational passage Paul uses *ex autou* - of Him, to identify Jehovah as the Source of all things. In Colossians where the context is apologetic, the parallel expression in regard to Christ is *en autoi* - in Him, a variation intended to counter Gnostic error. It emphasizes the truth that divine creative power resides in the Son *Himself* - in His essential being. He is therefore Jehovah's equal and not some emanation from God. This is altogether convergent with the truth declared in chapter 2, that the fulness of the Godhead dwells in Christ bodily.

Romans 11:34-36	Colossians 1:16-19
Who can know the mind of God (Jehovah) or who can be His counsellor? (Isa 40:25)	The Son of God is His equal.
for all things are of Him (divine power) through Him (divine prerogative) to Him (divine pleasure)	*for all things are* in Him through Him unto Him

Jehovah is Christ. Both have power, prerogative and pleasure in "all things" (cf Jn 1:3). Again we have the truth of the oneness in being yet plurality of Persons within the Godhead.

Before we conclude this section, observe that three portions of Scripture, Romans 11:36, Colossians 1:16, and Revelation 4:11 verify that the divine attributes, prerogatives and glory are inextricably linked and belong to the Son of God. He did what only God could do; he chose to do what only God could choose to do; He receives pleasure and glory as God, having acted as only God could act, revealing His undiminished and unceasing deity.

The Firstborn of all creation

We noted earlier that Scripture identifies Christ as the only begotten Son, using the term *monogenes*. This is not the same as Him being the Firstborn - *prototokos*. The former reveals Him to be *the only one of a kind*; the latter speaks of His *pre-eminent position among a kind*. Accordingly, He is revealed as the Firstborn among many brethren (Rom 8:29) and the Firstborn from among the dead (Col 1:18; Rev 1:5).

The term "firstborn" can refer to a person born first in *time*.

Luke uses it in this way in regard to Christ (Lk 2:7). But this is not the sense in which Paul applies it to Him in Colossians 1:15. The context is not the family of Mary, but the realm of creation, notably *all* creation. It is obvious, too, that Christ was not the first man born in time. When the pre-incarnate Son was born of Mary through divine conception, God stepped into time and He entered the ranks of creation as man. A new *relationship* began between God and creation. How then must God as the divine *Man* be viewed in this relationship? As God He is uncreated so he cannot be regarded as part *of* creation, as one who was "born through creation". This is why the Spirit of God informs us here that the Son is the Creator of all things, that He is before all things and that by Him all things consist (v.17). He must as the Creator-God have a title that represents His uncreated glory, yet acknowledge His real humanity as man among the ranks of creation. This is accomplished in the title "Firstborn of all creation". As the Firstborn of all creation the Son has the pre-eminent *rank* in regard to it. He holds this position of priority *because* of His deity. The use of Firstborn to represent rank is well illustrated in the case of Jacob and Esau (Gen. 27:19; cf Ex 4:22; Rom 9: 12-13).[28] Though not the firstborn in time, Jacob was by divine election deemed the firstborn. The title represented his new and superior *relationship* to Esau.

We note again the "alls" in Colossians 1:16-17. The Son is the Firstborn of *all* creation and the Creator of *all* things. If He is the Creator of all things then He cannot be created, He is eternal, Deity. Scripture never refers to the Son as the "first-created" - *protoktistos*, which is quite distinct from *prototokos* - firstborn. Nowhere in the Word of God is Christ said to have been created. Surely, if such an event had occurred it would be at least as noteworthy as the creation of the heaven and earth!

Similarly, the Son is the Firstborn from among the dead - in dignity and rank! His divine work and glory in redemption is set before us in verse 18, in Him bringing the new creation into being through His Person, power and prerogative. His pre-eminence is as the risen and glorified Head of the Church, His Body. The Son cannot be one of the Church - redeemed, for He is their Redeemer;

---

[28] Israel is the Lord's son and His firstborn among the nations of the world (Ex 4:22). Israel was not the fist nation in time, but it ranks first in God's order of things in *relation* to all other nations.

He cannot be one of creation – the created, because He is their Creator. Because He is the Redeemer, He is however the *Head* of the Church; because He is the Creator, He is *Firstborn* of all creation.[29]

"All the fulness"

Verse 19 gives us another categorical statement of the Son's deity. "For it pleased *the Father* [God] that in him should all fulness dwell."[30] The expression "all the fulness" - *pan to pleroma*, refers to "the totality of the Divine powers and attributes" (Lightfoot). All the divine attributes reside in Him and do so *permanently*. This statement refutes Gnosticism because it denies any diminution or accumulation of the divine attributes in the Son.

Some are perplexed that God should be "pleased" that in the Son all the fulness dwells. Deity cannot cease to exist where it does exist, and it cannot begin to exist where it did not previously exist. It is not therefore that the Son "took on" the fulness and pleased God. Rather, it is that the Son who *possesses* the fulness of deity took on humanity (cf Phil 2:7-9). It is God's divine pleasure derived from the *divine Son* becoming Man to condemn sin. The incarnation was according to the co-operative will and holy delight of the Godhead. There is a similar sentiment expressed in regard to the Son's crucifixion. It "pleased" the Lord [Jehovah] to bruise Him (Isa 53:10). It expresses God's holy delight in the Son because of His obedient sacrifice undertaken to vindicate God's holiness and to put away sin.

Colossians - chapter 2

Here redeemed hearts are again directed to the glories of the Second Person of the Godhead, but now He is the Christ, the

---

[29] The four occasions where the title Firstborn is used in regard to the Son, correspond with the four aspects of the glory of God we noted in chapter 1. He is the Firstborn: among many brethren (Rom 8:29) - His personal glory; of every creature (Col 1:15) - His creatorial glory; from among the dead (Col 1:18; Rev 1:5) - His redemptive glory; into the world (Heb 1:6-9) - His judicial glory.

[30] That it is *God* rather than the *Father* who is pleased, is in keeping with the representative and essential nature of the Son given in this discourse - the dear Son who is the image of the invisible God (Col 1:13-15); so, too, He is the brightness of God's glory and the express image of God (Heb 1:1-3). "The subject of *was well pleased, God*, is omitted as in Jas i. 12, and must be supplied; so that literally, the passage would read, *God was well pleased that in Him, etc*". ..The *fullness* denotes *the sum total of the divine powers and attributes*. In Christ dwelt all the fullness of God as deity." Vincent *Word Studies* Vol III p 472-478.

Anointed of God rather than the dear Son. Again the divine portrait is eminently suited to defend the truth of Christ's deity. The practical life of the Colossians was in danger of being undermined by Gnostic philosophy. Paul presents the practical worth of the divine glories of Christ to those who are complete in Him. Christ is - the Repository of all wisdom and knowledge, *learn* of Him (2:3); the Refuge of faith, *lean* on Him (2:5); the Reviver in walk, *live* in Him (2:6-7). All these bounties are also possessed in God, who is all wisdom, light and life, and the sole object of faith.

Defending Christ's deity against Gnosticism

A section of Gnosticism believed in the existence of beings that, in various degrees, "emanated" or "issued" from God.[31] The greater the emanation from God the greater is the devolution in deity.[32] Christ, they asserted, was one such being. He was *a* god, a "lesser" deity. It is vital to note, that the core contention between the Spirit of God and Gnosticism was not over the *degree* of deity that was said to exist in Christ, but whether such degrees of deity or emanations existed *at all*. Either the Gnostics are correct and Christ is an emanation from God and therefore such emanations exist, or Christ is very God and such emanations are non-existent. The divine cause the Holy Spirit takes up is that emanations from God do not exist *because* Christ is God. Paul does *not* put the case that emanations do not exist *therefore* Christ is God. This line of inquiry invites speculation. Paul's course was, as ours must be, always according to divine revelation.

When the Spirit inspires Paul's defence of Christ's deity, He cannot allow therefore the minutest intimation that His deity can exist in degrees. This is achieved in the declaration that in Christ *dwells all the fulness of the Godhead bodily*. All the divine consolations and assurances to man are gathered up in this ineffable truth, our focus in chapter 6. The fulness of the Godhead, the entire essence of God *dwells* in the *real* Man Jesus Christ. The Greek word dwell is *katoikei*, meaning a continuous and a permanent residence.[33] It

---

[31] The Gnostics split into two broad groups. The Docetic Gnostics denied Christ was truly human - He partook of a "phantom" body. The Cerinthian Gnostics accepted Christ's real humanity but regarded Him as an aeon or an emanation from God. Judaism, which became mingled with Gnosticism, is also opposed by Paul in this Epistle.

[32] Like the diminishing ripples when a stone is cast into a pond.

is the fulness of the Godhead - *theotetos*. All that gives God His essence dwells permanently in Christ.[34] Therefore Christ possess the divine attributes entirely, equally, eternally and exclusively. All three marks of deity abide in Him. We see again why it is important to discern the undiminished and unceasing deity of Christ revealed in Scripture.

The distinction between the Greek words *theotes* and *theiotes*, deity and divinity respectively, have already been noted. Both refer to God but from different standpoints, the latter referring to His divine attributes, the former to His essential nature. To the Christians at Colossae who were being seduced by the doctrine that Christ is less than God, it was prudent to employ *theotetos* rather than *theoites*, because it speaks of essence, and thus it categorically declares that Christ the Man is all that God is (cf Jn 10:30). He cannot therefore be *a* god.

The fulness of the Godhead dwells in Him in human form, "in a bodily way, clothed with a body".[35] This statement confronts and controverts the Docetic notion that Jesus of Nazareth did not possess a real human body. We must repeat, it is not taught here or elsewhere in Scripture, that God took up "residence" in a human body. The Word *became* flesh. It was never a case of the Word inhabiting flesh.[36]

This chapter delivers a fatal blow to Gnosticism and to every doctrine it spawns.[37] It complements the truth of Christ's deity and perfect humanity revealed in the Gospels and elsewhere in

---

[33] "Because in Him there is continuously and permanently at home all the fullness of the Godhead in bodily fashion". The compound verb *katoikei* (to dwell permanently) was used to distinguish between permanent residents of a town with temporary residents. Wuest *Word Studies*, Ephesians and Colossians Vol 1 p 201. The present tense dwelleth, denotes an eternal and essential characteristic of Christ's being. "The indwelling of the divine fullness in Him is characteristic of Him as Christ, from all ages to all ages." Vincent *Word Studies* Vol III p 487. Cf *paroikeo*, a passing or impermanent residency.

[34] *Theotetos*: "Here Paul is speaking of the essential and personal deity as belonging to Christ." Vincent *Word Studies* Vol III p 486. "Not the divine attributes, but the divine nature.", Bengal. "He was, and is, absolute and perfect God." (Trench).

[35] Vincent *Word Studies* Vol III p 487.

[36] In Hebrews 10 Christ's body is seen in "preparation" in regard to sacrifice and redemption - not habitation. "Wherefore when he cometh into the world, he saith, Sacrifice and offering thou wouldest not, but a body hast thou prepared me: In burnt offerings and *sacrifices* for sin thou hast had no pleasure" (vv. 5-6). The failure of such sacrifices and offerings meant that God in His holiness purposed to take on manhood in order to reconcile the world unto Himself.

[37] Arianism, Sabellianism, Socinianism, Unitarianism, Mormonism, Christadelphianism, the cult of the JWs, and the Kenosis teaching that Christ partially (or totally) emptied Himself of His deity etc. Appendix 1.

Scripture. The *existence* and *nature* of Gnostic error, and the opposition to it by Paul, confirms that the early Church believed in Christ's deity and defended it against the error of the day.[38]

Associated truths

Precious positional and practical truths rest upon Christ's undiminished, unceasing deity and perfect humanity. In chapter 1 it is the "body of His flesh through death" in reconciliation, whereby believers are presented holy, blameless and unreproveable in God's sight (1:22). In 2:10 our sanctification in Him is in view: "And ye are complete in him [the pre-eminent, risen and glorified divine *Man* Jesus Christ] which is the head of all principality and power". *Because* the fulness of the Godhead dwells bodily in Christ, those united with Him in His death and resurrection, have in Him all that they require, positionally and practically. What need then do we have for Gnostic philosophy, the rituals of Judaism and angelic worship and all the contemporary developments of them? What a blessed assurance this gives, prompting everlasting praise and adoration unto Him.

Dear reader, if you are among those who deny Christ His deity, you know nothing of the blessings of reconciliation and even less of the bounties of sanctification, all of which are in Christ by virtue of His uncreated, unceasing and undiluted divine Person.

The grandeur of Christ's person presented in Colossians 2:9 can be identified as follows:

in Him	- the *Person*	- an exclusive identity
dwelleth	- the *manner*	- an abiding permanency
all the fulness	- the *extent*	- an undiluted totality
of the Godhead	- the *essence*	- ineffable deity
bodily	- the *form*	- perfect and real humanity.

This five-fold presentation of the glory of Christ through its insistent declaration of Christ's deity lies at the heart of the truth that "God was, through Christ, reconciling the world unto Himself", and it predicates and provokes that soul-saving confession of Christianity, that Christ is "my Lord and my God".

---

[38] Appendix 14

Paul - chief among idolaters?
We have observed the resolute testimony of Paul regarding Christ. The Colossian Epistle is his Spirit-led epic assault on the false teaching that denied Christ's deity and perfect humanity. From his inspired pen and life of absolute subjection to Christ, we conclude that Christ was to Paul what God was to Saul of Tarsus and the faithful patriarchs and prophets of old. It was *Christ* who was to be magnified in Paul's body, whether in life or in death. For him to live was *Christ* (Phil 1:20,21). In his sincere penitence, Paul declared himself to be the chief of sinners (1 Tim 1:15). Is he, in his equally sincere total subjection to Christ, the chief of idolaters, or is Christ very God? One or the other has to be true!

> *In Thee, most perfectly expressed,*
> *The Father's glories shine,*
> *Of the full Deity possessed,*
> *Eternally Divine.*
> *(Josiah Conder)*

Hebrews 1

1. God, *who* at sundry times and in divers manners spake in time past unto the fathers by the prophets,
2. Hath in these last days spoken unto us by *his* Son, whom he *hath* appointed heir of all things, by whom also he made the worlds;
3. Who being *the* brightness of *his* glory, and *the* express image of his person, and upholding all things by the word of his power, when he had by himself purged our sins, sat down on the right hand of the Majesty on high.
4. Being made so much better than the angels, as he hath by inheritance obtained a more excellent name than they.
5. For unto which of the angels said he at any time, Thou art my son, this day have I begotten thee? and again, I will be to him a father, and he shall be to me a son?
6. And again, when he bringeth in the firstbegotten into the world, he saith, And let all the angels of God worship him.
7. And of the angels he saith, Who maketh his angels spirits, and his ministers a flame of fire.
8. But unto the Son *he saith*, Thy throne, O God, *is* for ever and ever: a sceptre of righteousness *is* the sceptre of thy kingdom.
9. Thou hast loved righteousness, and hated iniquity; therefore God, *even* thy God, hath anointed thee with the oil of gladness above thy fellows.
10. And, Thou, Lord, in the beginning hast laid the foundation of the earth; and the heavens are the works of thine hands:

MY LORD AND MY GOD

11. They shall perish; but thou remainest; and they all shall wax old as doth a garment;

12. And as a vesture shalt thou fold them up, and they shall be changed: but thou art the same, and thy years shall not fail.

13. But to which of the angels said he at any time, Sit on my right hand, until I make thine enemies thy footstool?

14. Are they not all ministering spirits, sent forth to minister for them who shall be heirs of salvation?

The Fourth Gospel invites us to believe in the divine Son of God who came down from above *to* settle the sin question. The Hebrews Epistle requires us to acknowledge God as the Son, who has gone up, the sin question *having* been settled. It is on this ground, that the Holy Spirit inspires the writer to the Hebrews to unveil the superior blessings of the New Covenant.

God *as the Son* is an edifying and instructive complement to *the Son as God* in the Fourth Gospel. In the latter, the eye of faith is directed to His eternal sonship, so that in believing we might have eternal life through His name (Jn 20:31). In the opening verses of the Hebrews Epistle, it is *God as the Son*, God in sonship. The eye of faith is to perceive and prove the greater blessings of the New Covenant, *having* eternal life in Him. Both portions speak of the eternal sonship of Christ. If God is revealed as the Son, then incontrovertibly the Son is eternal, and therefore an eternal relationship exists between the Son and the Father.

Like John, the writer necessarily begins with a revelation of the glory of the Person upon whom all divine blessings rest, the divine Son. The Son's deity is presented in five ways in chapter 1.

1. The Son in regard to God
   - *as His final Representative*
   - *as His Heir*
   - *as His Co-Creator*
2. The Son in regard to His own Person
   - *as the brightness of God's glory.*
   - *as the express image of God's Person [substance].*
3. The Son in regard to creation
   - *as the Sustainer*

164

4. The Son in regard to man[39]
- *as our Redeemer*
- *as our Advocate*
- *as our Great High Priest*
5. The Son in regard to angels
- *as having a more excellent name than they*
- *as the object of their worship*
- *as having a greater glory than they*

1. The Son in regard to God

Who spoke to men of the purposes of God once the OT prophets had come and gone? It was God Himself as the Son (v.2). The omission of the article before "Son" in verse 2 means that the text should read, "God.....has spoken unto us by [in] Son". It is "God the Son", as distinct from God the Father or God the Holy Spirit who spoke. This is a clear revelation of the Son's deity and of Him as the *Logos*. His eternal being is declared in that He was appointed Heir of all things in eternity past, given by the timeless tense of the term 'appointed'.[40] As the Heir of *all things*, He must possess the natural and moral divine attributes to fulfil the custodial responsibilities of an Heir to the possessions of an infinite God. "All things that the Father hath are mine" (Jn 16:15).

His deity is also revealed in that He is Co-Creator of the worlds with God. He possessed and exercised the divine power and prerogative involved in creation. If we are unconvinced, then observe the emphatic confirmation of equality and plurality of Persons within the Godhead in creation given in verse 10. Jehovah's personal and *direct* involvement in creation is explicitly declared. *He* "laid the foundation of the earth" and it was *His* hands that created the heavens. "I, even my hands, have stretched out the heavens" (Isa 45:12).

2. The Son in regard to His own Person

Verse 3 is the centre-point of this chapter, presenting the Son as the "brightness" of God's glory. God's glory is manifested through the exercise of His divine attributes and divine prerogatives, choosing to

---

[39] His advocacy is implicit in that He is seated at the right hand of God (the Father).
[40] See A T Robertson *Word Pictures* Vol V p 335; Vincent *Word Studies* Vol IV p 380.

do and doing what only He as God can do. These divine attributes and prerogatives were possessed and exercised by the Son, and He therefore radiated the glory of God. The tense of the word "being" - *on*, conveys that the brightness has a timeless and absolute existence in the Son.

As the "express image" of God, the Son is the distinct "impress" of His being. The meaning of "image" here is quite distinct from its use in Colossians. There it was emphatically employed as a mighty weapon of truth to slay Gnostic error. It was given by the term *eikon*, the Son as the manifestation and visible representation of the invisible God. Here it is *charakter*. With the same vigour of truth, it presents the Son as the very "stamp" of God's divine character and essence.[41] The Son is not the express image of God's appearance but of God's Person. The term person is properly rendered His *substance*, and the thought is reciprocal to *God the Son* in verse 2.[42]

To appreciate fully the Spirit's intentions in this portion, both expressions in verse 3 must be viewed according to the general purpose of the Epistle. The Epistle presents the relationship yet distinction between the Old and New Testaments, defining the superior blessings of the New Covenant over the Old. The writer necessarily begins with the divine glory of the One in whom these greater blessings rest. However, his message is essentially to Jewish Christians. Therefore he presents Christ, not as John presents Him to the world as the Son of God, nor as Paul does in Colossians as the pre-eminent One to the redeemed facing false teaching, but as God the Son. It was God who dwelt among His people under the Old Covenant, evident in His Shekinah glory. This same God who inspired their prophets and spoke to them in divers ways has now spoken - in the Son. God's divine glory was no longer veiled within the sanctuary, but "shone-out" in the brightness and express image of Deity in divine sonship.

3. The Son in regard to creation

The revelation of the divine Son continues through His divine

---

[41] A stamp, when applied to wax, was used to leave an exact reproduction of the original seal. "Here the essential being of God is conceived as setting its distinctive stamp upon Christ, coming into definite and characteristic expression in his person, so that the Son bears the exact impress of the divine nature and character." Vincent *Word Studies* Vol IV p 383.

[42] The term "person" is *hupostaseos (from hupostasis)*, and really means "substance" - the substance of God. "Thus it is the impress of the divine essence possessed by absolute Deity which is an exact reproduction of that essence. And that impress is the Son of God." Wuest *Word Pictures,* Hebrews Vol II p 38.

glory in creation. He upholds all things by the "word of His power". It is God, the Son, who is the Sustainer of "all things".[43] Once again it is the Second Person of the Godhead exercising His divine power and prerogative, revealing His deity. Those on the imperiled ship marvelled and exclaimed when, by His word He calmed the tempest. "What manner of man is this, that even the winds and the sea obey him" (Matt 8:27) - a man who possessed the prerogative and power of God. It is said of God as is seen in the Son, that "He walketh upon the wings of the wind" (Ps 104:3); "He treadeth upon the waves of the sea" (Job 9:8); "He walketh in the circuit of heaven" (Job 22:14).[44] By His *own* word, He brought all things into being and sustains them. The Spirit of God repeatedly brings to our attention the infinite and absolute realm of the Son's power in "all things", revealing His deity. He is:

- the Custodian of all things   (Matt 11:27)
- the Creator of all things   (Jn 1:3, Eph 3:9; Col 1:16; Heb 2:10; Rev 4:11)
- above all things   (Jn 3:31)
- the Heir of all things   (Jn 3:35; Jn 16:15; Heb 1:2)
- worker of all things   (Eph 1:11)
- the Fulfiller of all things   (Eph 4:10)
- the Head of all things   (Eph 1:22)
- the Subduer of all things   (Phil 3:21)
- before all things   (Col 1:17)
- the Upholder of all things   (Col 1:17; Heb 1:3;)
- pre-eminent over all things   (Col 1:18)
- the Reconciler of all things   (Col 1:20)
- the Renewer of all things   (Rev 21:5)

Note the divine attributes, divine prerogatives and divine glories encompassed in this resume about the Son.[45]

---

[43] "Not only with sustaining the weight of the universe, but also with maintaining its coherence and carrying on its development." Vincent *Word Studies* Vol IV p 383. Note, too, we have here teaching that defeats the claim of *deism,* that having created the universe, God takes no part in its operation, allowing "natural laws" to determine its course.

[44] "He is the principle of cohesion in the universe" (Lightfoot).

[45] If we are to insert the term "other" after the term "all" in the second case (Jn 1:3 etc) as we are told to do by some who deny Christ's deity, then to be consistent we must adopt the unscriptural course of inserting "other" after the term "all" in every one of these cases.

4. The Son in regard to man

The Son is the divine Redeemer who Himself purged our sins. The emphasis is upon the personal pronoun – *Himself.* It is to assure us here as elsewhere, that He inherently possessed and exercised divine prerogative, in this case in regard to redemption.

- He gave Himself for our sins   (Gal 1:4)
- He gave Himself for me   (Gal 2:20)
- He made One New Man in Himself   (Eph 2:15)
- He gave Himself for His Church   (Eph 5:25)
- He made Himself of no reputation   (Phil 2:7)
- He humbled Himself   (Phil 2:8)
- He gave Himself a ransom for all   (1 Tim 2:6)
- He gave Himself for us   (Tit 2:14)
- He offered up Himself   (Heb 7:27, 9:14)
- He put away sin by the sacrifice of Himself (Heb 9:26)
- He Himself bore our sins in His own body   (1 Pet 2:24)

Here are eleven glorious divine prerogatives exercised by the Son, each enabled by His divine attributes, all bearing resolute testimony to the three inextricable marks of deity in that blessed man, the Son of God Most High.

The Son is presented seated at the right hand of God. Though seated, He continues His work, not in regard to redemption, for this, praise God, is a finished work, having put away sin and obtained eternal security for the believer. Hebrews 9:26 declares the former truth and Ephesians 1:6 the latter truth. His present work is as the believer's Advocate and Great High Priest. In the Hebrews Epistle the Son's priestly work is in view, which is to do with our *communion* with *God* – not our sins. As our High Priest He *has*, on the ground of His divine holiness and redemptive work, enabled our access to God. He is a High Priest "*who is* holy, harmless, undefiled, separate from sinners". His absolute holiness is seen in that after He offered one sacrifice for sins He sat down forever at the right hand of God (Heb 10:12).

5. The Son in regard to the angels

Angelic beings played a vital role in the history of Israel (i.e. in the giving of the law, Acts 7:53; Gal 3:19), and because of this the Jews were inclined to venerate them above their divinely appointed station. The writer addresses this error by presenting the incomparable superiority of the Son over the angels. This entire passage, we observe, teaches the superiority of the Son *apart from* the angels, never *among* them.

The Son as the divine *Man* has a more excellent name than the angels. He who became a little lower than the angels (in His station) for the suffering of death (Heb 2:9), has become by virtue of His victory and vindication through that death, so much better than they. He has thus inherited a more excellent name than the angels (1:4). The divine Son who through the incarnation became man and became obedient unto death, has in glorification been given a name which is "above every other name" (Phil 2:9).

In verse 5 we have the eternal Son who came into the world through incarnation. His *relationship* to God as His Son is declared to distinguish the relationship between God and the angels. In verse 6 He is the "firstborn". As the Firstborn, the *Son* is worshipped by the *angels of God*. God declared that He will not give His glory to another, yet here He does this very thing allowing His angels to worship the Son. The angels are fully aware that God must be the sole object of worship (Rev 19:10; 22:8-9). The Son is seated at the right hand of God, "angels and authorities and powers being made subject unto him" (1 Pet 3:22). Verse 7 declares the Son's control over the angels, revealing His divine prerogative. He did not take the nature of angels, but the seed of Abraham (Heb 2:16), a clear censure to all who regard Him as an angel.

An explicit declaration of the Son's deity

An unassailable witness to the Son's deity is given in verse 8. "But unto the Son he *[God]* saith, 'Thy throne, O God, *is* for ever and ever: A sceptre of righteousness *is* the sceptre of Thy kingdom.'" God Himself addresses the Son as *ho theos*, as His equal. Who can the one and only God call God, but One who is His equal? Who other than God has an everlasting throne? We have another revelation of the plurality of Persons within the Godhead.

Every provision for man unfolded within this epistle rests on God the Son. He is the Captain of our salvation, the Mediator of the New Covenant, the Apostle and Great High Priest of our profession, and the Minister of the Sanctuary. The divine portrait in chapter 1 serves to invest each title, office and work of the Son with deity and sublime dignity, not only within this blessed Epistle, but throughout all Scripture.

Revelation 1:5-18

5. ...Jesus Christ, *who is* the faithful witness, *and* the first begotten of the dead, and the prince of the kings of the earth. "Unto him that loved us, and washed us from our sins in his own blood,

6. And hath made us kings and priests unto God and his Father; to him *be* glory and dominion for ever and ever. Amen."

7. Behold, he cometh with clouds; and every eye shall see him, and they *also* which pierced him: and all kindreds of the earth shall wail because of him. "Even so, Amen."

8. "I am Alpha and Omega, *the* beginning and *the* ending," saith the Lord, "which is, and which was, and which is to come, the Almighty."

9. I John, who also *am* your brother, and companion in tribulation, and in the kingdom and patience of Jesus Christ, was in the isle that is called Patmos, for the Word of God, and for the testimony of Jesus Christ.

10. I was in *the* Spirit on the Lord's day, and heard behind me a great voice, as of a trumpet,

11. Saying, "I am Alpha and Omega, the first and the last."

12. And I turned to see the voice that spake with me. And being turned, I saw seven golden candle sticks;

13. and in the midst of the seven candlesticks *one* like unto the Son of man, clothed with a garment down to the foot, and girt about the paps with a golden girdle.

14. His head and *his* hairs *were* white like wool, as white as snow; and his eyes *were* as a flame of fire;

15. And his feet like unto fine brass, as if they burned in a furnace; and his voice as the sound of many waters.

16. And he had in his right hand seven stars: and out of his mouth went a sharp twoedged sword: and his countenance *was* as the sun shineth in his strength.

17. And when I saw him, I fell at his feet as dead. And he laid his right hand upon me, saying unto me, "Fear not; I am the first and the last: I *am* he that liveth, and was dead; and, behold, I am alive for evermore, Amen; and have the keys of hell and of death."

18. I *am* he that liveth, and was dead; and, behold, I am alive for evermore, Amen; and have the keys of hell and of death.

The Son of man – Jehovah-God

The sum and substance of chapter 1 (indeed the whole Book), is predicated on and preoccupied with Jesus Christ. It is "The revelation of Jesus Christ" given to Him by God (v.1). Following the opening decrees and interdiction, we have the *personal* glory of *Jesus Christ*. He is the "faithful witness"; the "firstborn of the dead"; the "prince of the kings of the earth". Verse 7 gives Christ's *redemptive* and *judicial* glory. He has washed us from our sins in His own blood, and has made us kings and priest unto God and His Father. He is *Jesus Christ*, the Son of God who was "pierced", the One who "cometh with the clouds" in judgement, a sure reference to Him as the Son of man in Daniel 7:13, Matthew 24:30 (cf Zech 12:10). In verse 8 *Jesus Christ* Himself declares His *divine* glory as *Jehovah-God*. He speaks in person to define the authority with which *He* will execute the divine rule and judgements revealed in this Book. "I am Alpha and Omega, the beginning and the ending, saith the Lord [Jehovah], which is, and which was, and which is to come, the Almighty."

His deity seen in His titles

Five divine titles are claimed in verse 8 which identify Jehovah-God:

- Alpha and Omega
- the beginning and the ending
- the Lord (the Lord the God)[46]
- which is, and which was, and which is to come
- the Almighty

Christ claims the title "Alpha and Omega" (taken from the first and last letters of the Greek alphabet) to express His eternal being. He reiterates this truth by claiming to be the "beginning and the ending" - a title that "corresponds with the Hebrew name Jehovah".[47] Christ is frequently referred to as "the Lord" in the NT, and here He is the Lord who is God, who is the Almighty. Undoubtedly the One who speaks here is Christ, Jehovah-God.

Like the opening verses of John's Gospel and those of the Hebrews Epistle, verse 8 is inspired to declare the deity of the One whose Person and work is subsequently unfolded. In John's Gospel it was the Word and His divine work of salvation; in the Hebrews Epistle is was God the Son who is the basis and blessing of the

---

[46] *Kurios ho theos* - "The Lord the God", A T Robertson *Word Pictures*, Vol VI p 289. Common phrase in Ezekiel 6:3, 11; 7:2 etc.
[47] T Newberry *Newberry Reference Bible*.

better covenant. Here it is Jehovah-God as the man Jesus Christ and His work in divine judgement – His almighty judicial glory. God "hath appointed a day, in the which he will judge the world in righteousness by *that* Man whom He hath ordained...", whom He raised from the dead (Acts 17:31). That Man *Himself* now speaks from the excellent glory (v.8). It is not "this is my beloved Son hear ye Him" or 'God speaking as Son'. It is *Jesus Christ* who is Jehovah-God the "I am", "the First and the Last", who was dead but now alive for evermore (Rev 1:17-18; Isa 41:4; 48:12).

There is further revelation of Christ's deity in this chapter. We have a voice again from the excellent glory and the Speaker identifies Himself - "I am Alpha and Omega, the first and the last" (v.11). These titles belong to Jehovah, as noted earlier. On this occasion John is brought not just to hear, but also to *see* the Person who claims these divine titles. Who is the One who identifies Himself as Jehovah-God, the Alpha and Omega, who meets the eyes of John? It is the *Son of man*. The Old and New Testaments converge once again in their oneness of identity between Jehovah and Christ. Jehovah-God is indisputably the Son of man noted earlier. Christ takes this title exclusively to Himself in the NT. In verse 8 the titles 'the Almighty' and 'the Alpha and Omega' identify Jehovah-God. Verses 11 and 13 reveal that the Son of man is the Alpha and Omega. Who then can be the Almighty except Jesus Christ, the Son of man? The diagram below illustrates the link between verses 8, 11 and 13 through the common title "Alpha and the Omega" which, when taken together, complements the deity of Christ given independently in each of these passages.

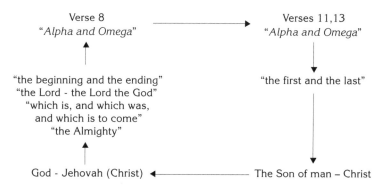

The revelation of Christ's deity presented here becomes even more emphatic when we observe that:

• in the OT Jehovah is exclusively referred to "the first and the last", and that this title specifically identifies His eternal being (Isa 41:4; 48:12). It is incontrovertible that the Son of man – Jesus Christ, owns this divine title (Rev 1:13-17), and it likewise identifies His eternal being.

• the "voice" of the Son of man was "as the sound of many waters" (Rev 1:15), which is also the voice of Jehovah-God, for His voice, too, "was like a noise of many waters" (Eze 43:2).

• the One who is the "First and the Last" - Jehovah, is said to have died. How can Jehovah die unless He became man? In the next chapter we will see why He had to become Man and die!

• in Revelation 21:6-7, Christ who is the Alpha and Omega is to be *God* to the overcomers, who are the children of God.

His deity seen in His judgements

The context of Revelation 1:10-18 confirms the deity of Christ, the Son of man. Where was the Son of man when John saw Him? In what capacity was He there? How did John respond when he saw Him? The Son of man is amidst the seven churches, His flowing vesture and solemn disposition speak of judgement, and John fell before Him in worship. There was no rebuke directed at John here as occurred when, in error, he bowed in homage to the angel, because the One here was God. He was, too, none other than Christ, the church's risen Head, who was dead but liveth, who is the "I am" and the "first and the last".

In these early passages in Revelation, we are truly blessed with an invincible revelation of the deity of the exalted Christ as the Son of man. The opening chapter presents the deity of Jesus Christ in His eternal and judicial glory, evident in the titles given to Him which speak of divine power and judgement - "the Almighty", "the Son of man", "the first and the last". His work as Divine Judge is predicated upon His eternal glory as Alpha and Omega, and also upon His personal and redemptive glory. They identify Him as One possessing the marks of deity – consistent with the record of His undiminished and unceasing deity in the Gospels.

The diagram which follows presents some of the golden threads that compose part of the sublime tapestry of Christ's deity revealed in Scripture. It comprises two sections corresponding to verse 8 and verses 10-18 respectively. The identity between Jehovah and Christ is taken up from (but not confined to) their shared divine titles, "I AM" and "Alpha and Omega". The first section refers to Jehovah-God. The second portion presents the divine Man, whose judicial glory must be seen in the light of His finished work of redemption, as One who in His absolute righteousness defeated sin and death (v.18). In this passage He claims not only to be the "Alpha and Omega", but also to be the *first and the last* (Rev 22:13). In the former title we have His divine *Person* - His eternal being. The latter speaks of His divine *prerogative*. As the Son of man He is Lord of all - the Initiator, Originator and Fulfiller of all things. In keeping with the purpose of this first chapter of Revelation, these titles direct us to acknowledge Jesus Christ as Jehovah. He is Jehovah in all His divine essence and in His pre-eminence as the kinsman Redeemer, the Son of man who came to give His life a ransom for many (Matt 20:28; Mk 9:31): "Thus saith the LORD [Jehovah] the King of Israel, and his [kinsman] redeemer the LORD of hosts; I *am* the first, and I *am* the last; and beside me *there is* no God" (Isa 44:6).

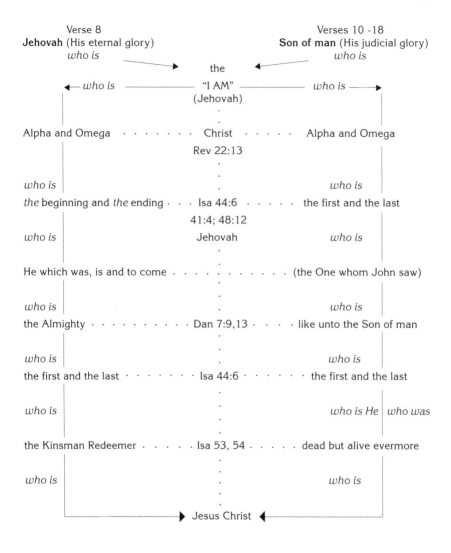

Verse 8
Jehovah (His eternal glory)
who is

Verses 10 -18
Son of man (His judicial glory)
who is

the

← *who is* ——— "I AM" ——— *who is* →
(Jehovah)

Alpha and Omega · · · · · · Christ · · · · Alpha and Omega
Rev 22:13

who is   *who is*
the beginning and *the* ending · · · Isa 44:6 · · · · · the first and the last
41:4; 48:12
who is   Jehovah   *who is*

He which was, is and to come · · · · · · · · · · (the One whom John saw)

who is   *who is*
the Almighty · · · · · · · · · · Dan 7:9,13 · · · · · like unto the Son of man

who is   *who is*
the first and the last · · · · · · · Isa 44:6 · · · · · · the first and the last

who is   *who is He* | *who was*

the Kinsman Redeemer · · · · · Isa 53, 54 · · · · · dead but alive evermore

who is   *who is*

Jesus Christ ◄

CHAPTER 6

Christ's Deity - its Absolute Necessity

It is evident from the foregoing study of Scripture, that belief in the deity of Christ is not baseless credulity. In addition to the explicit revelation of Christ's deity through His words, works and titles, Scripture gives us clear teaching as to why Christ *had* to be God in all His uncreated, undiminished and unceasing deity.

This is the biblical line of truth we examine in this chapter. It brings into view the holy character of God and the fallen condition of man. Here we enter into the great moral revelation of Scripture. It invites us to consider Christ not only as Emmanuel - God *with* us, but the exalted truth of Him as Jehovah our righteousness, Jehovah Tsidkenu - God *for* us. The moral reason for the divine Man has a unique strength, in that it is untouched by the quibbling of gainsayers over grammatical principles. This sublime subject is so vast it is difficult to know how best to proceed in order to do it justice. Let us begin by focusing upon two inseparable and pertinent questions:

1. Why did God in His undiminished and unceasing deity become man?

2. Why was this a matter of absolute necessity?

There are, as we shall see, a number of specific answers to these questions, but the general answer embraces two truths:
- The holy nature of God demanded it.
- The sinful nature of man required it.

The first truth reveals that God is Light, and it speaks of His infinite holiness (1 Jn 1:5-7). The second declares that God is Love, proclaiming His infinite grace to fallen man (1 Jn 4:8). God as Light and Love means that He is also Life - manifested in the Person of His Son the Incarnate Word, "the Word of Life" (1 Jn 1:1). The two truths above embrace the entire compass of Calvary, where mercy and truth met and righteousness and peace kissed each other.

God's righteous demands and man's salvation could never be met by a being of diminished deity or imperfect manhood. Those who deny Christ's deity, do so because they have little understanding of man's spiritual poverty and/or the absolute holiness of God. If we fail to acknowledge man's hopelessness in sin, then we see little necessity for a Saviour-God, and much less the need for salvation through divine grace. Failure to acknowledge God's holiness, is to deny that God Himself must be the One to put away sin and take away the sin of the world.

Ten reasons why God had to become man and why that Man was God

The list below identifies ten aspects of the *work* of Christ. Each one reveals why it was absolutely necessary for God to become man, and why that man must be God in all His undiminished and unceasing deity. This is one approach to apprehending something of the grand truth of Christ's deity based on its absolute necessity.

While each aspect of His work highlights a particular insight as to why God became man, their interdependence must not be overlooked in the divine work of reconciliation, particularly evident in regard to the defeat of sin, of death and of the curse of the law. The practical and dispensational distinctions between them is also vital to note, for they identify the *past*, *present* and *prospective* ministry of God as the man Christ Jesus (1-7; 8; 9-10 in the list, respectively). This is not our present task. However, as we consider these ten imperatives which reveal why God became man, the redeemed heart will rejoice in an absorbing truth in regard to them. The present and prospective ministry of the divine Man is predicated upon His past ministry that, gloriously, is a *completed* work, a work accomplished upon the *cross*. All manner of fearful heresies evolve from the failure to acknowledge and apprehend these two vital truths.

These imperatives also reveal why Satan opposes the truth about

Christ's Person. Deny His Person and we deny His all-sufficient work. If Christ is not the divine Man then He cannot be the perfect sacrifice for sin. The erroneous idea of salvation through works then follows, through which Satan continues seduce many souls into eternal ruin.

God, the divine Son, in His undiminished and unceasing deity, had to become man in order to:

1. declare the divine Father and the divine Son;
2. defeat sin;
3. defeat death;
4. defeat the curse of the law;
5. defeat Satan;
6. determine our sanctification;
7. destroy the "middle wall of partition";
8. declare our cause as our Great High Priest and Advocate;
9. declare God's perfect government on earth;
10. deliver the eternal kingdom to the Father.

1. To declare the divine Father and the divine Son
The revelation of God as Father to the children of God

In the OT God is revealed as Father to His earthly *nation* Israel (Deut 32:6; Jer 31:9; Mal 1:6 etc.). No individual Israelite could draw near and call God "my Father". They knew Him as God in His awesome power and covenant prerogative. Now however, to Jew and Gentile redeemed in His Son, He is God the *Father* having a paternal prerogative. He is unchanged in His Person and power as God, but now revealed in His infinite loving fatherhood through the Person of His own beloved Son. God is the *divine* Father, and through faith in the *divine* Son we become children of God (Jn 1:12). This brings into view the *fellowship* we as His children have with God as our Father. The nature and conduct of this fellowship depends upon:

• the Father's divine *Person*
• the Father's divine *purposes*
• the Father's divine *provisions*.

No voice pealing from the excellent glory, no prophet's inspired pen, angel or Theophany however vivid, could reveal such intimate and earnest matters dwelling in the heart of a loving and paternal God. The Father's very own Son, who possessed His divine nature and essence, had to come forth from His bosom and walk among men, so men may know first-hand of God as the divine Father. For this reason the Son declared to Philip, "He that hath seen me [the divine Son] hath seen the [divine] Father." The revelation of the divine Father cannot be undertaken by anyone but the divine Son, for then it becomes a revelation of something less than the divine Father. John declares the reality of it. They beheld the Son and saw the glory of the only begotten of [from] the Father, full of grace and truth (cf 1 Jn 1; Jn 12:38-41). Any glory of the Father must be the divine glory.

Scripture is clear concerning why the revelation of the *divine* Father's Person, purposes and provisions to men, could only be made by the *divine* Son.

• *Proximity*: No created man or celestial being has the required *eternal* nearness to God. The uncreated man Christ Jesus does, for He is the Son who is in the bosom of the Father eternally, as noted earlier (Jn 1:18). The Son (the Word) was with God in the beginning (Jn 1:1). He was "*that* eternal life which was with the Father" (1 Jn 1:1-2). It is not with *God* here (cf Jn 1:1), but with the *Father*, the emphasis being upon the unique *eternal relationship* between the divine *Father* and the divine *Son*.

• *Perception*: Seeing and knowing. "No man hath *seen* God at any time", that is, *God* as He Himself is, the *Eternal One* (Jn 1:18). The verb *to see* here refers to a physical act, and emphasizes an accompanying mental discernment. This is consistent with the Son "declaring" the Father, this word meaning to 'interpret' Him. Only deity has the capacity to see deity in this way.[1] Further, "no man knoweth the Son, but the Father; neither knoweth any man the Father, save the Son" (Matt 11:27). The word 'knoweth is "fully-known" in both instances'.[2] The Son has complete knowledge of

---

[1] See Vincent *Word Studies* Vol II p 59. In John 1:18 the object to be seen is not God's attributes or personality - *theiotes*, but His *eternal* essence – *theon*. This divine essence no man can see – only the Son, for He possesses that same essence. He is thus able to declare - 'interpret' the Father to men (cf I Jn 4:12, even a stronger word for 'seen'). In John 14:9 Philip was 'to see' the divine Father in Christ, in that Christ manifested the divine glory of the Father (cf Jn 1:14). Christ could not have done this unless he possessed the divine essence.

[2] See Vincent *Word Studies* Vol I p 67; A T Robertson *Word Pictures*, Vol 1 p 91.

the Father. This is corroborated in the reciprocity given in Jn 10:15; "as the Father knoweth me, even so know I the Father". The Father's knowledge of the Son cannot be less than total knowledge. Neither then can the Son's knowledge of the Father be less than total.

• *Prerogative*: No created being has the divine prerogative to *reveal* the Father. It is the Son revealing the Father to whomsoever the Son *will* reveal Him (Matt 11:27).

• *Personality*: The Father's divine nature cannot be appreciated apart from the divine nature of the Son. Conversely, we cannot appreciate the Son's divine nature apart from the divine nature of the Father: "I and *my* Father are one"; "the Father *is* in me and I in Him"; "If ye had known me, ye should have known my Father also: and from henceforth ye know him, and have seen him"; "he that hath seen me hath seen the Father" (Jn 10:30; 38; 14:7-11).

It was only through the Son who was man yet very God, that the *invisible, incomprehensible* and *inaccessible* divine Father became *visible, knowable* and *accessible* to fallen man. What ineffable grace!

> But the high myst'ries of His name,
> An angel's grasp transcend;
> The Father only (glorious claim),
> The Son can comprehend.
> *(Josiah Conder)*

The Person of the divine Father - the nature of the Father with whom we have fellowship

Whatever we know of God as our divine Father, is based upon the revelation of His paternity by the divine Son (Jn 1:12,14,18; 1 Jn 1:2-3). In the course of His Father's business, the Son revealed the Person and nature of the divine Father. "I have manifested thy name" (Jn 17.6); He is our "heavenly Father" – His character (Matt 6:14, 26; 15:13 etc). Only the divine Son can reveal the divine Father's *moral* attributes. He declared the divine Father's holiness and righteousness (Jn 17:11, 25); He taught and manifested the divine love of the Father (Jn 3:16; Jn 17:25-26; 1 Jn 3:1 etc). As the Son is the object of His Father's fellowship, so we come to appreciate "our fellowship *is* with the Father, and with his Son Jesus

Christ" (1 Jn 1:3). The Father's transcendent grace and truth is manifested *in* His Son (Jn 1:14). The parable of the prodigal son is a lesson of the heavenly Father's grace and truth as much as it is a lesson of restored man. The Son revealed the *natural* divine attributes of the Father, His omnipotence and omniscience. As man the Son engaged men, searched their hearts and worked miracles, evincing the heavenly Father. The divine Son "declared", or as we noted more appropriately, "interpreted" the divine Father to men (Jn 1:18). To do this the Son must possesses the divine attributes entirely, equally, eternally and exclusively.

The purposes of the divine Father - the nature of the fellowship
"I have given unto them the words which thou gavest me" (Jn 17:8). The divine Father is to be honoured and worshipped according to His character and Being. It is the Son who instructs how this must be done - "in spirit and in truth" (Jn 4:21-23); the Father is to be supplicated as "Our Father which art in heaven" (Matt 6:9). The divine Son teaches us as only He can, that the proper motive and manner of practical spiritual life is in regard to the "heavenly Father", who is God (Matt 6). Because the divine Man among men *personally* declared His Father unto men during the days of His flesh, John is fitted for inspiration and his pen enabled to write his precious First Epistle. He tells of the blessed intimate communion each believer can now have with God as his/her personal heavenly Father. No OT worthy could write John's testimony - "Behold what manner of love the Father hath bestowed upon us, that we should be called the children of God" (1 Jn 3:1). It required the coming of One among men as Man who had the divine prerogative to declare "he that hath seen me hath seen the Father".

The provisions of the divine Father - blessings in fellowship
Only the divine Son could reveal the paternal provisions of the divine Father unto His children. The Son having come from heaven can declare the Father as having sent the true bread from heaven, His provision for their *salvation* (Jn 6:32). He speaks of their *security* provided by the divine Father. "My Father, which gave *them* me, is greater than all; and no *man* is able to pluck *them* out

of my Father's hand. I and *my* Father are one" (Jn 10:29-30). He tells of the giving of the Holy Spirit by the Father, His provision for their *sanctification* (Jn 14:16). The divine Son reveals the existence of the Father's heavenly house containing many mansions, wherein a place is being prepared by the Son for the Father's children (Jn 14:1-2). As the beloved Son, he lovingly tells of their daily needs being supplied by the Father (Matt 6:8) and of their rewards from the Father (Matt 6:1).

How can the Son speak to man of such intimate things concerning the infinite Father if he were not of the same divine nature and essence of God the Father and yet truly man? If the Son is to reveal the Father as the Father *is*, then the Son must be God, for this is who and what the Father is, infinite in all His natural and moral attributes. It is through the divine Son as man that these blessed revelations of the Father become apparent and assured.

The revelation of believers as sons of God the Father

Apart from *fellowship* with God as His children, believers possess *sonship* as sons of God. We are no longer servants but sons (Rom 8:14-15; Gal 4:6-7). These are edifying and elevating truths. The fact of our sonship and our appreciation of it, had to wait until the fulness of time when God sent forth His Son into the world as man. In these last days God spoke to men "in Son". Why? Only God's Son among men could impart the essence and reality of sonship to redeemed sons.[3] Through His life of obedient dependence upon His Father, the Son as man revealed what it meant to be a son of the divine heavenly Father. The fulness of the Godhead did not dwell *bodily* in the Father or the Spirit, only the Son. It was during the days of His flesh that the Son promised the Comforter, the Spirit of adoption, whereby as sons of God we cry 'Abba *Father'*.

2. To defeat sin

When we speak of "the defeat of sin" or "sin as defeated", we mean that sin need no longer be a barrier to peace with God. It is in this sense, too, that we say sin has been "put away". Man can

---

[3] The absence of the article in Hebrews 1:2 ("God in Son"), and in verses such as John 1:12, 1 Jn 3:1 ("children of God") and Romans 8:14 ("sons of God"), place emphasis upon the "character" of the person or persons in view, rather than upon their identity.

be reconciled to God. How and why this is so, is our present subject. It is vital to note, that for those who have not been reconciled to God, sin remains an undefeated foe. They remain under its eternal condemnation and, in their unreconciled state, they will themselves in a day to come bear God's eternal wrath against their sin. "Be ye reconciled to God" (2 Cor 5:20).

The ministry of reconciliation

God was, through Christ, reconciling the world unto Himself. Three vital related elements are in this grand truth.

1. God was, in His heart, occupied with reconciliation.
2. God was, through Christ, undertaking a work of reconciliation.
3. God was reconciling the world unto Himself.

From these three elements, three aspects of the divine *work* of reconciliation are brought into view:

• The divine *means* of reconciliation. Christ was the Person through whom God was reconciling the world unto Himself. It invites us to consider the Son's *incarnation* – the *needed Sacrifice*, the holy Son of God coming into the world to enable reconciliation.

• The divine *matter* of reconciliation. In its broader aspect, reconciliation involves the settling of "all things" unto God through Christ, through the "blood of His cross" (Col 1:20). Then there is the particular aspect of it relating to the settlement of matters between the sinner and God through Christ. "When we were enemies, we were reconciled to God by the death of his Son" (Rom 5:10; Col 1:21). The underpinning truth here is Christ's *crucifixion* – the *perfect Sacrifice*.

• The divine *motive* of reconciliation. Peace! It brings before us God satisfying His holiness that was slighted by sin. It is peace consummated on the ground of divine righteousness. We have here Christ's *resurrection, ascension* and *glorification* – the *accepted Sacrifice*.

What is meant by "reconciliation"?

Reconciliation is the removal of the enmity between creation and the Creator. It requires a work that settles *forever* the matter which brought about that enmity. Peace with God is its eternal legacy.

Why was reconciliation needed?

Sin separated man and God and brought enmity between them, bringing God's righteous condemnation upon men and His curse upon the earth (Gen 3:17-18). Adam, the representative head of man sinned by disobeying God. He brought sin and its penalty of death among men (Rom 5:12). If reconciliation is to take place, then sin must be defeated. This necessarily involves the matter of an individual's sins, the work of sin-bearing, where a person's sins and condemnation before God are taken away forever.

While sin is the "precipitating" factor in reconciliation, the "initiating" factor in reconciliation is divine righteousness. God's holy nature demanded the defeat of sin. His righteousness however must not be considered apart from His love, for "he loved us, and sent his Son *to be* the propitiation for our sins" (1 Jn 4:10).

How was reconciliation to be undertaken?

Scripture makes it very clear that sin's penalty could only be met by death, the death of a *spotless* sacrifice, spotless because it is in accordance with God's holiness. The physically spotless sacrifices of the OT were typical of the holy *nature* and *character* of Christ.

Reconciliation in all its aspects requires the defeat of sin and this requires sin's penalty of death to be paid.[4] How was this to be

---

[4] Consider the divine moral principle involved. A judge may seek to be merciful and honourable by not requiring a person who has committed evil to make recompense for that evil. Such a decision is an anathema to the Righteous Judge. It may be considered merciful, but it is not according to truth, for truth condemns evil! It may be considered peaceable, but it is not according to righteousness, because righteousness hates evil and therefore cannot abide with it! For peace to exist, evil must be redressed, its penalty paid. Only then is righteousness given liberty to reign and peace will abide! Sin must be redressed! This divine holy standard is reflected in the rhetorical question posed by the prophet Habakkuk. "*Thou art* of purer eyes than to behold evil, and canst not look on iniquity: wherefore lookest thou upon them that deal treacherously, *and* holdest thy tongue?" (Hab 1:13). God's mercy is never at the expense of His righteousness! It is said of the Son, as it is of God, again reflecting the oneness in their divine moral nature, "Thou hast loved righteousness, and hated iniquity" (Heb 1:9). The divine standard of holiness requires mercy and truth to meet, and righteousness and peace to kiss each other (Ps 85:10). God's immutable righteous nature demands that the penalty for sin (death), must be paid. Sin must be defeated and only then will God's wrath against sin be appeased. Upon this righteous ground, appropriated by faith, a person's sins will be remembered no more. As noted, any one of God's moral attributes cannot be subordinated to another. His infinite righteousness that demands His wrath against sin must be met, is in perfect accord with His infinite love in that He has given His only begotten Son to bear such wrath, that we who believe in Him should be spared from the wrath to come (Rom 5:9).

accomplished? In the OT economy, sin was dealt with through *atonement* - the substitutionary death of a spotless animal. The life is in the blood. It is the blood that "maketh atonement for the soul" (Gen 9:4; Lev 17:11-13). These sacrifices however were only a 'covering' for sin, evident in their seemingly endless repetition. They could never completely satisfy God and defeat sin. Even in Solomon's opulent reign, where the animal sacrifices "could not be told nor numbered for multitude", sin could never be put away forever (1 Kings 8:5). "For *it is* not possible that the blood of bulls and of goats should take away sins" (Heb 10:1-4). "In burnt offerings and *sacrifices* for sin thou hast had no pleasure" (Heb 10:5-6; Ps 40:6-8).

What of man? What of the Law?

In his pride man believed he could meet God's righteousness and defeat sin through his works. So God brought in the law and demanded righteousness from him. The law is the standard God requires man to keep if man is to earn His righteousness before God. But as a sin-crippled victim of the Fall, man could never keep its righteous demands. The law therefore served to reveal him as hopelessly sinful and under divine judgement. In man's flesh dwells no good thing, for all his righteousnesses are as "filthy rags" (Isa 64:6; Rom 7:18). The law itself is perfect and holy, for it reveals God's moral demands upon men. But it "was weak through the flesh" (Rom 8:3). It can never make man righteous before God, because fallen man is incapable of keeping it (Jas 2:10). The law was given not to bestow life, but to reveal sin as sin, to expose man's helplessness in sin and to declare his absolute dependence upon God for salvation.

Christ the needed perfect Sacrifice

What hope was there for sinful man in the light of God's certain judgement upon sin? God in grace took up man's cause and God *Himself* became the perfect Sacrifice for sin. But it was not only man's cause that God took up. Sin affronted His glory. His absolute holiness had to be vindicated, and He alone as the absolutely Holy One could accomplish this. God is the Initiator, the Executor and Guarantor in reconciliation. Scripture *never* speaks of man reconciling God or of God being reconciled to man. God is not a pagan deity whose wrath is to be placated by man or some other created being – "we were reconciled to God" (Rom 5:10; 2 Cor 5:18-20). God was *Himself*, through Christ, reconciling the world *unto Himself*.[5] If God *alone* had to be the Sacrifice for sin as Scripture incontrovertibly declares, then Christ is God, because Scripture also teaches that Christ *alone* was the Sacrifice for sin.

To become that needed sacrifice, God had to become man, which He did through the Person of His Son. "For what the law could not do, in that it was weak through the flesh, God sending his own Son in the likeness of sinful flesh, and for sin, condemned sin in the flesh" (Rom 8:3).[6] And, given that God became man, that Man was undiminished and unceasing in His deity. Deity cannot cease to exist where it does exist.

The glorious work of creation did not require a body, but a body was needed for the gracious work of reconciliation. "Wherefore when he cometh into the world, he saith, 'Sacrifice and offering thou wouldest not, but a body hast thou prepared me'." That body of flesh was holy, spotless, undefiled, sin apart! Our salvation rests on Christ's perfect humanity as well as His deity. "The humanity of Christ guarantees the validity of His redemption, His deity its value."[7] When writing to the Corinthians concerning the ministry of reconciliation, Paul presents Christ as the needed perfect sacrifice for sin, the perfect Man. "For he [God] hath made him *to be* sin [a sin offering] for us, who knew no sin; that we might be made [become] the righteousness of God in him" (2 Cor 5:21). Peter also mentions the moral imperatives and the necessary death of the perfect Man. "For Christ also hath once suffered for sins, the just for the unjust, that he might bring us to God [not God to us], being put to death in the flesh" (1 Pet 3:18).

But we must consider again the matter of God's glory. Who could

---

[5] We should add, too, that Scripture does not teach that God was in Christ who *has* reconciled the world unto Himself (Why then would there be the need for a "ministry of reconciliation"?) There are those who have now been reconciled unto God - the believers in Christ who are of the new creation (2 Cor 5:17; Col 1:21). The enmity between Jew and Gentile too *has* been removed (Eph 2). There is, however, that which *will be* reconciled unto God in a day to come (Col 1:20). All these aspects of reconciliation depend on the defeat of sin through the death of Christ!

[6] Christ's sinless life bore testimony to the defeat of sin that was accomplished by His death on the cross.

[7] Wm Hoste, *Studies in Bible Doctrine* p48, Gospel Tract Publications

defeat sin and bring glory to a God whose holiness had been slighted by sin? Only One who was the perfect Sacrifice. Speaking of His impending sacrifice for sin, the Lord declared "Now is the Son of man glorified, and God is glorified in him. If God be glorified in him, God shall also glorify him in himself, and shall straightway glorify him" (Jn 13:31-32).

The following scriptures are among many that testify that reconciliation is wholly through the *death* of the *Man* Christ Jesus. When writing to the Romans concerning reconciliation and justification, Paul declares that though once enemies of God, they have been "reconciled to God by the death of His Son" (Rom 5:9-11). When writing to the Colossians of their sanctification and reconciliation unto God through Christ, he reminds them that it was through "the body of his flesh through death" that they are presented "holy and unblameable and unreproveable" in God's sight (Col 1:21-23). The broader matter of reconciliation also rests wholly on the death and shed of blood of Christ. "[God] having made peace through the blood of his cross [Christ's death], by him [Christ] to reconcile all things unto himself" (Col 1:20).

Such clear teaching compels us to consider both the *person* and the *process* required to defeat sin - the Man and His death. No sooner had sin entered creation than the righteous heart of the Creator responded in grace to put it away and reconcile all things unto Himself. The seed of the woman will bruise the head of Satan and He Himself will be bruised (Gen 3:15). In this blessed foundation prophecy we first come to know of God, through Christ, reconciling the world unto Himself.

Christ the Lamb of God, the needed perfect Sacrifice
"God will provide Himself a lamb" (Gen 22:8). It is not simply God providing a lamb, but God providing a lamb *for* Himself and He *Himself* is that Lamb. The Baptist's words marked the fulfilment of this divine provision and preogative, "Behold the Lamb of God which taketh away the sin of the world" (Jn 1:29 cf Rev 5:6-14). Peter speaks of the absolute holiness of the Lamb and His perfect sacrifice, when he declares that we are redeemed "with the precious blood of Christ, as of a lamb without blemish and without spot: Who verily was foreordained [in regard to His sacrifice] before the

foundation of the world, but was manifest in these last times for you" (1 Pet 1:19-20).

We have here, too, the infinite love of God. He did not send some extraordinary created being, some adopted son to bear His wrath against sin. It was His *own* Son, foreordained as the sacrificial Lamb whom He sent and gave (Jn 3:16). To deny the deity of the Lamb of God is to deny the eternal efficacy of the cross and to rob God of His love to fallen man. He "spared not his own Son, but delivered him up for us all" (Rom 8:32).

Christ the accepted Sacrifice

Sin *has* been defeated and God's holiness *has* been satisfied by Christ's sacrificial death. Christ therefore was also the *accepted* sacrifice. The Hebrews Epistle identifies three transcendent blessings that confirm this exalted truth. Their finality marks a striking contrast to the fleeting atonement obtained through the sacrifices and offerings of the OT. They also testify to the utter foolishness of man seeking salvation from the penalty of sin through his works. Together they compose a three-fold chord in the eternal anthem of those who are reconciled to God in Christ:[8]

1. There is no more *conscience* of sins (Heb 10:2).
2. There is no more *remembrance* of sins (10:17)
3. There is no more *offering* for sin (10:18).

These imperishable blessings rest on Christ as the accepted sacrifice. He who was God became man in order to defeat sin:
• by appearing *once* to put away *sin* by the sacrifice of Himself (9:26);
• by offering Himself *once* to bear the *sins* of many (9:28).

We have here the *necessity* and the *eternal efficacy* of the Man Christ Jesus. Scripture bears further testimony to this in that "after He [Christ] had offered one sacrifice for sins [He] forever sat down at the right hand of God" (10:12); He is exalted by God (Phil 2:9); "we are sanctified through the offering of the body of Jesus Christ once for all" (Heb 10:10); the redeemed are "accepted in the

---

[8] There is an important distinction between "sins" and "sin" here and elsewhere in Scripture that must be recognised.

beloved" (Eph 1:6), and they are "the righteousness of God in Him".

The divine Man, the suffering Sacrifice

Christ spoke of His suffering with the same deep conviction and inevitability with which He spoke about His death (Lk 22:15; 24:46). The sorrows and sufferings of Christ are as impenetrable as they are infinitely sacred. Scripture never encourages us to fathom their depth. But it does invite us to enquire reverently as to their cause. When we do, we are told that the suffering of Christ was due to man's sin and on account of the holiness of God. His suffering was not confined to the physical agony of the cross, horrendous though that was. It was also the suffering He willingly bore as One who was made sin, who knew no sin, in order that that we might become the righteousness of God in him.[9] Only the divine perfect Man could to bear the divine wrath against sin.

A young Buddhist student enquired, "What is the essential difference between Christianity and other religions?" Surely it is *Christ*, the divine Man who suffered for the sin of man at the hand of a thrice holy God. "*Is it* nothing to you, all ye that pass by? behold, and see if there be any sorrow like unto my sorrow, which is done unto me, wherewith the Lord [Jehovah] hath afflicted me in the day of his fierce anger" (Lam 1:12). Could such sublime words that foreshadow the divine love and grace of the Man Christ Jesus, emanate from the heart of Buddha, Confucius, Krishna, Muhammad or his god? Indeed not, for their deepest sentiments spring from the shallow hearts of fallen mortal men. In the light of Christ's infinite love, grace and truth, all men are constrained to confess, "Lord, to whom shall we go? thou hast the words of eternal life. And we believe and are sure that thou art that Christ, the Son of the living God" (Jn 6:68-69).

Christ - the needed and accepted Sacrifice typified in the OT
The Day of Atonement

The Day of Atonement, the tenth day of the seventh month, was an ordained day set aside each year to make atonement for the

---

[9] "The words 'to be' are not in the Greek. 'Sin' here is the substantive, not the verb. God 'treated as sin' the one 'who knew no sin'." A T Robertson *Word Pictures* Vol IV p 233.

sins of the people of Israel. Atonement rested on God meeting His *own* righteous demands in regard to sin.

The many procedures required on that day in their sum and in their parts, typify the Person and work of Christ. Our interest is in regard to that part involving the high priest bringing two goats before Jehovah. "And he [Aaron, the high priest] shall take of the congregation of *the* children of Israel two kids of the goats for a sin offering" (Lev 16:5). One goat by lot was for Jehovah - *Godward*, and the other for the people - *manward*. The goat for Jehovah was for a sin offering (v.9). It was slain and its atoning blood sprinkled on and before the mercy-seat by the high priest clothed in his holy garments. The blood sprinkled upon the mercy-seat speaks of what God is and what He demands, holiness and vindication respectively. *Sin* had been dealt with. Once this had been done, the high priest laid his hands upon the head of the live second goat confessing the *sins* of the nation. This goat was then released into the wilderness. It was the "scapegoat". It symbolized the bearing and carrying away of the peoples' *sins*, *in virtue* of the accepted shed blood of the first goat.

The first goat foreshadows the *propitiation* made by Christ, typifying the necessity and acceptability of His sacrifice before God in regard to the matter of *sin*.[10] This, we noted, was done "once for all', which marks the essential difference between Christ's propitiation and the atonement made in the OT. Christ's perfect sacrifice completely met the holy demands of God in regard to sin. As the divine Man, He was the needed perfect sacrifice for sin. He satisfied God's wrath against sin and, in so doing, vindicated the holiness of God forever. Sin therefore has been defeated, put away - Heb 9:26.[11] God sent His

---

[10] Did Christ make propitiation on the cross or when He ascended? "When was sin defeated?" There can be no doubt that it was on the cross. This is the conclusion we come to if we interpret the Day of Atonement in the light of Calvary, rather than Calvary in the light of the Day of Atonement. It is only when the Anti-type appears that we have a truer insight into the type! The Day of Atonement, like all OT types, is but a shadow of the true. The teaching from the NT, Romans in particular, refers in plain terms to the death of Christ (the cross) as the occasion when propitiation was made. God *sent*, not received His Son to be a propitiation for our sins (1 Jn 4:10). "I have glorified thee on the earth: I have finished the work which thou gavest me to do" (Jn 17:4). In Romans 3:25 propitiation is "mercy-seat", and in Romans 5:11 it is not "atonement" but "the reconciliation" which we have received. Propitiation is necessary for reconciliation.

[11] "It is God who is propitiated by the vindication of His holy and righteous character, whereby, through the provision He has made in the vicarious and expiatory sacrifice of Christ, He has so dealt with sin that He can shew mercy to the believing sinner in the removal of his guilt and the remission of sins." W E Vine *Expository Dictionary* p 223. We should note that God is not *changed*. Propitiation meets God's unchangeable nature and character.

own Son for *sin*, and His Son did not cover but *condemned* sin in the flesh.[12] This is the divine ground upon which God is able to show mercy to the guilty sinner.[13]

The second goat brings before us what man is and what he needs. He is a guilty sinner in need of a Sin-Bearer. This, the peoples' goat, typified the work of Christ in *substitution*, as the Scape-goat who bore our *sins* - Heb 9:28. Whereas propitiation is Godward and concerned with meeting God's holy nature and character, substitution is manward meeting man's need. Peter, addressing *believers*, speaks of "[Christ] who in His own self bore our sins in His own body on the tree".[14] The two goats as the one sin-offering foreshadowed one entire truth regarding Calvary. God became man, and as the Perfect Man He put away *sin* forever by the sacrifice of Himself. In so doing, He bore the *sins* in His own body on the cross for those who believe.

The above truths afford further insight to the two questions and their respective answers given at the start of this chapter. Why did God in His undiminished and unceasing deity become man? Why was this a matter of absolute necessity? The holy nature of God demanded it. The sinful nature of man required it. Isaiah declared that it "pleased the Lord to bruise Him" (Isa 53:10). What was it about the Son's death that brought pleasure to God? It was that God's holiness was satisfied by the death of His Son and sin was put away.[15] That same death enables fallen man to have peace and fellowship with God on the ground of divine righteousness. Surely, this brings pleasure to a holy God of love, grace and mercy!

Finally, the truth that God Himself was the needed Sacrifice pervades every aspect of Christianity. Paul writes to the overseers,

---

[12] Condemned sin in the flesh. "If the article *ten* had been repeated before *en tei sarki* Paul would have affirmed sin in the flesh of Jesus, but he carefully avoided that." A T Robertson *Word Pictures* Vol IV p 372.

[13] How often do we herald this blessed truth in the preaching of the Gospel? The 'good news' is predicated on the truth that God's holiness has been satisfied in the Person and work of His beloved Son.

[14] 1 Pet 2:24. In 1 Jn 2:2, the term "the sins" in the expression "for the sins of the whole world" (AV) is not found in the original text. It is a misleading interpolation conveying a wrongful meaning in regard to the truth of Christ's propitiation. Christ did *not* take away the *sins* of the world. His all-sufficient propitiating work enables all to have their sins taken away, if all accept Him as Saviour. The ground - Christ's shed blood, upon which God shows mercy to sinners is available to each and every sinner. It speaks against every shade of the Calvanist notion of limited atonement. However, only believers can say He bore our sins in His own body on the tree (cf 1 Jn 4:10).

[15] The death of Christ satisfied *every* attribute of God, as it must do in a God who possesses the divine attributes entirely, equally eternally and exclusively.

"Feed the church of God, which he [God] hath purchased with his own blood" (Acts 20:28). *God* is explicitly said to have purchased the church and He did so with His *own blood.* How can this be so except that Jesus Christ the perfect sacrifice is God blessed forever (Rom 9:5).[16]

The Passover
    The typical lesson from Leviticus 16 is *reconciliation.* God's wrath against sin has been appeased and His holiness vindicated. Whosoever will may now come unto Him, boasting excluded with pride abased. All this can instructively be brought into comparison with Exodus 12 in relation to our subject. Both portions converge at the cross of Christ, which imparts to them their particular glory. Whereas in Leviticus 16 we have the defeat *of* sin and *reconciliation* foreshadowed, in Exodus 12 we have man's deliverance *from* sin and *redemption* typified. It is God "coming down to deliver" enslaved man from the fetters of sin (Ex 3:8; Acts 7:34). Yet it was not without blood, because the lamb was slain and its blood applied. "When I see the blood I will pass over you" (Ex 12:13). Redemption, as with reconciliation, is on the ground of divine holiness, the shedding of blood. Whether it was the door post and lintel, the mercy seat or Calvary, it was necessary that God should look upon the blood. "O Lord, Who is like unto thee glorious in holiness?" (Ex 15:11). And, in each instance it was entirely *God's* estimate of the blood, not man's estimate of it that mattered. Hebrews 10 gives us the anthem of atonement, Exodus 15 the rhapsody of redemption. "The Lord is my strength and song, And he is become my salvation....Thou in thy mercy hast led forth the people *which* thou hast redeemed" (Ex 15:2-13). The lamb sacrificed had to be without blemish, an intimation of that perfect Sacrifice (Ex 12:5). When Paul wrote to the redeemed he declared "Christ our passover is sacrificed for us" (1 Cor 5:7). He had in view our *redemption* through the death of that perfect Man. God came down as man that sin should be

---
[16] When faced with the irrefutable testimony to the deity of Christ and the Trinity in this verse, some insert the expression "with the blood of his own [Son]". Such words are not found in any of the Greek manuscripts of the Bible.

defeated in the flesh through His death, and our redemption from sin be secured.[17]

In the light of these truths, may we appreciate that each and every redeemed person is a testimony to the deity and perfect humanity of Christ. When we look upon the symbol bread and wine at the Lord's Supper, may they be a blessed reminder that God in His undiminished and unceasing deity once walked upon the earth as the divine Man, Christ Jesus. What sublime grace! He did this to vindicate His slighted holiness and to redeem us from sin and judgement. What transcendent joy this imparts to the redeemed, when gathered to remember the Lord and show forth His death.[18]

To the joy and profit of our souls we should also embrace the other essential matter brought before us in the song of the redeemed. God is "glorious in power". He has dashed the enemy in pieces, his captains are drowned in the sea. (Ex 15:4). So, too, the gospel of Christ, for it is the "power of God unto salvation" (Rom 1:16).[19] Far greater than Israel's redemption is ours, for "If the Son therefore shall make you free, ye shall be free indeed" (Jn 8:36) – for the Son is the divine Redeemer! "Go ye therefore, and teach all nations" (Matt 28:19).

Christ - the needed divine Man typified in the OT
The divine Man as the Kinsman Redeemer

During the year of Jubilee, possessions lost through debt or hardship (with some exceptions) were restored to their original owner. It was a year of *rejoicing, release, restoration* and *rest* granted

---

[17] The defeat of sin speaks against the teaching of limited atonement, that Christ's death was only for an elect few. Neither does it mean, however, that all persons will be saved. As noted above, Christ did not bear the sins of all people on the cross. His putting away of sin makes it possible, "clears the way" for all to be saved and therefore for all to say He bore my sins in His own body on the cross - if all believe on Him! When Paul declares Christ died for our sins (1 Cor 15:3-4) and Peter states He bore our sins (1 Pet 2:24), they are referring to believers, those who have accepted Christ as their Saviour. There are many who sadly will die in their sins and reap the eternal wrath of a righteous God for they have not accepted Christ as their Lord and Saviour, never having availed themselves of the fact that sin has been put away!

[18] It is to *remember* the Lord and *show forth* His death, rather than remember His death and show forth the Lord (1 Cor 11:24-26). It is His Person - who and what He is, that gives value to His death. "This do in remembrance of me" (Lk 22:19).

[19] "To them that believe". Deliverance is given only to those who have applied the blood and are seen by God to be sheltering beneath it! When God saw the blood, the hand of death was stayed! (Ex 12:13).

by God to the Israelites (Lev 25). Lost possessions could be recovered prior to the year of Jubilee by a "kinsman redeemer" (vv.25-28). To be a kinsman redeemer, a person had to be a *near relative* and be *willing* and *able* to pay the redemption price. Boaz was Ruth's kinsman redeemer (Ruth 4:9-10).

Man needed to be redeemed from the bondage of sin. The price? Vindication of a Holy God through a perfect sacrifice! Only God Himself could pay this price. He became man to pay it and to become a near relative – the Seed of the woman. He did this willingly and became obedient unto death, even the death of the cross (Jn 4:34; 10:17; Phil 2:8). The man Christ Jesus was God and had to be God in all His undiminished and unceasing deity (1 Pet 1:18-19). "Blessed *be* the Lord, which hath not left thee this day without a kinsman [Redeemer]" (Ruth 4:14).

The divine Man as the Daysman between God and man

Job yearned for a "daysman" who "*is* not a man, as I am, that I should answer him, *and* we should come together in judgment"; a "daysman betwixt us, *that* might lay his hand upon us both" (Job 9:32-33). He saw himself as unjust and unworthy, in need of someone to arbitrate between himself and the unchangeable holy God – a daysman. Who but the divine Man – the Seed of the woman, can stand between God and man and arbitrate on man's behalf according God's absolute righteousness, laying His hand upon both man and God? "For Christ also hath once suffered for sins, the just for the unjust, that he might bring us to God, being put to death in the flesh" (1 Pet 3:18).

The divine Man as the Mediator between God and man

We must assert that which Scripture demands. Mediation involves man being brought to God, not God to man. Only a divine Person can identify with God's holy and righteous nature. Mediation, as with arbitration, is according to the unchangeable righteousness of God. Who among men could meet the divine requirement? Who can pledge eternal peace as the outcome of mediation due to sin? There is only One, the divine Man Jesus Christ the righteous. "For *there is* one God, and one mediator between God and men, the man Christ Jesus" (1 Tim 2:5). Christ the divine Man *has* "made peace through the blood of His cross" (Col 1:20). The mediation was made and accepted by God by the "blood of His cross" – the death of Christ. We who have believed have peace with God through Christ who is our peace (Rom 5:1; Eph 2:14).

Atonement, propitiation, reconciliation, redemption, arbitration and mediation, all rest upon the death of the perfect divine Man. Scripture consistently reveals the necessity of God becoming man and that Man is God in all His undiminished and unceasing deity.

Salvation solely by and in the divine Man our Mediator

If Christ is not God, then His death did not fully satisfy God, and man must do his part to appease Him. Those who deny Christ's deity are therefore obliged to preach a doctrine directly opposed to the *explicit* teaching of Scripture. When the Lord finished the work of salvation on the cross He cried, "It is finished." They must say it was *not* finished! Paul tells the Ephesians salvation is *not* of man's works (Eph 2:8). They must say it is! Titus, also guided by the Spirit, teaches that our salvation is *not* by our works of righteousness (Tit 3:5). They must again contradict the explicit teaching of Scripture and say that we are saved by righteous works. Paul exhorts the Philippians to "work *out*" their salvation with fear and trembling in regard to their practical Christian life (Phil 2:12). They interpret his words to mean "work *for* your salvation". James declares "faith without works is dead", referring to a Christian's *testimony* toward others (Jas 2:20). They must interpret his exhortation to refer to salvation. In the teaching of Christ, salvation is by faith, never through works.

Why have these people fallen into such blatant error? As noted above, they have little understanding of man's spiritual poverty and the absolute holiness of God. They have failed to acknowledge man's hopelessness in sin and therefore they see little necessity for a Saviour-God, and much less the need for salvation through divine grace. They have interpreted Scripture according to the vanity of their fallen minds. Conscience can only end its strife and the soul find blessed assurance in the all-sufficiency of the One who died at Calvary. God Himself has declared it to be so. Paul was a man who spoke, walked and taught as one who was eternally emancipated. He had no doubt that it was upon the middle cross where his salvation was secured. "For the preaching of the cross is to them that perish foolishness; but unto us who are saved it [the cross] is the power of God unto salvation" (1 Cor 1:18). His avowal that "we preach Christ crucified", is the inspired theme in his gospel (1 Cor 1:23). Not simply Christ, but Christ *crucified*. For this self-confessed chief among sinners, eternal assurance was never through Christ crucified complemented by his own righteous efforts (Eph 2:8; Tit 3:5). It is all of Christ! The blessed pledge granted to all who place their trust in Christ's death and shed blood is that they are the "righteousness of God in Him" (2 Cor 5:21); "complete in him [Christ]"; "accepted in the Beloved [Christ]" (Col 2:10; Eph 1:6). Self is excluded absolutely!

There are unfailing promises given to us through the Word of God in terms of our reconciliation (2 Cor 5:18; Col 1:21); redemption (Col 1:14); redemption and justification (Rom 3:24-25); justification and peace (Rom 5:1); perfection and sanctification (Heb 10:14); eternal life (Jn 3:16; 1 Jn 5:20); salvation (Eph 2:8). Absolute certainty and assurance abides because our standing before God is entirely the work of God. When God the Eternal Son became man to put away sin and to redeem man, it was a complete work. How foolish and fatal is the idea that man can add to what God Himself has done and declared complete. God in the divine Christ did only what God could do; He did only what God could choose to do; and He manifested the glory of God. To seek salvation through self-righteousness and ritual such as baptism in all its forms, is to regard God as a pagan deity who must be appeased by man.

Salvation is not through reformation or ritual, but by repentance and through the redemption in Christ. God justifies us according to faith, not its strength but according to the One upon whom it rests - Christ the divine Man (Rom 5:1). "Christ *is* the end of the law for righteousness to every one that believeth" (Rom 10:4).[20] The epic theme of Romans is of righteousness that comes not through the law and works, but by grace and faith. "*It is* of faith, that *it might be* by grace" (Rom 4:16). Salvation is *provided* by God through grace, *accepted* by man through faith, and *grounded* upon the precious

---

[20] "To everyone that believeth." Once again we are brought to consider the solemn fact that Christ's reconciliation is only unto them who believe. He does not bear the sins of the unbeliever. The wrath of God is not extinguished for the Christ-rejecter.

shed blood of Christ. May we assiduously avoid the error of preaching works *or* faith as the ground of salvation.

3. To defeat death

In the death of the divine Man we have the defeat of sin *accomplished*. In His bodily resurrection we have the *assurance* that sin has been defeated. It declares His *victory* over sin, death and hell. The eternal divine Son of God had no sin and death therefore had no dominion over Him. Only a Man of undiminished and unceasing deity could claim and consummate the divine prerogative that He lay down His life that He might take it up again (Jn 10:17).

Christ rising bodily from the grave declares too that God whose holiness was offended by sin has been vindicated. Sin had to be put away. The bodily resurrection of Christ is an eloquent testimony to the truth that there is therefore no more sacrifice for sin (Heb 10:18), because the death of the perfect Man fully satisfied God.

Paul champions the eternal worth of the bodily resurrection of Christ to the believer. "If Christ be not raised, your faith *is* vain; ye are yet in your sins. Then they also which are fallen asleep in Christ are perished. If in this life only we have hope in Christ, we are of all men most miserable" (1 Cor 15:17-19). If sin reigns then its penalty of death also reigns. The grave holds fast it prey. "Sin reigned unto death" (Rom 5:21). Death is the evidence of sin. The fact that Christ arose from among the dead *bodily* is the assurance that sin has been defeated, and the believer's dead body will arise incorruptible and immortal. Wondrous and glorious truth! God had to become man in order to *physically* die to put away sin, to deliver us from our sins, and to *physically* rise from the dead declaring that sin has been defeated. "Death is swallowed up in victory. O death, where *is* thy sting? O grave, where *is* thy victory? ...But thanks *be* to God, which giveth us the victory through our Lord Jesus Christ" (1 Cor 15:54-57). The sting of death *is* sin; and the strength of sin *is* the law, but His bodily resurrection proves He has defeated sin and death. The Spirit's *doctrine* of the resurrection is evident. "Christ died for our sins according to the scriptures; and that he was buried, and that he rose again the third day according to the scriptures" (1 Cor 15:3-4). His view of its *importance* is emphatic. Christ *must* rise again from the dead bodily (Jn 20:9). The believer's *estimation* of it is eternal. Jesus Christ our Saviour "hath abolished [nullified] death, and hath brought life and immortality to light through the gospel" (2 Tim 1:10).[21]

4. To defeat of the curse of the law

When he wrote to the Christians in Rome, Paul declared the emancipating truth that "now we are delivered from the law, that being dead wherein we were held" (Rom 7:6). He was speaking particularly to Jewish believers in Christ. But it is important to understand that the law curses both Jew and Gentile. This is because none of Adam's fallen race can meet its righteous demands (Rom 3:20).[22] It is equally vital to understand that anyone can be freed from curse of the law through faith in Christ. This is because of who Christ is and what He has done. "Wherefore my brethren, ye also are become dead to the law." How? It was "By the body of Christ", that sinless perfect sacrifice of the man Christ Jesus (Rom 7:4). Once again the necessity of God becoming man in all His glorious undiminished and uncreated deity is brought before us. The righteous claims of the law and the defeat of its curse upon man could only be achieved on the ground of divine holiness. Scripture repeatedly reveals this could only be secured through a perfect sacrifice for sin. The Galatians were seeking life and light among the dead things of Judaism. Paul reproves them by reminding them of Christ, the perfect sacrifice, crucified among them, who "redeemed us from the curse of the law, being made a curse for us" (Gal 3:1-13). Christ in His divine manhood as the perfect sacrifice for sin "*is* the end of the law for righteousness to every one that believeth".

---

[21] In 1 Corinthians 15:26 Paul states "The last enemy that shall be destroyed is death." Resurrection defeats death. This verse refers to the end of time when the unrighteous dead are resurrected for judgement (Rev 20). The righteous taken in death will have already been resurrected - they (and Christ who is the Firstfruits) are spoken of as being raised *from among* the dead (these dead are the unrighteous, who await their resurrection unto judgement - the *second death,* Rev 20:6). In the eternal state there will be no physical death. We should note in this connection, that Scripture does not teach a general resurrection. There is the first resurrection which involves all the righteous (at various stages), and the second resurrection involving all the unrighteous.

[22] The "law" here, is specifically the Mosaic law given by God to Israel. The Gentiles were never under the Mosaic law and, therefore, it had no hold upon them. However, the law is not dead. It reflects God's holy standard prescribed for man and it serves to condemn all men who are without Christ as their Saviour and all who seek justification before God through their own works.

5. To defeat Satan

The seed of the woman, "It [Christ] shall bruise thy head [Satan]" (Gen 3:15). This is the first prophecy in Scripture and it was wondrously fulfilled at Calvary. It transports us by faith to that sacred mount via Bethlehem's manger, to consider the One born of a woman who is God and perfect man. Once more we see that what God promises in grace He provides in His power.

The Hebrews Epistle gives us a further insight into this victory in Christ and its liberating legacy to those in Him. "Forasmuch then as the children are partakers of flesh and blood, he also himself likewise took part of the same; that through death he might destroy him that had the power of death, that is, the devil; And deliver them who through fear of death were all their lifetime subject to bondage" (Heb 2:14-15).[23] The word "destroy" in the AV is to "bring to nought".[24] The prince of the power of the air is alive and active, pending the day when he will be cast into the everlasting pit (Rev 20:10).

God became man in order to die and rise again from the dead that He might defeat sin and thus defeat him who had the power of death (Jn 12:31). Satan is the author of death through sin. He is a defeated foe to the believer, his power has been vanquished by Christ, the Captain of our salvation. Christ "hath delivered us from the power of darkness" (Col 1:13). "For this purpose the Son of God was manifested, that he might destroy the works of the devil" (1 Jn 3:8).

6. To determine our sanctification

Sanctification refers to a thing or person being set apart for a particular purpose. Typically it embraces *position* and *purpose*. Believers are "in Christ" (their position) and their life is to glorify God (their purpose). The moment we place faith in Christ as our Saviour we are set apart unto God. When the people in Egypt

---

[23] The Spirit of God again sedulously guards the deity of Christ. As human beings we are said to be "partakers" (*koinonia*) of flesh and blood, meaning we involuntarily share this in common with other human beings. Jesus Christ the Spirit says, 'took hold of' (*metecho*) flesh and blood. This refers to His incarnation, to Him taking hold of human nature - sin apart! See Wuest *Word Studies*, Hebrews Vol II p 62-63.

[24] From *katargeo* – to make idle or ineffective. A T Robertson *Word Pictures* Vol V p 349. It is not said that Satan had the power 'over' death, but the power 'of' death. He brought death through sin (Js 1:15).

sheltered under the blood of the slain lamb, they were set apart unto God. It was the blood of a spotless sacrifice that secured not only their redemption but also their sanctification.

The writer to the Hebrews presents the glorious truth in regard to the position and purpose of believers in Christ. "By the which will we are sanctified [set apart unto God] through the offering of the body of Jesus Christ once *for all*" (Heb 10:10). We have here again the *necessity* of the divine Man – His death as the ground of our sanctification. We also have the eternal *efficacy* of the death of the divine Man in our sanctification. "For by one offering he hath perfected for ever them that are sanctified [set apart unto God]" (10:14). Our sanctification is not probationary nor prospective, because it has been accomplished through divine *purchase*, through Christ as the spotless, perfect and accepted Sacrifice - the divine Man.[25]

7. To destroy the middle wall of partition

In the OT economy God decreed that His earthly nation Israel was to be separate from the Gentiles. It was an "'unclean" thing for Jews to mix with the Gentile races. In the NT, the church (the Body of Christ) comprises God's heavenly people, among whom racial distinctions do not exist. "There is neither Jew nor Greek, ...bond nor free...male nor female: for ye are all one in Christ Jesus" (Gal 3:28). What enabled this unity within the Church? It was Christ and His death. "But now in Christ Jesus ye who sometimes were far off [the Gentiles] are made nigh by the blood of Christ. For he is our peace, who hath made both one, and hath broken down the middle wall of partition *between us*; Having abolished in his flesh the enmity, *even* the law of commandments *contained* in ordinances; for to make in himself of twain one new man, *so* making peace; And that he might reconcile both unto God in one body by the cross, having slain the enmity thereby" (Eph 2:13-16). Again we see the necessity *and* the efficacy of the death of the divine Man – the accepted sacrifice. The blessed unity of the church, which is His Body, is only possible because of

---

[25] When speaking of a believer's sanctification, is correct to employ the typical explanation that a person is "set apart unto God", for it aptly declares his/her *position* and *purpose* as a new creation. But to say that the believer "having been *purchased* is set apart to God", brings to the fore the necessity of the divine Man in regard to that new creation. It reminds us in relation to our practical sanctification, that before we can live in regard to what it is we are brought into in Christ, we need to first apprehend what it is we have died to in Christ (Rom 5-8). (Our practical sanctification refers to how we walk unto God.)

Christ's death on the cross, His death and His shed blood. All those in Christ's Body, whatever their race, stand accepted in *Him* before God on the ground of His perfect sacrifice for sin (Eph 1:6). On this ground, the middle wall of separation – the Mosaic economy, was made inoperative.

8. To declare our cause, as our Great High Priest and Advocate
Our Great High Priest

Though redeemed and accepted in the Beloved we are pilgrims in the wilderness and prone to the spiritual trials therein. Our High Priest is the risen, glorified Son of God who, through His very Person and work, helps us in our infirmities (*not our sins*). He upholds us before God. This is the *nature* of the Son's work as our High Priest. It is unto God *for* us, unceasingly and in regard to every believer.[26]

He is *able* to be our High Priest because of His deity and perfect humanity. He must be God in all His unceasing and undiminished deity. How else can He possess the necessary divine attributes to intercede continually on behalf of *each* and *every* believer before God and, do so according to divine holiness? The Epistle to the Hebrews especially presents Christ as our High Priest. It begins therefore with an emphatic declaration of His deity. Chapter 2 follows with a presentation of His blessed humanity. This is because He must also be man to effectively sympathize with our trials and intercede before God on our behalf. The Word who was God became flesh. His life as man among men was necessary to become a fitting High Priest. "Wherefore [because of this] it behoved him to be made like unto *his* brethren, that he might be a merciful and faithful high priest in things *pertaining* to God" (Heb 2:17). As man, God the Son experienced the path of trial, sorrow, hunger, thirst, humiliation, unjust accusation and rejection. He is able therefore to succour those who are likewise tempted (v.18). He knew what it was to walk as the perfect Man in the wilderness. He is thus able to uphold those who walk in the wilderness and who are perfected in Him.

The Lord's absolute superiority as our High Priest rests in His deity and perfect humanity. He is our *Great* High Priest, because of His -

• *person* - He is God the Son, the Son of God (Heb 1:1-2; 4:14);

---

[26] As our Apostle, His work is from God *unto* us (Heb 3:1)!

- *pedigree* - His divine priesthood is declared in that He is a High Priest forever after the *order* of Melchisedek - without a beginning and end, without father or mother, and without descent (Gen 14:18-20; Ps 110:4; Heb 5:6,10; 7:1-20);[27]
- *place* - He is our High Priest who has passed into the heavens from whence He had come (4:14);
- *position* - He is at the right-hand of God (8:1);
- *posture* - He is seated (10:12).

What is the blessing to us? It is that we can "come boldly unto the throne of grace, that we may obtain mercy and find grace to help in times of need" (Heb 4:16). This blessed provision is secured because our Great High Priest sits at the right-hand of God. Why is He seated there? Because of who He is and what He has done. Here again we see the necessity and efficacy of the divine Man. The high priestly service of Aaron required access to God, and access to God could only be undertaken when sin had been dealt with on the basis of shed blood.[28] Aaron could never sit down, having to repeat his work because of the inadequacy of the animal sacrifices. But the Son of God as the divine perfect Man, was the perfect and accepted sacrifice, who through His precious shed blood "put away" sin. He opened the way unto God for us, which is kept open because of the all-sufficiency of His perfect sacrifice. "But this man, after he had offered one sacrifice for sins for ever, sat down on the right hand of God" (10:12). "Having therefore, brethren, boldness to enter into the holiest by the blood of Jesus, By a new and living way, which he hath consecrated for us, through the veil, that is to say, his flesh; And *having* an high priest over the house of God; Let us draw near..." (10:19-22). The terms "this man", "the blood of Jesus" and "his flesh" in these verses, clearly teach that Christ's high priestly work is based upon the necessity not only of His incarnation, but also of His crucifixion. It has been truly

[27] Christ is also a High Priest after the *pattern* of Aaron, because He is, as was Aaron, the man who could sympathize with the infirm and who was called of God (Heb 5:1-5).
[28] It is now as it was in the pattern of the Tabernacle, the high priest interceding between *God* and man. The high priest is ordained for men in things pertaining to *God* (Heb 5:1). It is before *God* because it is unto God that reconciliation had to be made - *God* (not the *Father*) was in Christ reconciling the world unto Himself - "in all things it behoved him to be made like unto *his* brethren, that he might be a merciful and faithful high priest in things *pertaining* to God, to make reconciliation for the sins of the people" (Heb 2:17). And, having done the work of reconciliation (Rom 5:10; 2 Cor 5:18; Col 1:21 - God, not the Father in this latter verse), He takes up His rightful position at the right hand of *God* - His place of glorification and exaltation as the Man Christ Jesus (Mk 16:19; Acts 2:33, 7:55; Rom 8:34; Col 3:1; Heb 1:3; 10:12; 1 Pet 3:22).

202

stated, there can be no priesthood without manhood. But another grand truth of Christianity is that there can be no *true* priesthood without Godhood. Christ's perfect manhood is indispensable to His *suitability* as our Great High Priest. His Godhood is essential for His *legitimacy* to be our Great High Priest. In the former He has the required human sympathy; in the latter, he has the needed divine fidelity!

Our Advocate

As children of God we are accepted in the Beloved. We have become the righteousness of God in Him. His precious blood has blotted out our sins, past, present and future. Sin can never be imputed to the redeemed in Christ. Glorious truth! It is vital to understand therefore, that the advocacy of Christ is *not* in regard to our *union* with the Father, which is unassailable. It is to do with our *communion* with the Father. *If* a child of God sins, communion with the Father is broken, because the Father is holy and He cannot have fellowship with sin. That lost communion must be restored. It is Christ our Advocate who restores it by pleading our cause before the righteous *Father*.[29] An advocate is one who is called to speak on behalf of another.

On what ground does Christ act as our Advocate? Sin can only be dealt with on the ground of *divine* righteousness. Our assurance of continuing fellowship with the Father rests therefore on the advocacy of One who is the Father's equal in righteousness, the Anointed Man "Jesus Christ the righteous" (1 Jn 2:1). He is as the Father is, inherently righteous (Jn 17:25). It is Jesus Christ the righteous who is "the propitiation for our sins" (1 Jn 2:2). When He pleads on behalf of the believers, it is not according to extenuation or mitigation, but upon the abiding efficacy of His blood shed in propitiation on the cross. We observe again the absolute necessity and efficacy of Christ's deity and perfect humanity.

As our Advocate and High Priest, Christ meets the spiritual need of each and every child of God. To do this He must search their hearts and discern their thoughts according to divine righteousness. This can only be possible if He possesses the natural and moral attributes of God.

9. To display God's perfect government on earth

Divine righteousness is the moral ground upon which God deals

---

[29] Not before *God* as is the case when His high priestly work is in view.

with man. In this church dispensation, it is *grace* reigning through righteousness; in the Tribulation it will be *judgement* reigning through righteousness and, in the Millennium, *government* will reign through righteousness. Our focus is the Millennium, the literal, halcyon one thousand year reign of Christ, that theocratic kingdom of perfect government upon earth (Rev 20:4,7). No angel will rule over this kingdom. "For unto the angels hath he not put in subjection the world to come, whereof we speak" (Heb 2:5). Christ then cannot be an angel. God Himself must reign as King. To what end?

To fulfil His sovereign purposes among men and all nations

Only Jesus of Nazareth the divine Man, is able to restore God's glory among the nations and accomplish the reality of God walking among men as Sovereign. Angels are explicitly excluded in such a work. "But to which of the angels said he at any time 'Sit on my right hand, until I make thine enemies thy footstool?'" (Heb 1:13). Man is also excluded because he carries the seed of sin and rebellion from his fallen head Adam. Biblical and secular history chronicle the abject failure of all kingdoms headed by man.

There is only one Person who can fulfill the millennial prophecy of righteous rule upon earth, the divine Man Jesus Christ. Isaiah speaks of His government in righteousness. "And righteousness shall be the girdle of his loins" (Isa 11:5). So too Jeremiah! "Behold, the days come, saith the LORD, that I will raise unto David a righteous Branch [a Man], and a King shall reign and prosper, and shall execute judgment and justice in the earth" (Jer 23:5). The righteous Branch is Jesus Christ the righteous in His undiminished and unceasing deity. He shall be called "Jehovah Tsidkenu", "the Lord our Righteousness" (Jer 23.6). "Who is the King of glory? The LORD [Jehovah] strong and mighty, the LORD mighty in battle...the LORD [Jehovah] of Hosts" (Ps 24).

The eternal Word who became flesh to redeem man, is the Man who *must* reign on earth (1 Cor 15:24-25). The earthly reign of the Son of God is part of a number of imperatives in regard to His work.[30] He is the Last Adam and the Second Man who will restore unto God a righteous Kingdom on earth (1 Cor 15:24-25). Through divine grace the first man Adam was given dominion (Gen 1:26),

---

[30] His mission (Lk 2:49; 4:43); His death and resurrection (Jn 20:9, Acts 17:3); His glorification (Acts 3:21).

but he failed and unrighteousness and strife were brought in. There must be another man to restore God's honour in government among men. The Last Adam (1 Cor 15:45), the Man Christ Jesus is that Man. Through divine *right* He will exercise divine *might* over all the earth, again, demonstrating that which God promises in divine grace He delivers in divine power. Through Him righteousness and peace will "kiss each other" in government.

To fulfil the inheritance of the divine Son in government.
The Millennium is the kingdom in which the once despised and rejected King, the Man Christ Jesus, will reign in universal majesty. He is not only a High Priest after the order of Melchizedek, but as Melchizedek, the king of Salem, He is also the King of righteousness and peace. Jesus of Nazareth will leave that heavenly place which He entered and return as King of kings and Lord of lords to the place of His humiliation. As the Son of man He will rightly receive unto Himself glory and honour on earth.[31] He is given dominion over all because He made Himself obedient unto death, even the death of the cross. "Wherefore God also hath highly exalted him, and given him a name which is above every name: That at the name of Jesus every knee should bow - of *things* in heaven, and *things* in earth, and *things* under the earth; And *that* every tongue should confess that Jesus Christ *is* Lord, to the glory of God the Father" (Phil 2:9-11). The divine Man, the Lion of the tribe of Judah will return to establish the kingdom reign of God on earth. "The sceptre shall not depart from Judah, nor a lawgiver from between his feet, until Shiloh come; and unto him *shall* the gathering of the people *be*" (Gen 49:10).

To fulfill His covenant promises to His earthly people Israel
The divine Man is required to fulfill the covenants that God made with Israel. They will rule over the nations under their divine Messiah-King, who will inaugurate and sustain peace and prosperity among them.[32] God, as the Man Christ Jesus will -

---

[31] Those who deny the "literal" one thousand year reign of Christ on earth, are in fact denying this imperative display of the personal glory of God through His Son on earth.
[32] Seen in the Abrahamic covenant (Gen 12:1-3; 17:8) the Davidic covenant (2 Sam7:12); the New covenant (Jer 31). The term covenant here does not refer to an agreement between separate parties. It refers to God unilaterally determining His manner of dealing with man.

- possess the land *for* His people - Abrahamic covenant;
- reign *over* and *with* His people - Davidic covenant;
- create a new heart *within* His people - New covenant.

Christ is the Mediator of the New Covenant (Heb 9:15). This New Covenant is superior to the Old Covenant because it offers man eternal promises secured by the shed blood of Christ, who was the perfect sacrifice for sin - the blood of the covenant (10:29).[33]

10. To deliver up the kingdom to the Father

Having subdued all things unto Himself and having established the kingdom of God on earth, the Son will then deliver up the Kingdom to the Father and into eternity (1 Cor 15:24). "Then shall the Son also Himself be subject unto him that put all things under him [God, the Father], that God may be all in all" (1 Cor 15:28). Reading this statement in the light of verse 24, we have Christ as the obedient and faithful Son who restores into the hand of God the Father that which belongs to Him, the Son always having before Him the glory of the Father - that God, the Father, and the Son and the Holy Spirit, may be all in all. The divine Man is the "Father of Eternity" - the "Everlasting Father" (Isa 9:6 cf Heb 1:8, "Thy Throne O God is for ever and ever").

The necessity of Christ's deity – its practical importance

The Trinity, the deity of Christ and His perfect humanity, are not mere dogma, but truths that are to sanctify our life and service unto God. The next table presents some key verses on the practical aspects relating to some of the reasons why God became man.

The truth that God took on perfect flesh, and that flesh was Deity in all His undiminished and unceasing nature, is the confession of genuine Christianity. Why He did so is its glorious profession. If the man Christ Jesus is not God in His undiminished and unceasing deity, then Christianity has as

---

[33] The Old (Mosaic, conditional) Covenant, was not in itself faulty. It was, as noted, "weak through the flesh" (Rom 8:3). The New Covenant is with Israel (Jer 31) and it will be fulfilled literally in the Millennium. In this dispensation of grace, all men through faith in Christ are able to partake of the eternal blessings of the New Covenant (1 Cor 11:25). The church partakes of the spiritual blessing under this Covenant because of its standing in Christ, who is the Mediator of it on the ground of His shed blood.

much to offer fallen man as any other religion - nothing at all!

To declare the Father and the Son	"For ye have not received the spirit of bondage again to fear; but ye have received the Spirit of adoption, whereby we cry, Abba, Father" (Rom 8:15)
The defeat of sin	"Likewise reckon ye also yourselves to be dead indeed unto sin, but alive unto God through Jesus Christ our Lord. Let not sin therefore reign in your mortal body, that ye should obey it in the lusts thereof" - "Walk in the newness of life" (Rom 6:11-12)
The defeat of death	"O death, where *is* thy sting? O grave, where *is* thy victory?...Therefore, my beloved brethren, be ye stedfast, unmovable, always abounding in the work of the Lord, forasmuch as ye know that your labour is not in vain in the Lord" (1 Cor 15:55-58)
The defeat of the law's curse	"But now we are delivered from the law, that being dead wherein we were held; that we should serve in newness of spirit, and not *in* the oldness of the letter" (Rom 7:6)
The defeat of Satan	"Through death he [Christ] might destroy him that had the power of death, that is, the devil; And deliver them who through fear of death were all their lifetime subject to bondage" (Heb 2:14-15)
To destroy the "middle wall of partition"	"Now therefore ye are no more strangers and foreigners, but fellow-citizens with the saints, and of the household of God" (Eph 2:19 - also 4:1-6; 1 Cor 12:13; Gal 3:27)
To declare our cause as our Great High Priest	"Having therefore, brethren, boldness to enter into the holiest by the blood of Jesus, By a new and living way, which he hath consecrated for us, through the veil, that is to say, his flesh; And having an high priest over the house of God; Let us draw near with a true heart in full assurance of faith, having our hearts sprinkled from an evil conscience, and our bodies washed with pure water" (Heb 10:19-22)

CHAPTER 7

Misused Texts in Regard to Christ's Deity

Certain passages of Scripture have been singled out by some in a vain effort to disprove Christ's deity and perfect humanity. We have already observed the consistent witness of the Spirit of God to the divine Man in Scripture. The Gospel narratives figure largely in this because they record Christ's personal testimony to His deity before heaven and earth. The Epistles, too, present a clear and convergent witness to the fact and necessity of Christ's undiminished and unceasing deity, as do His names and titles. When we interpret the passages below in regard to Christ's Person, we are entitled therefore to have His abiding deity before us as an unassailable truth! These passages can then be interpreted having confidence in what they *do not* say. On the other hand, when we take up these passages and examine their statements according to grammatical propriety and context, we will see that there is nothing inherent in them that detracts from the deity of our blessed Lord. Rather, there is much in them that reveals His deity and perfect humanity.

Jn 20:17; Matt 27:46; (Mk 15:34)

"Touch me not; for I am not yet ascended to my Father: but go to my brethren, and say unto them, I ascend unto my Father, and your Father; and *to* my God, and your God" (Jn 20:17)

"And about the ninth hour Jesus cried with a loud voice, saying, 'Eli, Eli, lama sabachthani?' that is to say, 'My God, my God, why hast thou forsaken me?'" (Matt 27:46).

It is alleged that Christ is not God because He refers to God as "my Father" and "my God". The broad point to make here is that there is nothing unusual in God speaking with God. It is consistent with the existence and revelation of the plurality of Persons within the Godhead. The compound unity in the divine title *Elohim* in Genesis 1:1, is consistent with the record of God speaking with God in verse 26, "Let us make man in our image." We noted the conversation between the Persons of the Godhead in Psalm 110, and God speaking to God in Hebrews 1:8 - God said unto the Son, "Thy throne O God, is for ever and ever." Here God calls the Son God. Why then should we have difficulty with the Son calling God - God?

Consider firstly John 20:17. The expression "my Father" reveals the special intimacy He has with God as the only Begotten of the Father. He is the Eternal Son of the Eternal Father. The intimacy and the distinction in His *sonship* is seen in that He takes care to employ the discriminating words, "my Father and your Father". There is a similar discrimination in the expression "my God and your God".

But in what sense does Christ refer to God as "my God"? He cried "my God, my God" as the One who fulfilled Psalm 22, the *man* Jesus Christ. This Messianic Psalm presents Christ prophetically not as the Beloved Son of the *Father*, but as the *man* who in subjection lays down His life as a sin-offering unto *God*. All the fulness of the Godhead dwelt in Him bodily, yet it was as the man entering into the dark, unfathomable suffering for sin that He cried, "My God, my God, why hast thou forsaken me." These words mark that supreme occasion when that obedient and perfect Man willingly bore the wrath of God against sin in all its unmitigated force. He is the *man* Christ Jesus, who is the Mediator between God and man by virtue of the cross (1 Tim 2:5). In John 20:17 He is to ascend to the *Father* as the Beloved Son who had revealed the Father. But He is to ascend to His *God*, speaking here again as the man who had been well pleasing to God, having put away sin by the sacrifice of Himself. When the Lord uses the expression "my God", it reveals His real manhood and His subjection unto God as man.[1] How contrary to the first man Adam!

---

[1] It was as *man* that the Son of God was ministered to by the angels ("For he shall give his angels charge over thee, to keep thee in all thy ways", Ps 91:11; Mk 1:13; Lk 4:10 etc).

Mark 10:17-27

17. And when he was gone forth into *the* way, *there came* one running, and kneeled to him, and asked him, "Good Master, what shall I do that I may inherit eternal life?"

18. And Jesus said unto him, "Why callest thou me good? *there is* none good but one, *that is*, God.

19. Thou knowest the commandments, Do not commit adultery, Do not kill, Do not steal, Do not bear false witness, Defraud not, Honour thy father and mother."

20. And he answered and said unto him, "Master, all these have I observed from my youth."

21. Then Jesus beholding him loved him, and said unto him, "One thing thou lackest: go thy way, sell whatsoever thou hast, and give to the poor, and thou shalt have treasure in heaven: and come, take up the cross, *and* follow me."

22. And he was sad at *that* saying, and went away grieved: for he had great possessions.

23. And Jesus looked round about, *and* saith unto his disciples, "How hardly shall they that have riches enter into the kingdom of God."

24. And the disciples were astonished at his words. But Jesus answereth again, and saith unto them, "Children, how hard is it for them that trust in riches to enter into the kingdom of God.

25. It is easier for a camel to go through the eye of a needle, than for a rich man to enter into the kingdom of God."

26. And they were astonished out of measure, saying among themselves, "Who then can be saved?"

27. And Jesus looking upon them saith, "With men *it is* impossible, but not with God: for with God all things are possible."

"Do not call me good, because only God is good" (v.18). Is this a denial by the Lord of His moral perfection and deity as some assert? We recall that the Lord referred to Himself as the "Good Shepherd" (Jn 10:11-14).

This matter being discussed between the Lord and this young man involved the way into the Kingdom of God. Some believed entrance into it and eternal life would be by observing the law, as instructed by the teachers of the law. The people held these teachers in high regard giving them the title "good master (teacher)". It would appear that the young man held such a view. He refers to the Lord as "good Master", regarding Him as one of the venerable rabbis, while at the same time he professes his diligence in the law (Mk 10:20). But the Lord was not about to encourage such a belief, neither in the law or its teachers, and he repels it in three ways. First He directs the young man to have hope in One to whom the Kingdom belongs - God, who is good. Second, He exposes the man's failure in regard to a moral principle of the law - charity. Third, He calls upon the young man to put his faith in Him, Jesus of Nazareth, and follow Him.

The rich young man rejected all three exhortations and went away grieved. He valued his earthly goods above heavenly possessions. Worldly riches proved a hindrance to entering the kingdom of God. Through an idiomatic proverb, the Lord declared that for anyone who trusts in riches (by implication, one who covets riches above all), it is impossible to enter the Kingdom of God (v.25). But with God all things are possible. The Gospel of Christ if obeyed, is the power of God unto salvation. It can convert the materialistic heart to confess to the infinitely greater riches in Christ, even life eternal.

There are three observations here that relate to the deity of Christ. First, the Lord challenges the young man regarding His identity. The young man knew the Lord merely as a "teacher", and he had no knowledge of His divine Person. The titles Son of God, Son of man, etc are absent. The Lord redresses this by stating a fact and letting it settle into the young man's heart. His question is not, "Why do you call me good *teacher?*" He asks - "Why do you call me *good?*" He isolates the moral attribute and places it within a divine context, for He declares that God is the only one who is good. No mere *man* is "good", no not one (Ps 14:3; Rom 3:10-12). The confession He desires is that if Jesus of Nazareth the man is good, then He must be more than a mere man, more than a teacher of the law. He must be God, for only God is "good". No such confession was forthcoming, for the young man's heart was pledged to the law and riches. The Lord in no manner rejects the recognition given that He is "good". "You call me teacher and Lord for *so* I am" (Jn 13:13). Second, the Lord exercises a *prerogative* of God in that He exhorts the young man to follow Him in order to gain eternal life. Finally, He exercises an *attribute* of God in that He is able to search the heart of this young man and discern the root of his failure. There is nothing in this passage that detracts from the deity of Christ.

Mark 13:32

"But of that day and *that* hour knoweth no man, no, not the angels which are in heaven, neither the Son, but the Father."

It is said that in these verses Christ admits to a limitation in His knowledge and therefore He cannot be omniscient Deity.[2] The rule regarding the marks of deity and possession of the divine attributes serves to dismiss such a claim. There are explicit statements in Scripture that tell us of the complete and unfailing knowledge of the Son in all things. In Christ "are hid all the treasures of wisdom and knowledge" (Col 2:3). The Father's knowledge of the heart and mind of the Son cannot be less than total knowledge. Neither then can the Son's knowledge of the Father be less than total, for the Son declared, "As the Father knoweth me, even so know I the Father" (Jn 10:15). This is plain testimony to the Son's possession of the divine attributes and, that the fulness of the Godhead dwelt in Him bodily.[3] He "knew all *men*" (Jn 2:24); "knew what was in man" (Jn 2:25); "He knoweth all things" (Jn 16:30; 21:17).

What then is the meaning of the Lord's disclaimer in this verse? It was not made in regard to His *capacity* as God, but in regard to His *commission* as a servant of God unto men. It is the Son speaking as the Servant, telling men that He professed not to know the day or hour when the Son of man shall come in glory and in power. Both Matthew and Mark record this statement. Mark in his preoccupation with the Son as the lowly servant unto men explicitly states the disclaimer - "neither the Son". It was not within the prerogative of the Servant unto men (though He is the Son), to profess to know such a thing. Therefore He claims in accordance with this humble position not to know it. He took on the essence of a servant (Phil 2). "The servant knoweth not what his lord doeth" (Jn 15:15).[4]

---

[2] Mark 6:38, "How many loaves have ye", and John 11: 34, "Where have they laid him", were not asked by the Lord out of ignorance, but as a way of prompting the sequence of events in each case. In the latter case, a "kindly design to kindle their expectations" W E Vine *Collected Writings* Vol 1 p 297. Questions are not always asked out of ignorance as any teacher and preacher knows. They can be used to create comment, convict a conscience, clarify a subject, or convey a standing. The Omniscient God asked Adam, "Where art thou?" (Gen 3:9). He asked Cain, "Where is Abel thy brother?" (Gen 4:9).

[3] Who but righteous omniscient Deity can know and judge the secrets of men? The omniscient knowledge of the Persons of the Triune Godhead is clearly taught in such verses as John 10:15, Romans 2:16; 8:27 and 1 Corinthians 2:11

[4] The Lord speaks similarly in Acts 1:7. Note that Paul, too, in his service unto God before the Corinthians, declared with discretion "I determined not to know anything among you, save Jesus Christ, and Him crucified" (1 Cor 2:2).

Scripture records many instances where the Son exercised subjection to the obligations associated with His obedient ministry as a servant. As a servant He was "sent" to do the Father's will (Lk 4:18; Jn 4:34; 5:30 etc). The word He spoke was not His but the Father's (Jn 14:24). As a servant He receives commandment from the Father (Jn 14:31). The Father is greater than He (Jn 14:28). Such statements reflect the obedient submission of the Son as a servant. It was obedient positional subjection and not personal inferiority, in order that God be glorified.

We must not discount the prolific revelations of His abiding deity in Scripture just because His work as a servant is in view. Though the Son was "sent" He also "came" (Jn 5:43; 9:39; 10:10; 18:37). He received commandment from the Father but He also spoke of His own, "my" commandments (Jn 14:21). He issued commandments of His own, a "new" commandment (Jn 13:34; 15:12). He claimed authority over the Sabbath law. We hear Him declare frequently in regard to the rule of law and life, "But I say unto you" (Matt 5:22-39). He declared His Father to be greater than Himself but He also said, "I and my Father are one," an equality in being, acknowledged by His opponents, by Himself, and through the Spirit-inspired pages of the Epistles.

Luke 2:51-52

51. And he went down with them [Mary and Joseph], and came to Nazareth, and was subject unto them: but his mother kept all these sayings in her heart.

52. And Jesus increased in wisdom and stature, and in favour with God and man.

These verses must be viewed similarly to those in Hebrews 5 examined below. The wisdom of the Lord here is not His divine eternal wisdom, which as Deity He always possessed in its fulness (Col 2:3). It is the wisdom (*sophiai*, not knowledge) He was acquiring as a man walking among men. As He grew in years and moved among men, He was exposed at each stage of His life to a multitude of different situations as a *man*, a hitherto unfamiliar realm of experience for Him. He dealt with them as they arose, revealing His increasing wisdom. This is a witness to His real manhood, the glory He brought to God through it, and the blessing to us in having such a Person as our Great High Priest.

John 14:28
"My Father is greater than I"

This verse is eagerly employed by those who seek to deny the Lord's deity. They vaunt it as an explicit denial of it by Him. When we examine this statement in context we see that the Lord is not denying His deity at all. It is another instance where as the Servant-Son He expresses His subjection to His Father.

When Christ came into the world, He experienced for the first time the obligation to walk in obedient and dependent service before God. "Mine ears hast thou digged... I delight to do thy will O my God" (Ps 40:6). The Father is greater in the sense that the Son is His faithful and obedient servant, who must do the will of the Father who sent Him, "For I came down from heaven, not to do mine own will, but the will of Him that sent Me" (Jn 6:38).

Scripture presents the Son of God as the servant of God *prophetically*, *historically* and *doctrinally*. Isaiah, we recall presents Him as the divine Servant-Messiah. It is proper therefore that Scripture records the Son's conduct and conversation as the willing and obedient servant of God. The verse before us is an instance of it. We noted above and will do so again, the many statements of subjection made by the Lord as the Servant-Son, none of which contradict His deity revealed in Scripture. The Spirit of truth places John 14:28 within the Gospel which begins and ends with the clearest of declarations of Christ's deity, intending that all matters concerning His person in this Evangel be interpreted according to the truth that in the beginning the Word was with God and was God, and that He is "my Lord and my God".

1 Corinthians 8:6
"But to us *there is but* one God, the Father, of whom *are* all things, and we in him; and one Lord Jesus Christ, by whom *are* all things, and we by him".

Some use this verse to claim that only the Father is God. Firstly, this assertion is a flagrant contradiction to the record of Scripture.

Paul explicitly applies the title "God" to Christ (Rom 9:5; Tit 2:13). It also ignores the fact that the title "Lord" given to Christ is a divine title, as noted above. Secondly, it mishandles the context. In this portion Paul notes that there are entities among the heathen that are called *gods* and *lords* (v.5). Gods are associated with matters of 'origination' and lords with matters of 'administration'. As far as Christians are concerned, when we speak of matters relating to origination, we acknowledge that there is but one God, the 'Originator', God the Father of whom are all things. When we speak of divine administration, we acknowledge that there is only one Administrator, the Lord Jesus Christ by whom are all things. The distinction here is not in regard to the essential nature of the Father and Christ, but in regard to their role in the divine scheme of things in Christianity. The administrative role of Christ in regard to such things as creation, reconciliation, redemption and intercession, require Him to possess the divine attributes entirely, equally, eternally and exclusively.

Ephesians 1:3, 17
"Blessed be the God and Father of our Lord Jesus Christ"; "The God of our Lord Jesus Christ"

"Christ cannot be God because God was His God and Father." What we have already noted repudiates such a claim. But let us examine these verses and address the allegation that is based upon them.

In the Roman Epistle we are given the sanctified walk of the man *justified* in Christ. In the Colossian Epistle we have the life of the man *risen* with Christ. The Ephesian Epistle deals with the sanctified walk of the man in Christ *seated* and *perfected* in Him before *God* and the *Father* (1:6; 2:6). It alerts us to the fact that those who are perfected in Christ walk before *God* and before the *Father* (2:10;18). The expressions "the God and Father of our Lord Jesus Christ" and "the God of our Lord Jesus Christ" (also "the Father of our Lord Jesus Christ", 3:14), are aptly suited to this truth.[5] They identify Christ in *His* relationship to *God* as *man* and

---

[5] Cf 1 Peter, the life of those in Christ, begotten unto a living hope through 'the God and Father of our Lord Jesus Christ', who are experiencing trials of faith, but who have an incorruptible inheritance, one that is undefiled and never fades away (1 Pet 1:4-7).

to the *Father* as His *Son.* In this He is our example and our blessing. We are to see Christ as the *man* who walked in total subjection to God, and lived as the Son in blessed unbroken fellowship with the Father. In such a Man believers are blessed with all spiritual blessings in heavenly places. The love of God, we say reverently, is not revealed in the existence of God, but in the coming and the dwelling of God as man among men and giving His life at Calvary. He who was with God could have remained with God and never have come in the likeness of men. We would then never have known divine redeeming love and its eternal blessings, and never have known what it is to walk in the world before God and the Father.

Christ's cry from the cross, "My God, my God," was the cry of the *man* suffering for sin before God, the man who was the sin offering figured in Psalm 22. In the compound titles before us we have Christ in His manhood as the meal offering. This offering typified what He was as a man and the blessing we have because of it - the perfect man, in His *life* of perfect obedience before God and of perfect fellowship with the Father as the Son![6]

There is also a dispensational matter to be noted. Israel's blessings are *under* the Messiah in *earthly* places and from *God-Jehovah.* The blessings of the believer are *in* Christ in *heavenly* places and from *God* and the *Father.* These distinctions are marked and brought into relief by the expressions, "the God and Father of our Lord Jesus Christ" and "the God of our Lord Jesus Christ". Their dispensational relevance is confirmed in the light of the fact that Christ has broken down the middle wall of partition between Jew and Gentile, making one new man (Eph 2:14-15).

Philippians 2:3-8

3. "Let nothing *be done* through strife or vainglory; but in lowliness of mind *let each* esteem other better than themselves.

4. Look not every man on his own things, but every man also on the things of others.

5. Let this mind be in you, which *was* also in Christ Jesus:

6. Who, being in *the* form of God, thought it not robbery to be equal with God:

---

[6] The composite of fine flour, frankincense and oil, speak of His *life* as the anointed man, which was a sweet savour unto God and to the Father.

7. But made himself of no reputation, and took *upon him* the form of a servant, and was made in the likeness of men:
8. And being found in fashion as a man, he humbled himself, and became obedient unto death, even *the* death of the cross. "

An incorrect interpretation of this passage has given rise to the *Kenosis* doctrine. Broadly stated, it claims Christ "emptied" Himself of His deity in order to become a man and die.[7] Some say He regained His deity upon His resurrection and exaltation.

The first and obvious question in objection to such an assertion is, "How can God cease to be God?" How can all the divine attributes exist in a person and then cease to exist in Him? The divine attributes are eternal and absolute and cannot be limited by time or space. If possessed, they are possessed entirely, equally, eternally and exclusively. The Gospel narratives provide us with the *historical* argument against the kenosis doctrine. They record the claims and acts of deity by Christ on earth. The Epistles give us the *doctrinal* repudiation of it, teaching that the fulness of the Godhead dwelt in Christ continuously. The Revelation proclaims the *prophetical* denial of it, revealing Christ as the coming divine Judge, the Alpha and Omega, the First and the Last!

Rather than scrutinize the Kenosis doctrine, we are better served by exposing it to the biblical interpretation of this passage. Let us first identify the context. The essential teaching in this portion is practical rather than theological, although it is firmly grounded upon a theological truth, the undiminished and unceasing deity of Christ. The Philippians were esteeming themselves above others and beset by vainglory (2:2-4). Paul brings before them the virtue of Christian humility, presenting Christ as their Exemplar (v.5). This he does through seven sublime statements that reveal the mind of Christ (vv.6-7). He -
1. being in the form of God
2. thought it not robbery to be equal with God
3. made Himself of no reputation (He emptied Himself)
4. took on the form of a servant
5. was made in the likeness of men

---

[7] The Kenosis doctrine was the product of the "Higher Criticism". It was initially associated with a number of 19th century German theologians. They stripped Christ of many if not all of His divine attributes.

6. was found in fashion as a man
7. became obedient unto death.

The second statement is the first mark of Christ's humility. It reveals the prevailing self-less and obedient attitude that reigned in His mind. It was this fragrant disposition that enabled and led Him to take the next step of humility, that of emptying Himself.

Of what did He empty Himself and manifest perfect humility? There are some further preliminary matters to observe before we answer this question. The word *ekenose* is from *kenos* which is literally "to empty". Its use in Scripture takes on the meaning "to make of no effect" or to "bring into nothingness", as in the following:

- *kekenotai* (Rom 4:14) - faith is "made void" - comes to nothing if the promises of God were vested in the law;
- *kenothei* (1 Cor 1:17) - the cross of Christ is of "none effect" - made empty through wisdom of words;
- *kenosei* (1 Cor 9:15) - voiding, Paul's glory comes to no effect;
- *kenothe* (2 Cor 9:3) - refers to "empty" or valueless boasting.

In isolation, the statement that Christ emptied Himself is vulnerable to the interpretation that Christ lost His deity. But the Spirit of God presents clear teaching to guard against such a dire conclusion. Before we are shown anything of the Lord's humility in this passage, the Spirit gives us a categorical statement of Christ's undiminished and unceasing deity – "Who, being in the form of God"! It is not that Christ *was* in the form of God, but of Him *being* in the form of God. "Form" - *morphe*, "is the essence of a thing". Christ is the essence of God.[8] Taken with the tense of the verb *being*, the statement expresses Christ's abiding deity. How consistent with the revelation of Christ's deity in the Gospels and with Paul's declaration to the Colossians concerning the fulness of the Godhead abiding continually in Christ. When, therefore, we consider the humility of Christ, we never lose sight of its majestic

---

[8] R C Trench, *Synonyms of the New Testament* p 265. The term *schema* - fashion, relates to the "outward presentation" p 263. *Schema* - "What is visible and perceptible to men....the Lord's outward life as perceptible to men." W E Vine *Collected Writings* Vol II p 471. In contrast, "*morphe*, is 'properly the nature of essence, not in the abstract, but as actually subsisting in the individual, and retained as long as the individual itself exists..*morphe Theou* (the form of God) *is the divine nature actually and inseparably subsisting in the Person of Christ*...it includes the whole nature and essence of Deity.'" Gifford, *The Incarnation*, quoted in W E Vine *Collected Writings* Vol 2 p 469. Further, the word "God" here is "without the definite article in the Greek text, and therefore refers to the divine essence." Wuest *Word Studies*, Philippians Vol II p 63.

sweetness, revealed in that He who is equal with God became obedient unto death, even the death of the cross. All statements in this portion that speak of Christ's humility, are intended by the Spirit of God to be interpreted in the light of His perpetual deity declared in the first statement.[9]

The fourth statement declares that Christ took on the form of a servant. Here, too, the term "form" - *morphe*, refers to essence. Christ took on the essence of a servant. He was not a servant in appearance only. If the "form of a servant" means Christ is in essence a servant, then it must follow that "the form of God" must refer to Him being the essence of God.

The fifth statement refers to Him becoming the likeness (*homoiomati*) of the flesh of sin. He became what men are, as distinct from becoming an angel or some other being. The sixth declares that He was in "fashion" as a man (*schemati*). The word "fashion" - *schema*, refers to an outward presentation. It is that representation or exterior form which appears to the eyes of men. Finally, the Lord's profound humility is seen in that He became obedient unto death, even the death of the cross.

We may summarise the key terms used in regard to Christ's person in this portion as follows:

Greek term	Translation	Meaning	Application
Morphe	Form	Essential Essence/ nature	Christ is the essence of God (His deity) Christ is the essence of a servant (His humility)
Schema	Fashion	Appearance	To look upon Christ was to see man (not some celestial being)
Homoioma	Likeness	Similarity	Christ is what men are, but because He is not just man (i.e. He is also God), He is "like" men

---

[9] Cf Jn 13. John, like Paul, records the deliberate steps taken by the Lord in humility. The Master arises from supper; lays aside His garments; clothes Himself with a towel; and, after pouring out water, He washes the feet of His disciples. How figurative of Christ leaving the place of heavenly fellowship with the Father, divesting Himself of that outward presentation of majesty, and taking on the form of a servant to cleanse man from sin! Here, too, lest through carnal thought we fail to see the divine Man, the Spirit of God predicates this account squarely upon the deity of Christ. John declares in verse 3 that "he [Christ] was come from God", placing before us Christ's pre-existence and presence with God. His condescension is given in that He was sent from God, His glorification in that He went to God (cf Phil 2, "wherefore God hath highly exalted Him"). It is also predicated on the deity of the Word given in the Prologue.

What did Christ bring to nothing?

In what sense did Christ regard equality with God a thing not to be grasped at? We may refer to equality in the sense of essence or appearance. They are distinguished by *morphe* and *schema* respectively, "morphe" being the essence of a thing and "schema" the outward or exterior presentation of it. When Paul refers to Christ not grasping at equality with God, he does not mean the form of God, the essential divine nature. The first statement rules this out. He is referring to the outward presentation of equality with God. When Christ emptied Himself, He brought to nothing the exterior glory of His deity.

He did this by doing three things. Firstly, He took on the form of a servant. It was not that He was in fashion (schema) as a servant, but He was the very essence of one. And, being the very essence of a servant, He considered that holding on to the exterior appearance of deity not to be grasped at. To be the essence of a servant and not dispossess the outward presentations of deity would be inconsonant with and, what is more, impugn the very principle of humility. "He stripped Himself of the insignia of majesty" (Lightfoot), portrayed chiefly in Mark's Gospel where the Son is the servant of God unto men.[10] Secondly, He became the likeness of men, in the likeness of the flesh of sin. He is as men are yet sin apart on account of His divine being. Thirdly, He was found in fashion (*schema*) as man. He displayed the outward appearance of man, which is also consistent with Him bringing to nothing the outward appearance of deity.

The essence of Christ's humility

Christ's sublime humility is not in that He *gave up* His deity to become a servant or man. Rather, it is demonstrated in all its ineffable grace that *while being* the Almighty and Sovereign God He condescended to become a servant and man. Humility, as seen in the condescension of Christ, is that moral grace where a person *voluntarily* gives up what he *has* in order to benefit others. Paul is

---

[10] The Lord had been from the beginning the Son who was with the Father. In John 17:5 the Lord prays for that glory He had with the Father to be granted to Him now that He had become man and a servant of God, who had finished the work for that which He was sent. This glory He *requests*, which is in perfect compliance with the place of submission He took in becoming flesh. What exquisite humility! As the perfect Servant He never sought to glorify Himself!

not speaking of giving up what a person *is*, as some wrongly infer. A king expresses the deepest humility if he spends a term living among his subjects as one of them. He is still the king, but he has given up something He possessed. He brings to nothing those things by which others would see his sovereignty, his royal robes, carriage, entourage, etc; he is "clothed with humility", 1 Pet 5:5. That which marks the rank and office of a king is exchanged for that which marks the rank and office of a servant. Where is the humility if he has ceased to be the king?

May we press the illustration a little further. Suppose a benevolent king takes a place of humility and service in order to bestow a blessing to his people that only a king can provide. He must remain a king to draw upon his inherent sovereign power and authority to supply that blessing. This is what Christ did. He could only be the needed and accepted sacrifice if He was God manifest in flesh. Christ possessed the divine attributes in their totality, but He willingly exercised them in a manner that was consistent with Him being dependent upon and submissive to God, as a Servant and Man. What causes our hearts and voices to rise in praise and adoration of Jesus of Nazareth? It is because we see Him manifesting all the marks of deity as God-Incarnate, yet willingly serving God and giving His life for fallen man on a felon's cross. But more! How can God come to earth not only to redeem man, but to vindicate His holiness, and then empty Himself of those very divine attributes that were needed to accomplish it? If it were possible for Him to empty Himself of His deity, then we say most reverently, His cause was defeated before it began.

Yet, the humility of Christ is more than voluntarily relinquishing the outward presentation of sovereignty to benefit others. It is doing so in order to bestow a benefit to others who are *undeserving* of it. Here divine grace comes in. "While we were yet sinners Christ died for us" (Rom 5:8). Only as Sovereign over life and death could He bestow that eternal blessing to undeserving man, by Him laying down His life that He might take it up again. This is the sublime *moral* aspect of Christ's humility whenever the cross is in view (Phil 2:8). There is, too, the ineffable *judicial* aspect of His humility. He died, He was buried and He rose again for our justification. The Just One died that unjust man may be justified before God.

In verse 8 Paul shows Christ's humility reaching its noble climax. The divine Man humbled Himself and became obedient unto death, even the death of the Cross. There is here in every aspect, a mystery kept from man. To seek its depth is to sink into the mire of misdoubt. Again we observe the essential lesson of humility. It is not that Christ gave up His deity to die at Calvary. But *being* the Holy Divine and Righteous One, He who knew no sin was made sin that we might become the righteousness of God in Him. The unfathomable depth of His humility and its judicial aspect is brought into further relief. Christ is not just the Exemplar, but the Victim. He died, the Just for the unjust. Death is passed upon all men for all have sinned (Rom 5:12). But death had no claim upon Him for He is not a man of Adam's fallen line. Being sinless, holy, undefiled and spotless, He was never "subject" to death and the penalty of sin. But, blessed and glorious truth, He was obedient to it that He might through death, deliver us from sin. Note, too, it was "even" the death of the cross, the most ignoble and cruel of deaths, reserved for the lowest among criminals. He endured the contradiction of sinners as God. *This* is why we love Him - and we must confess, how little we so do in the light of it!

In our dullness we may fail to appreciate His humility. But the ineffable humility of the Victim has not eclipsed the glory of the Victor, for there is One, God the Father, who has highly exalted Him and given Him a name which is above every other name.[11]

The kenosis doctrine - flawed and fatal

The first flaw in the Kenosis doctrine is the vain belief that we

---

[11] What name is referred to here? Some say "Lord" for God has made this same Jesus both Lord and Christ (Acts 2:36) (we may assert, perhaps pedantically, that "Lord" is a title rather than a name). Others say Jehovah, acknowledging the unique reverence given to that divine title in Scripture. The name "Jesus" satisfies all claims since it means Jehovah-Saviour and, He is Lord. Jesus - Jehovah-Saviour is the name God gave Christ at His birth, which is associated with His *condescension*. Jesus is the name associated with His *humiliation*, even His crucifixion. This name was mentioned at His *ascension* (Acts 1:11). It is, too, the name that is associated with His *glorification* (Heb 2:9). It seems appropriate then, that Jesus should be the name associated with the *exaltation* of God, the Father, for Jesus, the man, is Deity. He is God who came down to reconcile man unto Himself. "Whosoever shall exalt himself shall be abased; and he that shall humble himself shall be exalted." (Matt 23:12). Jesus of Nazareth is now the exalted Man, the Servant who is arrayed in all the majestic glory of a victorious Sovereign. There was a blessed glimpse of something of His outward glory given to Peter, James and John on the Mount of Transfiguration. "And [He] was transfigured before them: and his face did shine as the sun, and his raiment was white as the light" (Matt 17:2; Mk 9:2-3).

must *explain* how the two natures of Christ abide in Him. The second spawned by the first, is the unwarranted assumption that it was necessary for Christ to empty Himself of His deity in order that He should take on the form of a servant; to take on the likeness of sinful flesh; to be found in fashion as a man and become obedient unto death. Apart from such a notion being pure presumption in the face of divine power and prerogative, it wrongly supposes a metamorphosis, a change in essential nature. The word indicating a change in form - *metamorphosis*, is not used here by Paul.[12] The third flaw is to ignore that we are exhorted to follow Christ's example of humility. Such an exhortation is absurd if His humiliation in any way referred to Him emptying Himself of His essential divine nature. We would need to become something other than human beings. Finally, the kenosis theory must be prepared to admit that the love of Christ was less than infinite – measurable, limited and not more than tongue can tell. For if it concedes that Christ's love was infinite, it must then admit to Him possessing the divine attributes entirely, equally, eternally and exclusively – His undiminished and unceasing deity!

1 Timothy 2:5
"For *there is* one God, and one mediator between God and men, the man Christ Jesus".

Some deny that Christ is God because He is the mediator *between* God and man: How can He be God if He mediates on behalf of God? The title "God" is representative of the "Godhead", as the term "men" is representative of "mankind". As a Person within the Godhead, Christ is able to mediate on behalf of God; as man He is able to mediate on behalf of men. How gloriously it answers the need expressed by Job for a daysman between man and God, that He might lay his hand upon us *both* (Job 9:32-33). Christ is not some detached and distant mediator who knows little of the parties between whom He mediates. He is the *only* mediator

---

[12] The word *metamorphothe* is employed by Matthew and Mark to tell us that the Lord's form changed at His transfiguration (Matt 17:2; Mk 9:2). Luke prefers to represent the transfiguration by the term *heteros* - His countenance "became altered" (Lk 9:29). He gives us what Matthew and Mark do not - what it was that changed, the subject of the metamorphosis - His *appearance*. It was His essential appearance (not inherent nature) that underwent a complete change - a metamorphosis.

between God and man because He only is the divine Man. How blessedly consistent with the plurality of the Persons within the Godhead and the necessity of God becoming man.

Hebrews 5:8-9

8. Though he were a Son, *yet* learned he obedience by the things which he suffered;
9. And being made perfect, he became *the* author of eternal salvation unto all them that obey him.

In what sense did the Son "learn obedience"? These verses can never be taken to mean that as man He learned *how* to obey. The Gospel narratives declare His perfect obedience throughout His life, even from His very early years. "Wist ye not that I must be about my Father's business?" (Lk 2:49). "My meat is to do the will of him that sent me, and to finish his work" (Jn 4:34); "For I do always those things that please him [the Father]" (Jn 8:29); "For I came down from heaven, not to do mine own will, but the will of him that sent me" (Jn 6:38); "I must work the works of him who sent me" (Jn 9:4). His compelling obedience is foretold in the OT and confirmed in the NT. "I delight to do thy will, O my God: yea, thy law *is* within my heart" (Ps 40:8; Heb 10:7-9). His absolute willing obedience throughout His life was acknowledged by the Father's approbation of Him. His prayer in Gethsemane's garden is an eloquent witness to His perfect obedience: "O my Father, if it be possible, let this cup pass from me: nevertheless not as I will, but as thou *wilt*." These words reveal the holiness of the One who knew no sin but was soon to be made sin. Unlike us, He was not of the root of Adam, whose offspring partake of his sinful nature being born in sin. We who are born with a disposition to disobey must learn how to obey.

It is not that the Son learned how to obey, but that He learned what it *was* to obey. The creature must learn to obey because he is a sinner. The Creator learned what it was to obey because He is the Sovereign - a further testimony to His undiminished and unceasing deity. As God, He is the Divine Law-Giver. In becoming man however, He had to undergo the *experience* of being obedient and submissive. This He did *willingly*, in order to put away sin by the sacrifice of Himself. His work as Saviour required Him to enter the school of obedient suffering that He might bring us unto God. We have a blessed and intimate expression of this in the days just prior to His passion. "With desire I have desired to eat this Passover with you before I suffer" (Lk 22:15-20). It reveals again the Son as the Servant, the Sin-Offering of Mark's Gospel. This in turn unveils that moving Psalm, Psalm 22. It speaks of the One who cried in the daytime and in the night season, so that those sublime words, "It is finished", could be uttered before the throne of grace and resound throughout the universe. The perfect man was thus "made complete", or "fitted" for the work of redemption through obedient suffering. So we have in Hebrews 5:9, "being made perfect, he became the author of eternal salvation".[13] Scripture reveals the necessary *experience* of Christ's obedience (Heb 5:8); the *extremity* of it – "even the death of the cross" (Phil 2:8); the *efficacy* of it – "by the obedience of one shall many be made righteous" (Rom 5:19).

There is a deeper truth here when considering why the *perfect Man* had to learn what it was to obey. He is the High Priest to those who have been perfected in Him through the body of His flesh. What Satan could not do to the perfect Man, he persistently seeks to do to those who are perfected in Him. As Priest, Christ intercedes on behalf of the "new man", and not the "old man" who has been crucified with Him (Rom 6:6). The failing of the latter comes under His advocacy (1 Jn 2:1). As the High Priest of the redeemed, God the Son became us, and He intercedes in regard to the trials of those who walk in the newness of life. "Yea, and all that will live godly in Christ Jesus shall suffer persecution" (2 Tim 3:12). To walk in the world according to the paths of righteousness is to encounter trials. How blessed then, that we have a Priestly Intercessor who is God, yet He learned what it was for a righteous Man to walk amidst sin.

The two men of Scripture – Adam and Christ

God created man innocent and gave him dominion on earth.

---

[13] The word "perfect" is *teleios*, which fundamentally means "the bringing of a person or thing to the goal fixed by God" Wuest *Word Studies* Vol II p 102; Christ's "divinely- appointed discipline for the priesthood. The consummation was attained in His death, Phil 2:8", Vincent *Word Studies* Vol IV p436.

Through self-will and disobedience Adam plunged mankind into sin. Death and eternal judgement came upon all men. The first man failed and he lost what God had destined for man. Another *man* – not an angel or some other celestial being was needed to restore fallen creation unto God. God's Son became that man and He willingly took the place rejected by the first man Adam, the place of obedience and dependence upon God. He brought infinite delight to God, and through Him God will reconcile all things unto Himself. When we see the divine Son in subjection God, we are invited to see Him as the *man* Christ Jesus, the Last Adam and Second Man.

James 1:13 (& Matt 4:1-11)
Let no man say when he is tempted, I am tempted of God: for God cannot be tempted with evil, neither tempteth he any man. (Jas 1:13)

The case advanced against Christ's deity from this verse is based on the following spurious argument:
• God cannot be tempted.
• Christ was tempted.
• Therefore Christ is not God.

The conclusion provokes three equally false assertions.
1. Christ *could* sin (even though He did not sin).
2. Christ's triumph over sin was necessary to enable Him to help us in our battle with sin.
3. Christ's conflict with sin proves that His manhood was real.

This entire matter regarding Christ and sin is settled by the biblical truth that Christ is God in all His undiminished and unceasing deity. As God He could not sin. But let us address the specific issues that seem to trouble many concerning this matter. Is the premise that God cannot be tempted true?

God can be tempted, and yet He cannot be tempted.
The mischievous nature of the premise is that it is true in one sense, yet quite false in another. Scripture teaches that God can be tempted. Israel tempted Jehovah. "Why chide ye with me? wherefore do ye tempt the Lord [Jehovah]" (Ex 17:2, 7; cf Num

11; Deut 6:16; Mal 3:15).[14] Scripture also declares with equal clarity, that God cannot be tempted. James says this very thing.

In what sense can God be tempted?

Opponents of Christ's deity and perfect humanity fail to make clear the *sense* in which God can and cannot be tempted. He cannot be tempted by sin. Scripture never in any shade speaks of a battle between good and evil *within* the heart and mind of God. James does not merely say, as some want us to believe, that God cannot be tempted. He says God cannot be tempted with *evil.* There is nothing in God that inclines to evil and, therefore, there can be no contest between sin and righteousness in Him. He is absolutely holy! *God* was tempted not with sin, but in His longsuffering and judgement by Israel. Ananias and Sapphira tempted the *Spirit of God* (Acts 5:1-9).

So it is with Christ, the *Son of God.* He cannot be tempted with sin because He, too, is absolutely holy. He possesses the divine attributes entirely, equally, eternally and exclusively. There could never be a contest between good and evil within Him. We have His witness to it. "The prince of this world [Satan] cometh, and hath nothing in me" (Jn 14:30). There was nothing in Him that could incline to Satan's evil designs. There is further direct testimony to this blessed truth in Scripture from the Spirit of God.

"He was tempted…yet without sin" (Heb 4:15)

He "was in all points tempted like as *we are, yet* without sin", i.e., apart from being tempted by sin. A sinful proposition could never prompt the slightest inclination within Him.

If the Lord has no inclination to sin then in what sense *was* He tempted? The term "temptation" means a testing or trial.[15] He was tried in all points as we are in regard to our *infirmities* - every trial and test, *except those involving sin*. This is the meaning of the expression in verse 15 "all points as we…yet without sin". It is in regard to *these* temptations that He sympathizes with us as our Great High Priest, His principal office in this Epistle. "Yea, and all

---

[14] Satan confronts God in regard to Job (Job 1:6; 2:4-5). Satan contests Jehovah (Zech 3:1-2). Satan confronts the Son of God (Matt 4 etc).
[15] *Peirazo* - to "try"; to "prove", as in "assay", cf Heb 2:18.

that will live godly in Christ Jesus shall suffer persecution" (2 Tim 3:12). His high-priestly work we noted is not in regard to our sins. He can never sympathize with our sins! But what about the believer's sins – *if* they sin? They come under His righteous advocacy and not within His high-priestly sympathy! Let us not forget too, the sanctifying work of the Spirit of God. He was given to indwell all believers and to help them in their resistance against sin (Gal 5;16-17). And further, are we to suppose that the Holy Spirit has to be capable of sinning for Him to be effective as our helper? The assertion that the Lord had to possess a sinful nature to help us in our inner contest with sin is therefore unnecessary and unscriptural.[16]

The reality of Christ's manhood is revealed in that He took part of flesh and blood, possessing body, soul and spirit. It is also seen in that He suffered hunger, thirst, tiredness, the sorrows of being forsaken, despised and unjustly accused, afflicted and rejected among men (Heb 2:18). His temptation by Satan was not endured in Eden, but under the dire deprivations of the wilderness. Consequently, as our High Priest, He can be "touched [have sympathy] with the feelings of our infirmities". It is also unnecessary and unscriptural therefore, to assert that Christ's real manhood could only be proved if He was tempted with sin.

It was the Spirit of God who led Christ into the wilderness *to be* tempted (Matt 4:1). If He did this to provoke a contest between good and evil within Christ – to prove He could triumph over sin as asserted by some, then God tempted Him with evil. This contradicts the truth of James 1:13, that God tempts no one with evil. Satan's provocations were indeed evil. But when the Spirit of God led Christ to be tempted by Satan, it was not with evil because there was nothing in Christ that could answer to evil.[17]

Satan's "proving" served to *manifest* the perfect humanity of

[16] As noted by another, those who suggest otherwise must admit that the Lord was not only sinful but also ignorant, for how then could He have real sympathy for the ignorant unless He, too was ignorant?

[17] Cf Matt 6:13, "Lead us not into temptation". The thought here is "preservation", which is consistent with the petition to the heavenly Father "deliver us from [the] evil". This prayer is the prayer of the Jewish remnant during the days of the Tribulation, a time of terrible trial, as they await the coming Millennial kingdom on earth. "In the Garden of Gethsemane Jesus will say to Peter, James, and John: 'Pray that ye enter not into temptation' (Lk 22:40). That is the idea here. Here we have a 'Permissive imperative' as grammarians term it. The idea is then: 'Do not allow us to be led into temptation'." A T Robertson *Word Pictures* Vol 1 p 54.

the divinely approved *Man* as the obedient and dependent Servant of God (Matt 3:16-17; cf Phil 2). It brought out what lay within – sinless perfection! The Lord's thrice repeated reply "It is written", was not the product of an inner conflict between good and evil. It was a response born of the abiding cooperation of His will with the will of God, so evident in the Gospel narratives. Through all this He "learned obedience". The Son as man experienced what it was to be obedient and dependant as a servant of God. There was never a conflict between obedience and disobedience, nor between dependence and independence within Him.

So the Spirit led the Son of God into the wilderness to be tempted. For his part, Satan knew that Jesus of Nazareth was the divine Son of God. But He was also *man* - God's own *man* in whom God expressed His delight and glory. The Adversary saw Jesus of Nazareth the *man*, a man who was untried. He had tempted the first man Adam and he fell. Could he cause this Man to fall too and slight God's glory?[18] Satan's evil enticements find no right of entry into the heart of God's Anointed! Jesus of Nazareth is revealed as the *perfect man*, the perfect Servant of God – sin apart! Because of His inherent holiness, this *Man* heads a *new* creation comprising all those perfected in Him. The first man *did* sin because he *could* sin. All in him stand unrighteous and condemned before God. The Second man is the very antithesis in His Person and posterity. He *did not* sin because He *could not* sin. All in *Him* stand righteous and justified before God.

Christ "overcame", but this does not mean He triumphed after a contest with sin, but that He overcame the trials and tribulations of the world (Rev 3:21). "In the world ye shall have tribulation: but be of good cheer; I have overcome the world" (Jn 16:33). These words, declared in the last week of His private ministry, comfort all who follow Him in a world that rejected and despised Him. As the Incarnate Son and Faithful Witness (Rev 1:5), He overcame the accusations and trials associated with doing His Father's will. He overcame all this as the "man of sorrows" acquainted with grief, the Sin-Bearer (Isa 53; Jn 1:29). Blessed be His name!

---

[18] Satan is not omniscient. Confronting the God-Man Jesus of Nazareth was a new experience for him. He was an "unknown quantity" to Satan. His temptation of the man Christ Jesus was a genuine one on his part, expecting no doubt to be successful in it.

"Made like unto His brethren in all things"

"Wherefore in all things it behoved him to be made like unto *his* brethren, that he might be a merciful and faithful high priest in things *pertaining* to God, to make reconciliation [propitiation] for the sins of the people. For in that he himself hath suffered being tempted, he is able to succour them that are tempted" (Heb 2:17-18). Some assert that the absolute likeness to men given in the expression "in all things", must mean that Christ possessed a sinful nature. To be consistent, the expression "in all things" must refer to *everything*, unless of course it is qualified grammatically, by the immediate context or by the inviolable truths of Scripture. There is no grammatical qualification here. We dare not resort to spurious interpolations using the word 'other' as some opponents of Christ's deity do elsewhere. There is however a clear qualification from the context and from the biblical doctrine of propitiation. We have it first in regard to Christ's high priestly ministry. This work we noted is *not* in relation to our sins for they come under His advocacy. To assert that the expression "in all things" must include man's sinful propensity is therefore unwarranted and unscriptural. This expression is also qualified here by His work in propitiation. This required a perfect Sacrifice – God Himself as man in His absolute holiness. To have the expression "in all things" include man's sinful nature is again shown to be unwarranted and unscriptural. This is consistent with the clear teaching of Hebrews 4:15 declaring Christ as sin apart.

The absolute holiness of Christ

There is a comprehensive composite witness by the Spirit of truth to the divine holiness of the Son of God. It serves to interpret every portion of Scripture that touches on His manhood. Christ *did no sin* and He *knew no sin*, because *in Him is no sin*. Can there be a more complete definition of *God's* holiness? We may refer to these truths as the "three marks of perfect humanity" - even Absolute Holiness!

These three truths transcend the testimony of those who made them. They can only be the witness of omniscient knowledge - the Spirit of truth Himself, whose work is to magnify Christ. Sin we know is committed in deed *and* in thought (Matt 5:28; cf Prov

23:7). For Peter himself to assert that Christ "did no sin", he would have had to witness everything Christ did and known all His thoughts. Further, He would have had to make a moral judgement in each instance according to God's holiness, because sin is coming short of God's glory. The statements of John and Paul above, and of Peter when He declared Christ as the Lamb without blemish and without spot (1 Pet 1:19), are endorsed by this same Omniscience.

In Him is no sin (1 Jn 3:5)
Christ's sinless *nature*

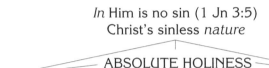

ABSOLUTE HOLINESS

He *knew* no sin (2 Cor 5:21)   Christ *did* no sin (1 Pet 2:22)
Christ's sinless *thoughts*   Christ's sinless *deeds*

Christ could not sin - a further consideration

During His temptation, the Lord rebuked Satan - "Thou shalt worship the Lord [Jehovah] your God, and him [Jehovah] only shalt thou serve" (Matt 4:10; Deut 6:13; 10:20). *Worship* and *service* belong exclusively to Jehovah. All else is blasphemy, as confirmed by the Lord Himself - "Thou shalt love the Lord thy God with all thy heart, and with all thy soul, and with all thy mind, and with all thy strength: this *is* the first commandment" (Matt 22:37-39); "No man can serve two masters: for either he will hate the one, and love the other; or else he will hold to the one, and despise the other. Ye cannot serve God and mammon" (Matt 6:24). Paul's teaching is vitally against serving the creature (Rom 1:25).

If Christ is *not* God, then He *did* commit a grievous sin, and He did tempt men with evil, in that He exhorted and accepted worship and service from men (Jn 8:31; 12:26 etc). In the Epistle before us, and without qualification, James declares himself to be the servant of the Lord Jesus Christ *and* of God. He was clearly serving two masters if Christ is not God, and Christ had enticed Him into evil. Paul, too, while speaking much about *God* and the *Father*, pledges himself (and Timothy) unreservedly to the service of *Christ* (Rom 1:1; Phil 1:1; cf. Tit 1:1). He did this while claiming in good conscience to serve the God of his forefathers (2 Tim 1:3). In his

Second Epistle Peter pledges service to Christ whom he refers to as the Sovereign Lord – *Despotes*, (2 Pet 1:1; 2:1). Those who say Christ could sin but did not sin, must accept Christ is God (and therefore He could not sin), or in contradiction to their own assertion, admit that He did indeed sin by exhorting men to worship and serve Him.

It was while Christ was in the womb before He had committed any deed at all, that the angel declared Him to be "holy". This could only be in reference to His *nature*, meaning that He could do no sin. The Lord was not just sinless in His life but inherently holy! The Holy One became Man, and because of His undiminished and unceasing holiness that Man is ever holy. A Christ in moral and emotional conflict is not the Christ of Scripture, which is unvarying in its witness of Him as the sure yet submissive Servant of God. He faced and passed through the deepest of trials, yet never do we read of any irresolution in Him or retraction from Him. It is not that He was able to sin but did not sin. Rather, He did no sin because He was unable to sin.

The teaching of James

James 1:13 is not a sullen mote in the radiant glory of Christ's deity. He was writing to Jewish Christians facing evil temptations. These circumstances were not the fault or design of God. "Let no man say when he is tempted (solicited) to do evil, he has been tempted (solicited) to it by God." He gives the reason for this. If God tempts (solicits) a person to do evil, then God must have an evil nature, prone to being tempted (solicited) by evil. Evil begets evil. But God does not possess such a nature and cannot be tempted (solicited) by evil. He is holy. There is nothing within Him that can respond to evil solicitations - in Him is no sin. It is so with Christ!

God never tempts us with evil, but tempts (tests) us in regard to our faith unto patience, as seen in His way with Abraham (Gen 22:1). "My brethren, count it all joy when ye fall into divers temptations [trials]; Knowing *this*, that the trying of your faith worketh patience" (Jas 1:2-3). It is not 'count it all joy when we fall into *sinful* temptations'! We are to flee these, avoid the very appearance of them and ask God to deliver us from them!

How precious is the truth is that Christ did not sin, that He knew no sin and that in Him is no sin. The eternal hope of man depends upon it. God's holy character is declared and vindicated by it.

A warning!

To claim Christ could sin is to deny His deity, defame His perfect humanity and decry God's demand for a perfect Sacrifice. It asserts that God's holy Son who was conceived by His Spirit possessed a latent lust to do evil, that He had an appetite for sin. It means that there is a High Priest and Advocate at the right hand of God and the Father who is capable of sinning. Our very salvation and access to God would therefore be in continual jeopardy (cf Heb 4:16; 10:22). Every divine purpose that rests on the moral rectitude of the Son of God becomes conditional. Moreover, if Christ could sin He must have a sinful nature. In the Person of God's Son therefore, sin abides in the very presence of God – in the Person whom God has "highly exalted" and "crowned with glory and honour".

Some say He "regained" His deity and holiness upon His resurrection. Upon what Scripture is this based? The assertion contradicts the truth that the Man "Jesus Christ is the same yesterday, and today, and forever" (Heb 13:8) – the unchangeable One. It controverts the witness to His perpetual deity and holiness in Scripture. The fullness of God dwelt in Christ bodily - permanently. "It dwelt in Him *during* His incarnation. It was the Word that became flesh and dwelt among us, full of grace and truth, and His glory which was *beheld* was the glory as of the Only begotten of the Father (John 1:14; 1 John 1:1-2). The fullness of the Godhead dwells *in His glorified humanity* in heaven"[19] – glorious and ineffable truth!

The claim that Christ could sin means, too, that Satan, the author of sin, stalks the very throne of God! What diabolical treachery abides in the doctrine that Christ could sin! What Satan failed to accomplish against the perfect Man while He was on earth, he seeks to achieve by having those who profess to belong to Him deny His moral perfection.

---

[19]See Vincent Vol III p 487.

CHAPTER 8

The Virgin Birth and the Deity of Christ

Who is He at yonder stall,
At whose feet the shepherds fall?
'Tis the Lord, O wondrous story,
'Tis the Lord, the King of Glory!
At His feet we humbly fall –
Crown Him, crown Him Lord of all!
(B R Hanby)

The Virgin Birth is among the most known and revered credal truths of Christianity. It is also one of the more misunderstood and misappropriated doctrines within Christendom. There are some among the professing Church who vehemently deny it, some who view it with sceptical indifference, and there are others who accept its truth but prefer to minimise its importance. It is vital therefore to ascertain what Scripture has to say concerning it.

What is meant by the Virgin Birth?

We noted in chapter 2 that God becoming man is referred to as the *Incarnation*. The Virgin Birth was the *way* in which the incarnation was achieved. Scripture reveals four inseparable truths concerning the Child born of the virgin. He was:

1. a pre-existing Person, the *divine* Son of God (Isa 9, Jn 1:1 etc);
2. holy (Lk 1:35);
3. born naturally by Mary (Lk 1:31; 42; 2:5,7);
4. conceived through the power of God. (Lk 1:35).

234

The first truth means that no new Person came into being through the Incarnation. The Virgin Birth does not involve a "miraculous creation" but a miraculous "incarnation". The pre-existing eternal Son of God took up a "new mode of existence". He became something that He was not previously - man. But in doing so He never abandoned what He was previously - very God. The second truth declares the child to be holy. As God, the child was holy for God is holy. The third truth reveals that the child had a human mother, which speaks of His real humanity. He came in flesh (not into flesh). The fourth teaches us that Christ did not have a human father. There was no human generation involved in Him coming into being as man. It means He was not of Adam which brings into view His sinless manhood.

Who came through the Virgin Birth?

Clearly it was no angel or other celestial creature, since the Person who came was of the seed of the woman and truly man. He was also the pre-existent holy Son of God who is Emmanuel, God with us, very God. Therefore He is the perfect, sinless man. Both Matthew and Luke refer to Christ being born of a virgin and conceived of the Holy Ghost. He is "Son of God". In these inspired narratives we are given the *identity* and *nature* of the divine Man, so evident in the days of His flesh. In Him humanity and deity are distinguishable yet combined into an inseparable oneness.

The Virgin Birth in the Word of God

From its very first intimation in Scripture, we learn that the Virgin Birth was ordained by God to vindicate His holiness and, in divine love, meet the need of man in his sin. Genesis reveals the origin of sin in man, indeed in the whole world, and the offence it brought to a holy God. "And I will put enmity between thee and the woman, and between thy seed and her seed; it shall bruise thy head, and thou shalt bruise his heel" (Gen 3:15). In this leading prophecy, we have the first lines of the eternal anthem of reconciliation - the coming of One who appeared at "end of age to put away sin by the sacrifice of himself". The Seed that will bruise Satan and will be Himself bruised, is not the seed of the man, which would be according to natural law. He is the *seed* of the woman, according

MY LORD AND MY GOD

to supernatural power. Here we have our first lesson of Christ's divine conception yet His humanity. As the seed of the woman He is not of Adam's generation, which means He is not a partaker of Adam's sinful nature. We have an intimation of the perfect humanity and the deity of the coming Saviour of men, who came in the *likeness* of the flesh of sin – man but sin apart.

These intimations are confirmed by the prophet Isaiah through the Holy Spirit (Isa 7:13-14). He draws aside the veil a little further, and we see the coming Seed as the *Son*. His name is mentioned to avoid mistaking who He is when He does come - very God, "Emmanuel", "God with us". But more! We are told how He will come among men. He will be born of a *virgin*, confirming Him as the seed of the woman declared in Genesis, and consistent with His divine conception recorded in the Gospels. We are informed, too, that the seed of the woman will come unto the house of David (v.13). He is indeed the Saviour of all men. But as the Son of David He must first come unto the children of Israel, to fulfil the promises given to them by Jehovah. God had preserved a remnant among them for this very purpose.

Then in chapter 9 the Spirit of God draws aside the veil even further. He is the child born and the son given. It is now appropriate that His names are given - Mighty God, the Prince of Peace, etc. We noted that the distinction between the Child born and the Son given, speaks of Christ's humanity and pre-incarnate being respectively.

In the Gospels, we have the consummation of all this in the ineffable splendour of the Incarnation. The holy and redeeming God steps into time as the seed of the woman and He is revealed as the *Son*, the *Saviour*, the *Sacrifice*, and the *Sovereign*. Divine Promise and prophecy are fulfilled, the child is born to the virgin Mary; His name is Emmanuel, God with us (Matt 1:23); He is born a Jew unto the house of David, and He is called Jesus, for He will save His people from their sins (Matt 1:21; Lk 1:27, 31). "God sent forth his Son, made [come] of a woman, made [come] under the law" (Gal 4:4). But He came not only as a Jew under the law and unto Israel, but also as the Son of God - "a light to lighten the Gentiles" (Lk 2:32). The gospel of Christ is the power of God unto salvation, to the Jew first and also to the Gentiles (Rom 1:16). The biblical account of the Virgin Birth is not poetical, allegorical nor mythical. It is historical and doctrinal.

The necessity of the Virgin Birth
As a sign to the house of David

It is clear from the first intimation of it in Scripture, that the Virgin Birth is a truth relevant to all men (Gen 3:15). It has, however, a particular significance to Israel. A virgin bearing a child was to be a sign to the house of David (Isa 7:13-14). The Jews were a sign-seeking people (1 Cor 1:22). Of what was the Virgin Birth a sign to them?

Firstly, it represented a fulfilment of prophecy and testified to Jehovah's faithfulness to Israel. The Messiah had come according to divine promise to offer the kingdom of God to the nation. He is the seed of the woman, the seed of Abraham and the Son of David. Matthew's Gospel was particularly inspired to declare this.

Secondly, it was a monumental demonstration of the almighty power of God. The Virgin Birth defies every natural law of procreation, contradicting the greatest of natural laws relating to the generation of life. When a woman bears a child without any human paternal or biological involvement, *and* that child was a Person who eternally pre-existed, only one conclusion remains concerning the birth of the child. He was divine and conceived by divine power. Who but God can move so exceptionally in regard to His natural laws? Divine conception is indispensable to the *credibility* of the virgin birth.

The deity of the Messiah is taught here and sign-posted by Israel's own prophet to every Jew in every age. It is through the divine Messiah that all the divine covenants in regard to Israel will be fulfilled. But, He came unto His own and they received Him not. They rejected the prophets and stoned them that were sent unto them (Matt 23:37). A day is coming however, when they shall look upon Him whom they pierced and worship Him as their divine Messiah-King (Zech 12:10; Isa 53), He who was born of a virgin.

The need for a perfect Man and a perfect Sacrifice

God required another *man* to restore what the first man Adam lost. He had to be a *perfect* Man to be that perfect sacrifice needed to satisfy God's holiness. Only when we accept these truths, will we come to appreciate the necessity of the Virgin Birth and its relevance to all men, for all have sinned and come short of God's glory.

The Virgin Birth with its vital connection to divine conception, means that the child who was born is the Son of God. So said the angel - "He shall be called the Son of God", a divine title. If His birth was by a woman who was not a virgin, with what plausibility could it be said that His birth was divinely conceived; that He is the Son of God, Emmanuel (God with us); not of Adam's fallen seed; the perfect Man and perfect sacrifice"?[1] We noted that divine conception is indispensable to the credibility of the Virgin Birth. We now note that the Virgin Birth is indispensable to the credibility of divine conception and the perfect Man. It determines the *identity* and *nature* of the Child born and Son given. It establishes absolutely the truth of divine conception, which in turn substantiates all that rests upon it, the deity of Christ, His *perfect* humanity and Him as the perfect and accepted sacrifice for sin. There is only one man who is excepted from the divine decree that all have sinned and fallen short of the glory of God. Jesus of Nazareth is that Man as revealed by His incarnation and Virgin Birth.

An opposing view

Some within Christendom accept the fact of the Virgin Birth but deny its importance. They regard it as an "unnecessary truth". The first reason given is that no other doctrine depends upon it. Clearly, those making this assertion have not fully understood the absolute necessity for a perfect *Man* in the matter of divine reconciliation.

The second reason given, in support of the first, is that the Virgin Birth appears so infrequently in Scripture. It fails to appear where we "expect" it to appear, if it were in fact a vital truth. We must be guided by biblical revelation rather than intellectual expectation. It is true the narratives of Christ's birth contain the only explicit references to the Virgin Birth in the NT. The Virgin Birth is not

---

[1] Credibility would be compromised, too, if she was in a situation in which she could have known a man. Mary was "betrothed" to Joseph, and the biblical record of His angst when she was found to be with child serves as evidence of the moral rectitude in their relationship.

explicitly mentioned when Christ declared His deity. It is not mentioned in the polemics of the Roman Epistle. Neither is it employed by the Spirit of God in the apologetic Christology of the Colossian Epistle or in presenting the superiority of Christ in Epistle to the Hebrews.

Let us note first, that if Scripture employed the Virgin Birth in the cause of Christ's deity, it would give occasion to elevate the virgin rather than the Child she bore. Also, where men are captivated by Babylonian creeds and ceremonies, such a course would undoubtedly encourage the unwarranted homage bestowed to Mary. Second, the matter foremost in the heart of Christ was His death, not His birth. In His death sin was defeated and from His death all blessings flow to man. It is His death we are enjoined to show forth on the first day of each week (1 Cor 11:24; Lk 22:19). It is not the Babe in Bethlehem, but Christ and His saving work on the cross that the Holy Spirit unceasingly elevates before us, as worshippers and as evangelists of the ministry of reconciliation.

Satan is always seeking to depreciate the Person and work of Christ. He sees in Christ's birth an opportunity to do this very thing. What blasphemy is perpetuated by the worshipping of the virgin Mary, her role as a mediatrix and the errant doctrine of the "Immaculate Conception".[2] When the world speaks of the "Christian Festive Season", it refers principally to the celebration of Christ's birth. His birth and the virgin are revered in unwarranted prominence. Where Scripture would have us show forth the Lord's death, men would rather give prominence to His birth.

It is true that there are only a few references to the "Virgin Birth" in Scripture. However, the number of times a matter is mentioned in Scripture is not to be taken as indicative of its degree of importance. God speaks once yea twice, but man perceives it not (Job 33:14). Besides, the progressive revelation of the Virgin Birth in the OT, reaching its fulfilment in the NT, shows it was no minor matter in the eternal counsels of God.

We must understand that the Virgin Birth, the Incarnation and Christ's deity are inseparable truths. Only then will we come to

---

[2] The doctrine that Mary was, by divine power excepted from original sin so God's Son could be born by her. The Romanist notion that Mary was "the mother of God" is not biblical and is essentially pagan. Mary was the mother of Him who was God.

acknowledge that wherever we have reference to Christ's deity and Incarnation in Scripture, there we have an intimation of the Virgin Birth. Wherever we have a revelation of all or one of the three marks of deity in Christ, we are to acknowledge the Virgin Birth. Wherever the truth of Christ as the perfect and accepted sacrifice is brought before us in Scripture in title, type or teaching, we have the necessity of the Virgin Birth. Where Scripture speaks of the righteousness of God, that He Himself must be that sacrifice for sin, there, too, we have the Virgin Birth.[3] The Spirit however is pre-occupied with the Incarnation, not the actual birth. Nor is it with Mary, the virgin that gave birth. It is with God becoming *man*, because in this we have the holiness of God and the love of God to man revealed (Jn 3:16). It is not a case therefore of the insignificance of the Virgin Birth, but of the sedulous hand of the Spirit of God guarding the pre-eminence of the holy One to whom the virgin gave birth.

---

[3] When correcting the Galatians, Paul brings the Virgin Birth into view in that Christ is the One who was the seed of the woman (Gal 4:4).

APPENDIX 1

A brief chronology of early error relating to the Person of Christ and contemporary manifestations of it

Date c. AD	The Error	Its Christology	Its Repudiation	Contemporary manifestations of it - various degrees
1st	Gnosticism	Christ was an emanation from God	(Paul in his Epistle to the Colossians and John's 1st Epistle)	New Age Movement
2nd	Ebionitism	A Jewish sect within Christianity that believed Christ was the Messiah, but they denied His deity and Virgin birth		Mormonism (Latter-Day saints)
4th	Arianism (Arius)	"Christ was created by God"	Council of Nicea 1, 325	Jehovah's Witnesses Mormonism Christadelphianism Brahamism Hinduism - many gods of which Brahman is the supreme god
	Sabellianism (Sabellius)	"God is a single entity but He 'manifested' HImself initially as the Father and Creator, then as the Son and the Holy Spirit." (Modalism)		
	Apollinarianism (Apollinaris)	"Christ was divine but not a real man"	Council of Constantinople 1, 381	
5th	Nestorianism (Nestorius)	"Christ was both divine and human, but these two natures were quite separate"	Council of Ephesus, 431	
	Eutychianism (Eutyches)	"Christ possessed one essential nature, which was divine."	Council of Chalcedon, 451	
16th	Socinianism (Socinus)	Denial of Christ's deity, and anti-Trinitarian		Unitarianism Jehovah's Witnesses Mormonism Christadelphianism

APPENDIX 2

Further notes on the term *logos*

"Logos" was a term used by Alexandrian Judaism to express the manifestation of the invisible God, His Absolute Being in creation and government. Alexandrian Judaism (cf the orthodox Judaism of Palestine), was an admixture of allegorised Jewish OT doctrines and Platonic philosophy. Philo, the principal proponent of the Alexandrian school, regarded logos as an intermediate "agency" through which God created material things and communicated with them. Just what this agency was in terms of its essential substance Philo himself was uncertain.

Lightfoot states the term *logos* itself refers to reason and speech. Dods remarks that *logos*, a common expression used to express God's connection with the world, was taken by John to "denote the Revealer of the incomprehensible and invisible God" (M Dods, "The Gospel of St. John"; - *Expositors*, Vol 1, p 684). This would be consistent with the Prologue of the Hebrew Epistle, that reveals that in these last days God has "spoken" to us through Himself as the Son, and concordant with the Word of John's Gospel, who is the "image of the invisible God" (Col 1:15). John's *Logos* is clearly the Second Person of the Trinity - the Eternal Son of God.

If John were influenced at all by contemporary language, it would surely be the language of the Jewish Targums (Jewish paraphrases of the OT). He was, after all, a simple local fisherman, who would be more familiar with contemporary Judaism than abstract theories and philosophy. In the Targums, the Aramaic term *memra* or "Word of God", is often used to represent communication between God and man. In Genesis 3:8-9 for instance, the rendering is "they heard the voice of the *Word* of the Lord God". The expositors tell us the term *memra* is not just an utterance or voice, for this the Targums use the term *pithgama*. Barnes remarks, the term *Mimra* - i.e.

"Word", was used by the Jews to represent the Messiah - "Ye have appointed the Word of God a king over you this day, that he may be your God" (Targum). Other scholars note that *memra* was used to represent the term "word" as it is used in the OT in regard to God as the Creator and the Saviour. Therefore, when John looked for the most suitable Greek word to represent the term and concept of *memra* in contemporary Jewish theology, he chose the term *logos*.

In the final analysis Scripture is our rule. The Bible is not silent on the meaning of John's *Logos*, as we have noted. In John's Gospel alone there is ample evidence that his *Logos* has a divine and distinct personality. The diagram below illustrates the thematic presentation of John's *Logos* in his Gospel, revealing the convergent lines of truth that make known His identity.

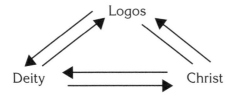

TOPICAL INDEX

INDEX OF KEY VERSES

Hebrew and Greek Words and Expressions